the complete book of
juicing

the complete book of juicing

REVISED AND UPDATED

your delicious guide to youthful vitality

michael t. murray, N.D.

Clarkson Potter/Publishers
New York

Published in the United States by Clarkson Potter/
Publishers, an imprint of the Crown Publishing
Group, a division of Random House LLC, a
Penguin Random House Company, New York.
www.crownpublishing.com
www.clarksonpotter.com

CLARKSON POTTER is a trademark and POTTER
with colophon is a registered trademark of
Random House LLC.

Early versions of this work were previously published,
in significantly different form, by Prima, an imprint
of Random House LLC, New York, in 1992, and by
Three Rivers Press, an imprint of the Crown Publishing
Group, a division of Random House LLC, New York, in
1997.

WARNING—DISCLAIMER
Random House LLC has designed this book to provide
information in regard to the subject matter covered.
It is sold with the understanding that the publisher
and the author are not liable for the misconception or
misuse of information provided. Every effort has been
made to make this book as complete and as accurate
as possible. The purpose of this book is to educate.
The author and Random House LLC shall have neither
liability nor responsibility to any person or entity
with respect to any loss, damage, or injury caused
or alleged to be caused directly or indirectly by the
information contained in this book. The information
presented herein is in no way intended as a substitute
for medical counseling.

Library of Congress Cataloging-in-Publication Data
Murray, Michael T.
  The complete book of juicing / Michael T.
  Murray.—First revised edition.
  "Revised and updated."
  Includes bibliographical references and index.
  1. Fruit juices—Health aspects. 2. Vegetable
juices—Health aspects. 3. Fruit juices.
4. Vegetable juices. I. Title.
  RA784.M84 2014
  641.3'4—dc23   2013009513

ISBN 978-0-385-34571-2
eISBN 978-0-385-34572-9

Printed in the United States of America

Book and cover design by Ashley Tucker
Cover photograph: Stockbyte/Getty Images

10 9 8 7 6 5 4 3 2 1

First Revised Edition

contents

acknowledgments

I would especially like to thank my wife, Gina, not only for the tremendous impact she has made in my life but also for the wonderful person that she truly is.

To my children, Lexi, Zach, and Addison, for being so incredibly magnificent and for teaching me so much about life. I am blessed.

foreword

Dr. Michael Murray is the first person I call when I have a question about health or nutrition. He is one of the most knowledgeable and respected doctors in the country. I have known Dr. Murray for more than 22 years. He served on the Nutritional Board of Advisors for my company, Trillium Health Products, back in the early 1990s. Our mission was simple back then: to educate people about good health and proper nutrition and provide them with quality products and programs to live a healthful lifestyle. Along with Jay Kordich, we were really responsible for the juicing craze through our infomercials, juice machines, and educational materials. Together we introduced millions of people to the benefits of juicing.

Educating people about good health is still a cause I hold dear to my heart. As I travel the country speaking and consulting, I find more and more people who are run down and out of energy. I am often asked, "What do you recommend to help me get healthy again?" My answer is always the same: Start juicing and read *The Complete Book of Juicing* by Dr. Michael Murray. This updated edition of the book has been researched with the latest and best nutritional information available today. We are starting to see some of the long-term effects of what we taught people more than twenty years ago, with additional support from the scientific and medical communities. Fresh fruits and vegetables as part of a low-fat, high-fiber diet help promote health and prevent disease. Specifically, the American Cancer Society, the American Institute for Cancer Research, the United States Surgeon General's Office, the American Heart Association, and many more all agree that various diet-related diseases may be prevented if the quality of our food choices were improved.

Health brings us a freedom very few appreciate until we no

longer have it. We have an absolute health crisis going on right now. More than one million Americans will die this year from heart attack, stroke, or cancer. Childhood obesity and juvenile-onset diabetes are at an all-time high. Medical professionals say that for the first time in history, this generation of children might not outlive their parents. But there is hope. Public health experts say that more than 75 percent of these issues can be remedied by simply improving the quality and quantity of the food we eat, and one of the best things we can do is to increase our intake of raw fruits and vegetables.

Juicing has changed my life and the lives of countless other people. I am 58 years young and work out five times a week. I feel great, look great, and—God willing—will live a long and healthy life, and juicing is a big part of it. Over the past twenty years, I have received e-mails and phone calls from people with terminal cancer and other debilitating diseases, who were sent home "to get their house in order," who started juicing as part of a healthy lifestyle and are still here today. There is story after story of weight loss, increased energy, healthier complexions, increased clarity, decreased medications, pain relief, and much more.

Dr. Michael Murray has gathered a wealth of information from respected scientific sources. His tireless research and past experience working with patients prove that a preventive approach to health care—using nutrition as the basis—is the best way to achieve optimum wellness. His recommendations are both clinically relevant and scientifically proven. The information he shares in this book is eye-opening, fascinating, and gives you everything you need to live a healthy, nutritionally sound lifestyle.

With health and vitality,
STEVEN CESARI, president and CEO, Vital Visions Inc.

foreword
to the first edition

I've been sharing my personal story about juicing for more than 60 years. My message has been the connection between diet and health, and how by decreasing intake of meat and dairy products, and increasing consumption of fresh fruits, vegetables, grains, and legumes, people can help prevent diet-related diseases. Juicing is a great way to add more fresh fruits and vegetables to the diet, plus it's easy and delicious. I'm living proof that a good diet pays off in good health. I'm almost 90 years old and I've never felt better.

Dr. Michael Murray's *The Complete Book of Juicing* goes beyond the simple fact that juicing offers many health benefits; it takes an in-depth look at the scientific side of the juicing phenomenon. This book is a "must read" for anyone interested in juicing to improve or enhance the quality of life.

When I first started sharing my message, I was one of the very few people out there talking about how more fresh fruits and vegetables in the diet could help prevent diet-related disease and premature aging. Today health and medical professionals are accepting and acknowledging what I've been saying all along: Fresh fruits and vegetables as part of a low-fat, high-fiber diet do help promote health and prevent disease. Specifically, the American Cancer Society, the American Institute for Cancer Research, the U.S. Surgeon General's Office, heart disease specialist Dr. Dean Ornish, the American Heart Association, and many more all agree that various diet-related diseases may be prevented if the quality of our diet is improved. Scientific studies show that cancer, heart disease, arthritis, diabetes, and stroke could be prevented or lessened if certain components found in a plant-based diet (fruits, vegetables, grains, and legumes) are consumed on a regular basis.

Dr. Murray has gathered a wealth of information from respected scientific sources. His tireless research and practical experience working with patients proves that a preventive approach to health care using nutrition as the basis is the way to achieve optimum wellness. His recommendations are both clinically relevant and scientifically proven. The data he shares and the education he provides are eye-opening, fascinating, and completely support what I have been proposing all my life: Including more fresh fruits and vegetables in your diet is one of the most important things you can do for your body, and juicing is one of the easiest ways to do this. This book deserves a space in each and every home in America.

Dr. Murray adds the second edition of *The Complete Book of Juicing* to his impressive collection of health- and nutrition-oriented publications: *The Encyclopedia of Natural Medicine, The Encyclopedia of Healing Foods,* and *What the Drug Companies Won't Tell You and Your Doctor Doesn't Know.*

Yours in health,
JAY KORDICH
The Juiceman

preface

Health is a term that is difficult to define: Many definitions place unnecessary boundaries on its meaning. But I like the way the World Health Organization defines health as "a state of complete physical, mental, and social well-being, not merely the absence of disease or infirmity." This definition stretches well beyond the absence of sickness. My life and this book are about helping people attain a higher level of health.

Many of our health practices and lifestyle choices are based on habit and marketing hype. Time, energy, and money are spent marketing bad health practices. The mass media constantly bombards us with messages promoting unhealthful choices. In addition, the health practices and lifestyle of our parents usually become intricately woven into the fabric of our own lifestyles. No wonder so many Americans live at the lower end of the health spectrum.

The first step in achieving and maintaining wellness is taking personal responsibility. In this context, responsibility means choosing a healthful alternative over a less healthful one. If you want to be healthy, you must make healthful choices. This may seem too simplistic, but if we look at the cumulative effects of our routine choices on attitude, diet, lifestyle, and exercise, it is quite apparent that we do, in fact, control the level of health we will experience. The reward for most people who maintain a positive mental attitude, eat a healthful diet, and exercise regularly is a life full of energy, joy, vitality, and a tremendous passion for living.

It is often difficult to "sell" people on health. It is usually not until the body fails us in some manner that we realize that we haven't taken care of it. Ralph Waldo Emerson said, "The first wealth is health." I urge you to take action now.

1

why juice?

Quality of life begins with the quality of the foods that sustain it. The surest path to health and energy, strong bones, and beautiful skin begins with a diet rich in natural foods such as whole grains, legumes, fruits, and vegetables. Especially important on this road to health are fresh fruit and vegetable juices. Fresh juices provide vital proteins, carbohydrates, essential fatty acids, vitamins, minerals, and other nutrients critical to good health in one serving.

The Surgeon General, the U.S. Department of Health and Human Services, the National Cancer Institute, and many other experts have long agreed that fresh fruits and vegetables are the key to good nutrition. Juicing is the most fun and efficient way to increase your consumption of these life-giving foods as it provides the nutritional advantages of plant foods in a concentrated form that is easily absorbed by the body.

The advantages of increased energy, strengthened immunity, reduced risk of disease, strong bones, and the glowing complexion that is the evidence of great health can all be yours when fresh fruit and vegetable juices play a key role in your daily diet.

what do americans eat?

The so-called Standard American Diet, or SAD, does not provide adequate levels of fruits and vegetables. According to National Health and Nutrition Examination surveys conducted by the U.S. National Institute of Health over the past 20 years, French fries or potato chips notwithstanding, fewer than 10 percent of Americans meet the minimum recommendation of 2 fruit servings and 3 vegetable servings a day—in fact, the average number of daily servings of dark green or orange vegetables in American adults is 0.3 servings per day.

Instead of eating foods rich in vital nutrients, most Americans focus on refined foods high in calories, sugar, fat, and cholesterol, filling up on cheeseburgers, French fries, ice cream, and chocolate chip cookies and washing them down with artificially colored and flavored fruit drinks or colas. More and more food additives (such as preservatives, artificial colors, artificial flavorings, and acidifiers) have been shown to be extremely detrimental to health. Many have been banned because they were found to cause cancer and a great number of synthetic food additives are still in use that are being linked to such diseases as depression, asthma and other allergies, hyperactivity and learning disabilities in children, and migraine headaches. Synthetic food additives need to be avoided. It is a "SAD" fact that diet has replaced cigarettes as the number one contributor to premature death, and that 8 out of every 10 Americans over the age of 25 are now overweight or obese. Diet and obesity contribute to heart disease, cancer, strokes, diabetes, and virtually every other major disease afflicting our society. It's little wonder when you take a look at what we eat.

Based on detailed national health and nutrition surveys, it has been estimated that in one year, the average American consumes 100 pounds of refined sugar and 55 pounds of fats and oils in the form of:

- 300 bottles of sugary beverages
- 18 pounds of candy
- 5 pounds of potato chips
- 7 pounds of corn chips, popcorn, and pretzels
- 63 dozen doughnuts and pastries
- 50 pounds of cakes and cookies
- 20 gallons of ice cream

On top of this, nearly one-third of our adult population smokes and at least 10 percent are alcoholics. And what about the health effects of the more than 4 billion pounds of additives, pesticides, and herbicides added to our foods each year? It is no wonder that as a nation, according to the World Health Organization and the United Nations Department of Economic and Social Affairs, the United States ranked lower in life expectancy than 39 other industrial nations in 2012, despite the fact that we spend more money on health care than any nation in the world.

antioxidants and the battle against free radicals

Throughout this book, many key benefits of consuming fresh juices will be pointed out, but perhaps the greatest benefit is that they provide high levels of natural plant compounds known as antioxidants, which can protect the body against aging, cancer, heart disease, and many other degenerative conditions. The cells of the human body are constantly under attack. The culprits? Compounds known as free radicals and pro-oxidants. A free radical is a molecule that contains a highly reactive unpaired electron. A pro-oxidant is a molecule that can promote oxidative damage. These highly reactive molecules can bind to and destroy other cellular components. Free-radical damage is a cause of aging and is also linked to the development of cancer, heart disease, cataracts, Alzheimer's disease, and arthritis, among others.

Most of the free radicals zipping through our bodies are actually produced during normal and necessary metabolic processes like energy generation, detoxification reactions, and immune defense mechanisms. The major source of free-radical damage in the body is actually the oxygen molecule, the very molecule that gives us life! Just as oxygen can rust iron, when toxic oxygen molecules are allowed to attack our cells free-radical or oxidative damage occurs.

Although the body's own generation of free radicals is significant, the environment contributes greatly to the free-radical load of an individual. Cigarette smoking, for example, greatly increases an individual's free-radical load. Many of the harmful effects of smoking are related to the extremely high levels of free radicals being inhaled, depleting key antioxidant nutrients like vitamin C and beta-carotene. Other external sources of free radicals include ionizing radiation, chemotherapeutic drugs, air pollutants, pesticides, anesthetics, aromatic hydrocarbons, fried food, solvents, alcohol, and formaldehyde. These compounds greatly stress the body's antioxidant mechanisms. Individuals exposed to these environmental factors need the additional nutritional support that fresh juices can provide.

With the help of antioxidants and enzymes found in the plant foods we consume, including carotenes, flavonoids, vitamins C and E, sulfur-containing compounds and many other phytochemicals, our cells can protect against free-radical and oxidative damage. Free radicals must be broken down by enzymes or be chemically neutralized before they react with cellular molecules. Examples of the free-radical scavenging enzymes produced by the body are catalase, superoxide dismutase, and glutathione peroxidase. Taking enzymes as an oral supplement has not been shown to increase enzyme tissue levels. However, ingesting antioxidant nutrients—such as manganese, sulfur-containing amino acids, carotenes, flavonoids, and vitamin C—has been shown to increase tissue concentrations of the enzymes.

The other way the cell can protect itself against free radical or oxidative damage is by chemical neutralization, or antioxidants binding to or neutralizing the free radical or pro-oxidant. Dietary antioxidants block free-radical damage by chemically reacting with the free radical or pro-oxidant to neutralize it. Ingesting fresh juices can increase tissue concentrations of antioxidant phytochemicals, thereby supporting normal protective mechanisms and blocking free-radical and oxidative damage to cells of the body.

the role of the diet in disease prevention

An extensive body of research has clearly established the link between the SAD and the development of the primary "diseases of civilization" such as heart disease, cancer, strokes, high blood pressure, diabetes, gallstones, arthritis, and many more. Likewise, one of the best bets in preventing virtually every chronic disease is a diet rich in fruits and vegetables of assorted colors. The evidence in support of this recommendation is so strong that it has been endorsed by U.S. government health agencies and by virtually every major medical organization, including the American Cancer Society.

Fruits and vegetables are so important in the battle against cancer that some experts believe that cancer is a result of a maladaptation over time to a reduced level of intake of fruits and vegetables. As a study published in the medical journal *Cancer Causes and Control* put it, "Vegetables and fruit contain the anticarcinogenic cocktail to which we are adapted. We abandon it at our peril."[1]

A vast number of substances found in fruits and vegetables are known to protect against cancer. Collectively they are referred to as chemopreventers, but they are better known as phytochemicals. Phytochemicals include pigments such as carotenes, chlorophyll, and flavonoids; dietary fiber; enzymes; vitamin-like compounds; and other minor dietary constituents. Although they work in harmony with nutritional antioxidants like vitamin C, vitamin E, and selenium, phytochemicals exert considerably greater protection against cancer than these simple nutrients.

Among the most important groups of phytochemicals are pigments such as chlorophyll, carotenes, and flavonoids responsible for the color of many fruits and vegetables. One of my key dietary recommendations is for people to consume a "rainbow" diet; they need to focus on colorful fruits and vegetables (see table 1.1). Regularly consuming the full spectrum of fruit and vegetables—red, orange, yellow, green, blue, and purple—provides the body the full contingent of pigments with powerful antioxidant effects as well as the nutrients it needs for optimal function and protect against disease. Juicing provides a great way to color your diet with these life-giving foods.

Drinking at least 12 to 16 ounces of juice each day is as easy as swapping your morning coffee for juice. If you work away from home, make enough juice to fill your thermos and take it to work with you. A midmorning or midafternoon juice pick-me-up is a healthful way to keep your energy level high. At lunch and dinner, start your meal with a "salad in a glass." Once you start experiencing some of the benefits of juicing, incorporating fresh fruit and vegetable juice in your daily routine will become second nature.

fresh juice vs. whole fruits and vegetables

You may ask, "Why juice? Aren't we supposed to eat whole fruits and vegetables to get the fiber?" The answer: Of course you are, but juice gets you more, faster. Juicing fresh fruits and vegetables

table 1.1. the rainbow assortment

RED	Apples (red) Bell peppers (red) Cherries Cranberries	Grapefruit (pink) Grapes (red) Radishes Raspberries	Plums (red) Strawberries Tomatoes Watermelon
ORANGE	Apricots Bell peppers (orange) Butternut squash	Cantaloupe Carrots Mangoes Oranges	Papaya Pumpkin Sweet potatoes Yams
YELLOW AND LIGHT GREEN	Apples (green or yellow) Avocado Banana Bell peppers (yellow) Bok choy Cabbage	Cauliflower Celery Fennel Kiwi fruit Lemons Lettuce (light green types)	Limes Onions Pears (green or yellow) Pineapple Squash (yellow) Zucchini (yellow)
DARK GREEN	Artichoke Asparagus Bell peppers (green) Broccoli Brussels sprouts Chard	Collard greens Cucumber Grapes (green) Green beans Honeydew melons Kale	Leeks Lettuce (dark green types) Mustard greens Peas Spinach Turnip greens
BLUE/ PURPLE	Beets Blueberries Blackberries Currants	Cabbage (purple) Cherries Eggplant Onions (red)	Grapes (purple) Pears (red) Plums (purple) Radishes

does provide some fiber, particularly the soluble fiber that has been shown to lower cholesterol levels. Think about it—fiber really refers to indigestible material found in plants; while this is important for proper bowel function, the juice of the plant ultimately contains the nutrients that nourish us. Our body actually converts the food we eat into juice so that it can be absorbed, so juicing actually saves the body energy, resulting in increased energy levels. Juicing also helps the body's digestive process and allows for quick absorption of high-quality nutrition. Juicing quickly provides the most easily digestible and concentrated nutritional benefits of fruits and vegetables.

fresh juice vs. canned, bottled, or frozen juices

Fresh juice not only contains greater nutritional values than its canned, bottled, or frozen counterparts, but it also contains enzymes and other "living" ingredients. In contrast, canned, bottled, and packaged juices have been pasteurized, which keeps them on the shelf longer, causing the loss of identifiable vitamins and minerals as well as the loss of other factors not yet fully understood.

A group of researchers at Health Canada designed a scientific study comparing the antiviral activity of fresh apple juice to commercial apple juice from concentrate, apple cider, and apple wine.[2] The most potent antiviral activity was found in fresh apple juice. Why? Commercial apple juices are produced using methods like pasteurization that destroy enzymes and alter many key compounds. In doing so, a great deal of the antiviral activity is also lost.

The compounds that are responsible for the antiviral activity of fresh apple juice are various flavonoid molecules. More will be discussed regarding these valuable compounds in chapter 3; the point being made here is that they are found in the highest quantities in fresh, not commercial apple juice (see table 1.2).

Fresh apple juice also contains ellagic acid, a compound that exerts potent antioxidant and anticancer properties,[3] while commercial apple juice that has been cooked has been stripped of this

table 1.2. flavonoid concentration of fresh vs. commercial apple juice

FLAVONOID COMPOUNDS	FRESH JUICE (mg/l)	COMMERCIAL JUICE (mg/l)
Hydroxycinnamic acids	57–593	69–259
Flavan-3-ols/ procyanidins	50–393	14–124
Flavonols	0.4–27	4–14
Dihydrochalcones	10–171	9–87
Total flavonoids	154–970	110–459

Source: C. Gerhauser, "Cancer Chemopreventive Potential of Apples, Apple Juice, and Apple Components," *Planta Medica* 74 (2008): 1608–24.

enriching natural factor. Ellagic acid protects against damage to the chromosomes, while blocking the cancer-causing actions of many pollutants, such as polycyclic aromatic hydrocarbons found in cigarette smoke and toxic chemicals such as benzopyrene. Ellagic acid is not destroyed by freezing or freeze-drying, but it can be destroyed by heat. While fresh whole apples and fresh apple juice contain 100 to 130 mg ellagic acid per 100 g (roughly 3.5 ounces), the amount found in cooked or commercial apple products is at or near zero.[4] The flavonoid and ellagic acid content is exceptionally high in many berries, particularly raspberries and blackberries, which can contain up to 1.5 mg ellagic acid per gram. The levels in berries are approximately five to six times higher than those levels found in other foods.[5] But again, that only applies to the fresh fruit or juice.

Another example of how freshness impacts nutritional value is dietary glutathione. Glutathione is a small protein composed of three amino acids manufactured in our cells, which aids in the detoxification of heavy metals such as lead as well as in the elimination of pesticides and solvents. Whether our bodies can meet the demand for glutathione is contingent on how much fresh vegetation we consume. While fresh fruits and vegetables provide ample glutathione, processed foods do not (see table 1.3).[6] To derive the greatest benefit from our foods, we should consume them in their freshest forms.

At each step in the modern evolution of the orange, there is a loss of nutritional value. For example, the vitamin C content of pasteurized orange juice is extremely unreliable. As with most processed juices, the total nutritional quality is substantially lower than that of fresh juice. This is particularly true for juices stored in paperboard containers lined with wax or polyethylene. These products will lose up to 75 percent of their vitamin C content within three weeks.[7] Frozen juice concentrates fare no better, and orange drinks have no vitamin C unless it is added. This highlights the fact that in the latter stages listed below there is not only a decrease in nutritional value, there is also an increase in the number of synthetic additives.

the modern evolution of the orange

Raw, whole oranges or freshly prepared orange juice

↓

Refined, processed (pasteurized) unsweetened orange juice

↓

Refined, processed, sweetened orange juice or concentrate

↓

Refined, highly processed, sweetened, artificially colored, and flavored "orange" drinks

↓

Completely fabricated products (such as Tang)

table 1.3. comparison of glutathione in fresh vs. canned or bottled juice

Food	Glutathione mg/100 mg Dry Weight	
	FRESH	CANNED OR BOTTLED
Apples	21.0	0.0
Carrots	74.6	0.0
Grapefruit	70.6	0.0
Spinach	166.0	27.1
Tomatoes	169.0	0.0

Source: D. P. Jones, R. J. Coates, E. W. Flagg, et al., "Glutathione in Foods Listed in the National Cancer Institutes Health Habits and History Food Frequency Questionnaire," *Nutrition and Cancer* 17 (1995): 57–75.

fresh juice vs. processed food products

The best way to reduce exposure to preservatives and other synthetic additives is to consume as many fresh and natural foods as possible.

what is the difference between a vegetable and a fruit?

In 1893 this question came before the U.S. Supreme Court. It was then ruled that a vegetable refers to a plant grown for an edible part that is generally eaten as part of the main course, while a fruit is a plant part that is generally eaten as an appetizer, as a dessert, or out of hand. Some typical parts of plants used as vegetables are bulbs (garlic and onion), flowers (broccoli and cauliflower), fruits (pumpkins and tomatoes), leaves (spinach and lettuce), roots (carrots and beets), seeds (legumes, peas, and corn), stalks (celery), stems (asparagus), and tubers (potatoes and yams).

Juicing fresh fruits and vegetables is not only a great way to increase dietary intake of important nutritional components, it also circumvents the majority of harmful additives and preservatives. This is especially true if you juice only organic produce.

cooking: homey and healthy don't always equate

Although less ruthless than commercial processing methods, home handling and cooking also means loss of nutrients in fruits and vegetables. For example, leafy vegetables will lose up to 87 percent of their vitamin C content upon cooking, while carrots, potatoes, and other root vegetables will lose up to 33 percent of vitamin B_1, 45 percent of B_2, 61 percent of B_3, and 76 percent of vitamin C. However, cooking is not the only way fruits and vegetables lose nutritional value: Oxygen exposure can be just as detrimental. A slice of cantaloupe left uncovered in the refrigerator will lose 35 percent of its vitamin C content in 24 hours. Freshly sliced cucumbers, if left standing, will lose between 41 and 49 percent of their vitamin C content within the first three hours.[8]

From this information we can conclude that it is best to drink fresh juice as soon as it is prepared. If this is not possible, juice should be stored in a thermos or in an airtight container in the refrigerator.

juicing, obesity, and high blood pressure

Many Americans are overfed but undernourished. Estimates are that up to 80 percent of the adult population is overweight. Juice may help reset one's appetite control by providing the body with the high-quality nutrition it needs. This is always vital but never more so than during weight loss. If the body is not fed, it feels that it is starving, and metabolism will slow down. This means less fat will be burned.

Diets containing a high percentage (up to 60 percent of the calories) of uncooked foods are associated with significant weight loss and lowering of blood pressure in overweight individuals.[9] Raw-food diets produce these effects via the following ways:

- *A raw-food diet provides higher levels of many nutrients.* Cooking can cause the loss of up to 97 percent of water-soluble vitamins (B vitamins and C) and up to 40 percent of the fat-soluble vitamins (A, D, E, and K). Since uncooked foods such as juices contain more vitamins and other nutrients, they may help increase the feeling of satisfaction from food leading to a reduced calorie intake.
- *The blood-pressure-lowering effect of raw foods is most likely due to healthier food choices, fiber, and potassium.* When patients switch from a raw diet to a cooked diet (without a change in calorie or sodium content), there is a rapid increase of blood pressure back to prestudy levels.
- *A diet in which an average of 60 percent of the calories ingested comes from raw foods reduces the stress on the body.* Specifically, the presence of enzymes in raw foods, the reduced allergenicity of raw foods, and the effects of raw foods on our gut-bacterial flora are thought to aid digestion compared to a diet focused on cooked foods.

Juicing is a phenomenal way to reach the goal of ingesting 60 percent of total calories from raw foods. Juice helps the body's digestive process and allows for quick absorption of high-quality nutrition. The result: increased energy levels. This is one of the greatest advantages of utilizing fresh juice in a weight-loss plan.

Some juices are better than others for promoting weight loss. The most effective are those that are dense in nutrients but low in calories. Here, in descending order, are the most nutrient-dense fruits and vegetables suitable for juicing:

Bell peppers
Parsley
Kale
Broccoli
Spinach
Celery
Brussels sprouts
Cauliflower
Carrots
Cabbage
Beets
Pineapple
Cantaloupe
Watermelon
Tomatoes
Apples
Strawberries
Pears
Oranges
Grapes

The first eight vegetables listed are not only nutrient dense, but they are also very flavorful. Try mixing them with carrot, apple, or tomato juice. Notice that the fruits are farther down on the scale than the vegetables. Although fruits are full of valuable nutrients, they contain more natural sugars than vegetables. This means they are higher in calories and can potentially stress blood sugar control. Eat them sparingly.

summary

Many medical experts and every agency of the U.S. government dealing with health, including the National Academy of Science, the Department of Agriculture, and the Department of Health and Human Services, as well as the National Research Council and the National Cancer Institute, recommend that Americans consume two to three servings of fruit and three to five servings of vegetables a day. Unfortunately, most Americans are not coming anywhere near these goals.

Juicing provides an easy and effective way to meet your dietary requirements for fresh fruits and vegetables, the most nutrient-packed form. One of the key benefits of fresh fruit and vegetable juices, beyond their nutritional superiority, is their rich supply of phytochemicals with exceptional antioxidant activity. Oxidative damage is a cause of aging and is also linked to the development of cancer, heart disease, cataracts, Alzheimer's disease, arthritis, and virtually every other chronic degenerative disease. The consumption of fruits and vegetables is known to offer significant protection against the development of these diseases.

2

what's in juice?

the nutrients

This chapter will describe the nutritional elements found in fresh fruit and vegetable juices and discuss their importance to our health. Juice is a source of natural water and provides the body with easily absorbed protein, carbohydrates, essential fatty acids, vitamins, and minerals. Fresh juice also contains numerous phytochemicals, including enzymes, and pigments such as carotenes, chlorophyll, and flavonoids, which are discussed in the next chapter.

water:
vital for optimal performance

First, fresh juice provides natural water. Water is the most plentiful substance in the body. It constitutes over 60 percent of body weight—that is, about 10 gallons of water for most of us. More than two-thirds of the body's water content is found inside the cells. The rest is found coursing through the body, carrying vital nutrients and blood cells. Water is also important to the body's natural chemical reactions, serves as a lubricant in joints, aids in maintaining body temperature, and serves as an insulator and shock absorber in body temperature.[1]

Each day your body requires an intake of over 2 quarts of water to function optimally. About 1 quart comes from food. This means you need to drink at least one quart of liquids each day to maintain good water balance. More is needed in warmer climates and for physically active people.

Not drinking enough liquids or eating enough high-water-content foods puts a great deal of stress on the body. Kidney function is likely to be affected, gallstones and kidney stones can form, and immune function will be impaired.

Based on research conducted primarily by the U.S. Environmental Protection Agency (EPA), there are reasons to be concerned about the quality of the U.S. water supply. Not only are chlorine and fluoride routinely added to water, there are numerous potential contaminants. Toxic organic compounds and chemicals, such as PCBs (polychlorinated biphenyls), pesticide residues, nitrates, and heavy metals such as lead, mercury, and cadmium are just some of the commonly found contaminants. The EPA estimates that lead alone may contaminate the water in the homes of more than 40 million Americans and has started an awareness campaign (see http://water.epa.gov/drink/info/lead/). The problem is that lead leaches into tap water through the corrosion of plumbing materials that contain lead, particularly in homes built before 1986.

Drinking fresh fruit and vegetable juices (especially those derived from organic produce) is a fantastic way to give your body the natural, pure water it desires.

acid-base value and human health

To function properly, the body must maintain the correct balance of acidity and alkalinity (pH) in the blood and other body fluids. Juicing is a phenomenal way to ensure the proper pH balance. In particular, it has a great alkalinizing effect to counteract the typical acid-forming diet consumed by many Americans. There is accumulating evidence that certain disease states like osteoporosis, rheumatoid arthritis, and gout, among other illnesses, are caused by too much acid-forming foods in the diet. For example, osteoporosis may be the result of a chronic intake of acid-forming foods consistently outweighing the intake of alkaline foods; this causes the body's bones to give up their alkaline minerals (calcium and magnesium) in order to buffer the excess acid.

For most people, the achievement of proper pH balance is quite simple—consuming more alkaline-producing foods than acid-producing foods. Basically, an alkaline diet is one that focuses on vegetables, fruit, and legumes while avoiding overconsumption of grains, meat, dairy, and most nuts.

Keep in mind that there is a difference between acidic foods and acid-forming foods. For example, while foods like tomatoes and citrus fruits are acidic, they actually have an alkalizing effect on the body. What actually determines the pH nature of the food in the body is the metabolic end products when it is digested. For example, the citric acid in citrus fruit is metabolized in the body to its alkaline form (citrate) and may even be converted to bicarbonate—another alkaline compound. Appendix A provides a brief food table on the acid or alkaline effect of common foods.

protein: essential to good health

The word *protein* is derived from the Greek *proteios,* or "primary." The name is fitting as, after water, protein is the next most plentiful component of our body. The body manufactures proteins to make up hair, muscles, nails, tendons, ligaments, and other body structures. Proteins also function as enzymes, hormones, and as important components to other cells, such as our genes. The human body contains somewhere between 30,000 and 50,000 unique proteins. The building blocks for all proteins are molecules known as amino acids.

The body strives to make good use of its protein. During a single day, about 1 pound of an adult's body protein is broken down into amino acids and reassembled into new proteins. The protein is either broken down or manufactured to allow us to maintain the integrity of proteins subjected to daily wear-and-tear. This protein turnover allows us to grow, heal, remodel, and internally defend ourselves on a continual basis. Cells are constantly remodeling themselves and the structures they make. Since there is some loss and although we can manufacture some amino acids, adequate dietary protein intake is essential in providing those amino acids that we cannot make—essential amino acids.

The government mandated recommended dietary allowance (RDA) for protein is based on body weight (0.36 g per pound or 0.8 g per kilogram of body weight). Take a minute to calculate your protein requirement. The amount is usually considerably less than the amount most Americans typically take in. The RDA is as follows:

Multiply 0.36 g by your weight in pounds. This will equal the grams of protein needed each day. For example, a woman who weighs 118 pounds would require 43 grams of protein each day (0.36 × 118 = 43 g). For a general approximation of protein needs based on age, see table 2.1.

table 2.1. recommended dietary intake of protein

AGE	U.S. RDA (in grams)
INFANTS	
Up to 6 months	13
6 months–1 year	14
CHILDREN	
1–3	16
4–6	24
7–10	28
MALES	
11–14	45
15–18	59
19–24	58
25–50	63
51+	63
FEMALES	
11–14	46
15–18	44
19–24	46
25–50	50
51+	50
PREGNANT	60
LACTATING	
First 6 months	65
Second 6 months	62

The average American easily reaches and often exceeds this protein requirement (without even being on a high-protein diet). Actual daily protein consumption ranges from 88 g to 92 g for men and from 63 g to 66 g for women.

There are many conditions in which extra protein is needed (0.8 g/day), including childhood/adolescence (growth), pregnancy, lactation, intense strength and endurance training, and dealing with diseases such as AIDS and cancer. Athletes and the elderly may also require additional amounts of protein to maintain muscle mass.

Since the body does not need or use excess protein, excess protein can become a burden for the kidneys and liver—the organs that are in charge of getting rid of wastes. Contrary to popular belief, you can get fat eating a high-protein diet. Excess protein intake increases the use of amino acids as a daily energy source, which then, in turn, decreases the breakdown and utilization of fat for energy thereby promoting an increased body fat content.

Proteins are composed of individual building blocks known as amino acids. The human body can manufacture most of the amino acids required for making body proteins. However, there are nine amino acids, termed essential amino acids, that the body cannot manufacture and must get from dietary intake: arginine, histadine, isoleucine, lysine, methionine, phenylalanine, threonine, tryptophan, and valine. The quality of a protein source is based on its level of these essential amino acids along with its ability to be utilized by the body.

A complete protein source is one that provides all nine essential amino acids in significant amounts. Animal products—meat, fish, dairy, poultry—are examples of complete proteins. Plant foods, especially grains and legumes, often lack one or more of the essential amino acids but become complete when they are combined. For example, combining grains with legumes (beans) results in a complete protein, as the two protein sources complement each other. With a varied diet of grains, legumes, fruits, and vegetables, a person is almost assured of consuming complete proteins as long as the calorie content of the diet is high enough.

Fresh fruits and vegetables often contain the full complement of amino acids and a relatively high percentage of calories as protein (see table 2.2). But because fruits and vegetables contain protein in lower quantities, they are generally considered poor protein sources. However, as previously mentioned, the nutritional qualities of fruits and vegetables become concentrated in their juice form, making juices an excellent source of easily absorbed amino acids and proteins. Because fruits and vegetables are poor protein choices, fresh juice should not be relied on to meet all your body's protein needs. You will need to eat other protein sources, such as lean cuts of meat and poultry or grains and legumes; or you can supplement your juice with a protein source such as whey, rice, soy, or hemp protein.

table 2.2. percentage of calories as protein of common fruits and vegetables

FRUITS	%
Lemons	16
Honeydew melons	10
Cantaloupe	9
Strawberries	8
Oranges	8
Blackberries	8
Cherries	8
Grapes	8
Watermelons	8
Tangerines	7
Papayas	6
Peaches	6
Pears	5
Bananas	5
Grapefruit	5
Pineapple	3
Apples	1

VEGETABLES	%
Spinach	49
Kale	45
Broccoli	45
Brussels sprouts	44
Turnip greens	43
Collards	43
Cauliflower	40
Parsley	34
Lettuce	34
Zucchini	28
Cucumbers	24
Green peppers	22
Artichokes	22
Cabbage	22
Celery	21
Eggplant	21
Tomatoes	18
Onions	16
Beets	15
Pumpkin	12
Potatoes	11

carbohydrates: the body's energy source

Carbohydrates provide us with the energy we need for body functions. There are two groups of carbohydrates, simple and complex. Simple carbohydrates, or sugars, are quickly absorbed by the body for a ready source of energy. The natural simple sugars in fruits and vegetables have an advantage over sucrose (white sugar) and other refined sugars in that they are balanced by a wide range of nutrients that aid in the utilization of the sugars. Problems with carbohydrates begin when they are refined and stripped of these nutrients. With the loss of the outer coat and bran in the refining of grains, virtually all the vitamin content has been removed from white breads and pastries, and many breakfast cereals. When high-sugar foods are eaten alone, the blood sugar level rises quickly, producing a strain on blood sugar control.

Too much of any simple sugar, including the sugars found in fruit and vegetable juices, can be harmful—especially if you are hypoglycemic, diabetic, or prone to candida infection. Since fruit juices are higher in sugars than vegetable juices, their use should be limited. Sources of refined sugar should be limited even more. Read food labels carefully for clues on sugar content. If the words *sucrose, glucose, maltose, lactose, fructose, corn syrup,* or *white grape juice concentrate* appear on the label, extra sugar has been added.

Complex carbohydrates, or starches, are composed of many sugars (polysaccharides) joined together by chemical bonds. The body breaks down complex carbohydrates into simple sugars gradually, which leads to better blood sugar control. Vegetables, legumes, and grains are excellent sources of complex carbohydrates.

fruit consumption and diabetes

There is no question that increased consumption of sugary drinks increases the risk of type 2 diabetes as well as increased body weight. But what about natural sugar from fruit or fruit juices? First, let's take a look at diabetes risk. Using data from 350,000 people in eight European countries, researchers found that every extra 12-fluid-ounce serving of sugar-sweetened drink raised the risk of diabetes by 22 percent compared with drinking just one serving a month or less.[2] However, fruit or vegetable juice consumption was not linked to diabetes incidence. These findings echo similar conclusions from research in the United States and Japan, where several studies have shown that intake of sugar-sweetened drinks is strongly linked with higher body weight and conditions like type 2 diabetes, but 100 percent pure fruit juice consumption is not.[3]

In regards to fruit consumption in patients with type 2 diabetes, the general recommendation is strict limitation to no more than 2 servings per day, but new research is challenging that advice. In fact, research shows that not only does moderate fruit consumption not adversely affect blood sugar control but it offers important health benefits to patients with type 2 diabetes.[4] Most important, fruit consumption in these patients is associated with higher antioxidant activity in the blood.

The bottom line is that you should not shy away from fruit consumption out of fear that it is going to adversely affect blood sugar control. Nonetheless, while I encourage moderate fruit or fruit juice consumption (2 to 3 servings per day), I do not recommend going above this level, especially in people with either type 1 or type 2 diabetes.

the glycemic index

Perhaps more important than labeling a sugar as a complex or simple carbohydrate is to consider the *glycemic index* and *glycemic load*. The glycemic index (GI) provides a numerical value that expresses the rise of blood glucose after eating a particular food to ingestion of 50 g of glucose, which is used as the reference standard and

table 2.3. glycemic index of some common foods

SUGARS		GRAINS	
Maltose	105	Rice, puffed	95
Glucose	100	Cornflakes	80
Honey	75	Bread, whole grain	72
Sucrose	60	Rice	70
Fructose	20	Bread, white	69
FRUITS		Wheat cereal	67
Raisins	64	Corn	59
Bananas	62	Bran cereal	51
Orange juice	46	Oatmeal	49
Oranges	40	Pasta	45
Apples	39	**LEGUMES**	
VEGETABLES		Peas	39
Potato, baked	98	Beans	31
Potato (new), boiled	70	Lentils	29
Beets	64	**OTHER FOODS**	
Carrot, cooked	36	Ice cream	36
Carrot, raw	31	Milk	34
		Nuts	13

given a value of 100. Table 2.3 provides the GI of some common foods.

While the GI is important, the major shortcoming is that it doesn't tell you how much of that carbohydrate is in a typical serving of a particular food. Another tool is needed. That is where glycemic load comes in. The glycemic load (GL) is a relatively new way to assess the impact of carbohydrate consumption that takes the GI into account but gives a fuller picture of the effect that a food has on blood sugar levels than does the GI alone. For example, let's take a look at beets—a food with a high GI but low GL. Although the carbohydrate in beets has a high GI, there isn't a lot of it, so a typical serving of cooked beet root has a GL that is relatively low (about 5). When we are judging GL, a value of 20 or more is high, 11 to 19 inclusive is medium, and 10 or less is low. Thus, eating a reasonable portion of a low-GL food has an acceptable blood sugar impact, even if the food is high in its GI. For example, a diabetic can enjoy some watermelon (GI of 72) as long as he keeps the serving size reasonable (e.g., 120 g has a GL of only 4).

In general, foods that are mostly water (e.g., apple or watermelon), fiber (e.g., beet root or carrot), or air (e.g., popcorn) will not cause a steep rise in your blood sugar even if their GI is high as long as you keep the portion sizes moderate. The same is true for juice. Typical GL scores for 6 to 8 ounces of higher sugar content juices like unsweetened apple, carrot, orange, and most fruit juices are typically in the 10 to 12 range while most vegetable juices like tomato, celery, beet, and kale would have a GL of only 4 to 5 at the highest.

using the glycemic index and glycemic load

Appendix B provides a list of the GI, fiber content, and GL of common foods. It is provided to help you construct a healthful diet. There are a few practical recommendations that go a long way in improving your health and in incorporating juicing into your diet:

1. Keep your GL below 20 for any 3-hour period. If you are diabetic or trying to lose weight, keep the value below 15.

2. When drinking juice, keep the amount of high-GL juices like apple, carrot, orange, and most fruit juices to no more than 8 ounces per 3-hour period.

3. Focus on high nutrient, low-GL fruits and vegetables to juice.

4. Use smaller amounts of higher-GL foods (most fruit and carrots) as a base to add flavor and palatability while focusing on higher nutrient, lower-GL choices.

fats and oils: important cellular components

There is very little fat in fresh fruit or vegetable juices, but the fats that are present are essential to human health. The essential fatty acids, linoleic acids, and linolenic acids provided by fruits and vegetables function in our bodies as components of nerve cells, cellular membranes, and hormonelike substances. Fats also help the body produce energy.

Animal fats are typically solid at room temperature and are referred to as saturated fats, while vegetable fats are liquid at room temperature and are referred to as unsaturated fats or oils. There is a great deal of research linking a diet high in saturated fat to numerous cancers, heart disease, and strokes. Both the American Cancer Society and the American Heart Association have recommended a diet containing less than 30 percent of calories as fat. Table 2.4 makes it clear that the easiest way for most people to achieve this goal is to eat fewer animal products and more plant foods.

vitamins: essential for life

Vitamins are essential to good health; without them key body processes would halt. Vitamin and mineral deficiencies may be preventing many people from achieving optimal health. There are 15 different known vitamins, each with its own special role to play. The vitamins are classified into two groups: fat soluble (A, D, E, and K) and water soluble (the B vitamins and vitamin C).

table 2.4. percentage of calories as fat

EGGS & DAIRY PRODUCTS	%
Butter	100
Cream, light whipping	92
Cream cheese	90
Egg yolks	80
Half-and-half	79
Cheddar cheese	71
Swiss cheese	66
Eggs, whole	65
Cow's milk	49
Yogurt, plain	49
Ice cream, regular	48
Cottage cheese	35
Lowfat (2%) milk/ yogurt	31

MEATS	%
Sirloin steak*	83
Pork sausage	83
T-bone steak*	82
Porterhouse steak*	82
Bologna	81
Spareribs	80
Frankfurters	80

	%
Lamb rib chops*	79
Salami	76
Rump roast*	71
Ham*	69
Ground beef, fairly lean	64
Veal breast*	64
Leg of lamb	61
Round steak*	61
Chicken, dark meat*	56
Chuck steak, lean only	50
Turkey, dark meat with skin	47
Chicken, light meat+	44

FRUITS	%
Grapes	11
Strawberries	11
Apples	8
Blueberries	7
Lemons	7
Pears	5
Apricots	4
Oranges	4

* Lean, with fat
+ With skin, roasted

Bananas	4	Turnip greens	11
Cantaloupe	3	Cabbage	7
Pineapple	3	Cauliflower	7
Grapefruit	2	Green beans	6
Papayas	2	Celery	6
Peaches	2	Cucumbers	6
Prunes	1	Turnips	6
VEGETABLES	**%**	Zucchini	6
Mustard greens	13	Carrots	4
Kale	13	Green peas	4
Beet greens	12	Beets	2
Lettuce	12	Potatoes	1

good fats vs. bad fats

What makes a fat "bad" or "good" has a lot to do with the function of fats in our cellular membranes. Membranes are made mostly of fatty acids. What determines the type of fatty acid present in the cell membrane is the type of fat you consume. After all, you are what you eat! A diet composed mostly of saturated fat, animal fatty acids, trans fatty acids (from margarine, shortening, and other sources of hydrogenated vegetable oils), and high in cholesterol results in membranes that are much less fluid in nature than the membranes in a person who consumes optimal levels of unsaturated fatty acids.

Modern pathology tells us that an alteration in cell membrane function is the central factor in the development of virtually every disease. For example, as it relates to diabetes, abnormal cell membrane structure owing to eating the wrong types of fats leads to impaired action of insulin.

Without a healthy membrane, cells lose their ability to hold water, nutrients, and electrolytes. They also lose their ability to communicate with other cells and be controlled by regulating hormones, including insulin. Without the right type of fats in cell membranes, cells simply do not function properly. Considerable evidence indicates that cell membrane dysfunction is a critical factor in the development of many diseases.

The type of dietary fat profile that is linked to many diseases is an abundance of saturated fat and trans fatty acids (hydrogenated vegetable oils) along with a relative insufficiency of monounsaturated and omega-3 fatty acids. On the flip side, just the opposite effect has been shown by diets high in monounsaturated fats and omega-3 fatty acids.

The traditional "Mediterranean diet" provides an optimal intake of the right types of fat and has shown tremendous benefit in fighting heart disease and cancer as well as diabetes. It has the following characteristics:

- Olive oil is the principal source of fat.
- It centers on an abundance of plant food (fruit, vegetables, breads, pasta, potatoes, beans, nuts, and seeds).
- Foods are minimally processed and there is a focus on seasonally fresh and locally grown foods.
- Fresh fruit is the typical daily dessert.
- Dairy products (principally cheese and yogurt) are consumed daily, but in low to moderate amounts.
- Fish is consumed on a regular basis.
- Poultry and eggs are consumed in moderate amounts (one to four times weekly) or not at all.
- Red meat is consumed in low amounts.
- Wine is consumed in low to moderate amounts, normally with meals.

Olive oil consists not only of the monounsaturated fatty acid, called oleic acid, but it also contains several antioxidant agents that may also account for some of the health benefits. Olive oil is particularly valued for its protection against heart disease. It lowers the harmful LDL (low-density lipoprotein) cholesterol and increases the level of protective HDL (high-density lipoprotein) cholesterol. It also helps circulating LDL cholesterol from becoming damaged.

Vitamins and enzymes work together in chemical reactions necessary for body functions, including energy production. Together they act as catalysts in speeding up the making or breaking of chemical bonds that join molecules together. For example, vitamin C functions in the manufacture of collagen, the main protein substance of the body. Specifically, vitamin C is involved in the joining of a portion of a molecule of oxygen to the amino acid proline to form hydroxyproline, a very important structural component of collagen. Since collagen is such an important protein for the structures that hold the body together (connective tissue, cartilage, tendons), vitamin C is vital for wound repair, healthy gums, and the prevention of easy bruising.

Fresh fruit and vegetable juices are rich sources of water-soluble vitamins and some fat-soluble vitamins (provitamin A carotenes and vitamin K), as juicing allows for concentration of nutrition providing key nutrients in their most natural form. Cooking destroys many of the B vitamins and vitamin C, so fresh fruit or vegetable juice is often higher in these nutrients than cooked fruits or vegetables.

While most people think of fruits as the best source of vitamin C, some vegetables also contain high levels, especially broccoli, peppers, potatoes, and Brussels sprouts (see table 2.5). For the B vitamins (except vitamin B_{12}), your best sources are grains and the green leafy vegetables, such as spinach, kale, parsley, and broccoli.

One vitamin that is often neglected is vitamin K. Vitamin K_1, the

table 2.5. vitamin c content of selected foods

Milligrams per 100 g edible portion (100 g = 3.5 ounces)

Peppers, red chili **369**	Turnips **36**
Guavas **242**	Mangoes **35**
Peppers, red sweet **190**	Asparagus **33**
Kale leaves **186**	Cantaloupe **33**
Parsley **172**	Swiss chard **32**
Collard leaves **152**	Green onions **32**
Turnip greens **139**	Liver, beef **31**
Peppers, green sweet **128**	Okra **31**
Broccoli **113**	Tangerines **31**
Brussels sprouts **102**	New Zealand spinach **30**
Mustard greens **97**	Oysters **30**
Watercress **79**	Lima beans, young **29**
Cauliflower **78**	Black-eyed peas **29**
Persimmons **66**	Soybeans **29**
Cabbage, red **61**	Green peas **27**
Strawberries **59**	Radishes **26**
Papayas **56**	Raspberries **25**
Spinach **51**	Chinese cabbage **25**
Oranges and juice **50**	Yellow summer squash **25**
Cabbage **47**	Loganberries **24**
Lemon juice **46**	Honeydew melons **23**
Grapefruit and juice **38**	Tomatoes **23**
Elderberries **36**	Liver, pork **23**
Liver, calf **36**	

form that is found in green leafy vegetables, has a major role in bone health by converting a special bone protein (osteocalcin) to its active form. Osteocalcin is the major noncollagen protein found in bone. Vitamin K is necessary for activating the osteocalcin molecule to join with the calcium and hold it in place within the bone.

A deficiency of vitamin K leads to impaired mineralization of the bone owing to inadequate osteocalcin levels. Very low blood levels of vitamin K$_1$ have been found in patients with fractures due to osteoporosis. The severity of the fracture strongly correlated with the level of circulating vitamin K. The lower the level of vitamin K, the more severe the fracture.

Vitamin K may be one of the protective factors of a vegetarian diet against osteoporosis. Green leafy vegetables (spinach, kale, mustard greens, etc.) are an excellent source of naturally occurring vitamin K.

minerals: necessary for blood, bone, and cell functions

There are 22 different minerals important in human nutrition. Minerals function, along with vitamins, as components of body enzymes. Minerals are also needed for proper composition of bone, blood, and the maintenance of normal cell function. The nutritional minerals are classified into two categories, major and minor, based upon the levels required in the diet. The major minerals include calcium, phosphorus, potassium, sodium, chloride, magnesium, and sulfur. The minor, or trace, minerals include iron, iodine, zinc, chromium, vanadium, silicon, selenium, copper, fluoride, cobalt, molybdenum, manganese, tin, boron, and nickel.

Because plants incorporate minerals from the soil into their own tissues, fruits and vegetables are excellent sources for many minerals, especially potassium (see table 2.6). The minerals as they are found in the earth are inorganic—lifeless. In plants, however, most minerals are usually bound to organic molecules. This usually means better mineral absorption. Juice is thought to provide even better mineral absorption than the intact fruit or vegetable because juicing liberates the minerals into a highly absorbable form. The green leafy vegetables are the best plant source for many of the minerals, especially calcium.

table 2.6. potassium content of selected foods

Milligrams per 100 g edible portion (100 g = 3.5 ounces)

Dulse **8,060**	Cauliflower **295**
Kelp **5,273**	Watercress **282**
Sunflower seeds **920**	Asparagus **278**
Wheat germ **827**	Red cabbage **268**
Almonds **773**	Lettuce **264**
Raisins **763**	Cantaloupe **251**
Parsley **727**	Lentils, cooked **249**
Brazil nuts **715**	Tomato **244**
Peanuts **674**	Sweet potatoes **243**
Dates **648**	Papayas **234**
Figs, dried **640**	Eggplant **214**
Avocados **604**	Green peppers **213**
Pecans **603**	Beets **208**
Yams **600**	Peaches **202**
Swiss chard **550**	Summer squash **202**
Soybeans, cooked **540**	Oranges **200**
Garlic **529**	Raspberries **199**
Spinach **470**	Cherries **191**
English walnuts **450**	Strawberries **164**
Millet **430**	Grapefruit juice **162**
Beans, cooked **416**	Cucumbers **160**
Mushrooms **414**	Grapes **158**
Potato with skin **407**	Onions **157**
Broccoli **382**	Pineapple **146**
Kale **378**	Milk, whole **144**
Bananas **370**	Lemon juice **141**
Meats **370**	Pears **130**
Winter squash **369**	Eggs **129**
Chicken **366**	Apples **110**
Carrots **341**	Watermelon **100**
Celery **341**	Brown rice, cooked **70**
Radishes **322**	

It has already been mentioned that vegetarians are at a lower risk for osteoporosis. In addition to vitamin K_1, the high levels of many minerals found in plant foods, particularly vegetables, may also be responsible for this protective effect. A trace mineral gaining recent attention as a protective factor against osteoporosis is boron. Boron has been shown to have a positive effect on calcium and active estrogen levels in postmenopausal women, the group at highest risk for developing osteoporosis. In one study, supplementing the diet of postmenopausal women with 3 mg boron a day reduced urinary calcium excretion by 44 percent and dramatically increased the levels of 17-beta-estradiol, the most biologically active estrogen.[5] It appears boron is required to activate certain hormones, including estrogen and vitamin D. Since fruits and vegetables are the main dietary sources of boron, diets low in these foods may be deficient in boron. The high boron content of a vegetarian diet may be another protective factor against osteoporosis.

potassium: key to blood pressure maintenance

One of the primary nutritional benefits of fresh fruit and vegetable juice is that it is very rich in potassium and very low in sodium. The balance of sodium and potassium is extremely important to human health: Too much sodium in the diet can lead to disruption of this balance. Numerous studies have demonstrated that a low-potassium, high-sodium diet plays a major role in the development of cancer and cardiovascular disease (heart disease, high blood pressure, strokes).[6] Conversely, a diet high in potassium and low in sodium is protective against these diseases, and in the case of high blood pressure it can be therapeutic.[7] Sodium restriction alone does not improve blood pressure control in most people—it must be accompanied by a high potassium intake.

Most Americans have a potassium-to-sodium (K:Na) ratio of less than 1:2. This means most people ingest twice as much sodium as potassium. Researchers recommend a dietary potassium-to-sodium ratio of greater than 5:1 to maintain health, which is ten times higher than the average intake. A natural diet rich in fruits and vegetables can produce a K:Na ratio greater than 100:1, as most fruits and vegetables have a K:Na ratio of at least 50:1. For example, here are the average K:Na ratios for several common fresh fruits and vegetables:

Bananas 440:1
Oranges 260:1
Potatoes 110:1
Apples 90:1
Carrots 75:1

functions of potassium

Potassium is one of the electrolytes—mineral salts that can conduct electricity when they are dissolved in water. Electrolytes are always found in pairs; a positive molecule like sodium or potassium is always accompanied by a negative molecule like chloride. Potassium, as a major electrolyte, functions in the maintenance of:

Water balance and distribution
Acid-base balance
Muscle and nerve cell function
Heart function
Kidney and adrenal function

More than 95 percent of the potassium in the body is found within cells. In contrast, most of the sodium in the body is located outside the cells in the blood and other fluids. How does this happen? Cells actually pump sodium out and potassium in via the *sodium-potassium pump* found in the membranes of all cells in the body. One of its most important functions is preventing the swelling of cells. If sodium is not pumped out, water accumulates within the cell, causing the cell to swell and ultimately burst.

The sodium-potassium pump also functions to maintain the electrical charge within the cell, which is particularly important to muscle and nerve cells. During nerve transmission and muscle contraction, potassium exits the cell and sodium enters, resulting in a change in electrical charge. This change is what causes a nerve impulse or muscle contraction. It is not surprising that a potassium deficiency affects muscles and nerves first.

Potassium is also essential for the conversion of blood sugar into glycogen, the storage form of blood sugar found in the muscles and liver. A potassium shortage results in lower levels of stored glycogen. Because glycogen is used by exercising muscles for energy, a potassium deficiency will produce great fatigue and muscle weakness. These are typically the first signs of potassium deficiency.

potassium deficiency

A potassium deficiency is characterized by mental confusion, irritability, weakness, heart disturbances, and problems in nerve conduction and muscle contraction. Dietary potassium deficiency is typically caused by a diet low in fresh fruits and vegetables but high in sodium. It is more common to see dietary potassium deficiency in the elderly. Dietary potassium deficiency is less common than deficiency due to excessive fluid loss (sweating, diarrhea, or urination) or the use of diuretics, laxatives, aspirin, and other drugs.

The amount of potassium lost in sweat can be quite significant, especially if the exercise is prolonged in a warm environment. Athletes or people who exercise regularly have higher potassium needs.

how much potassium do we need?

The estimated safe and adequate daily dietary intake of potassium, as set by the Committee on Recommended Daily Allowances, is 1.9 to 5.6 g. If body potassium requirements are not being met through diet, supplementation is essential to good health. This is particularly true for the elderly and the athlete. Potassium salts are commonly prescribed by physicians in the dosage range of 1.5 to 3 g a day. However, potassium salts can cause nausea, vomiting, diarrhea, and ulcers. These effects are not seen when potassium levels are increased through the diet only, highlighting the advantages of using juices, foods, or food-based potassium supplements to meet the body's high potassium requirements. Most fruit and vegetable juices contain approximately 400 mg potassium per 8 ounces.

Can one take too much potassium? Of course, but most people can handle any excess. The exception is people with kidney disease or those taking certain drugs. They do not handle potassium properly and are likely to experience heart disturbances and other consequences of potassium toxicity. Individuals with kidney disorders usually need to restrict their potassium intake and follow the dietary recommendations of their physicians. People taking the following drugs also have to be careful of too much potassium: amiloride, triamterene, and the ace-inhibitor drugs for high blood pressure (Captopril, Lisinopril, etc.).

summary

Fresh fruit and vegetable juices provide excellent nutrition in an easily absorbed form. They are rich in many vital nutrients, including pure water. Fresh juices are also nutrient dense in that they provide a high amount of quality nutrition per calorie. Proteins, carbohydrates, vitamins, and minerals are all found in natural forms in fresh juice. One of the key minerals provided by fresh juice is potassium, which is vital for many body functions and is especially important for heart, nerve, and muscle tissue.

3

what's in juice?

the phytochemicals

Fresh juice contains a range of substances often collectively referred to as phytochemicals: enzymes; pigments like carotenes, chlorophyll, and flavonoids; and a long list of other compounds often referred to as accessory food components. Nutrients are classically defined as substances that either provide nourishment or are necessary for body functions or structures.

In the past, phytochemicals were often referred to as *anutrients*. The placement of the prefix *a-* in front of nutrients was used to signify that these compounds were without nutritional benefit. While not technically nutrients, these substances have profound health benefits; in fact, anutrients are responsible for many of the known health benefits of fruits and vegetables. So the term *anutrient* is really a misnomer.

The key point is the "essential nutrients" are not the only important components of food in our diet. In fact, the phytochemicals may be even more effective in promoting health and protecting against diseases like heart disease and cancer. One of the American Cancer Society's key dietary recommendations for reducing the risk of cancer is to include cruciferous vegetables such as cabbage, broccoli, Brussels sprouts, and cauliflower in the diet. These foods have been shown to exert a protective effect against many types of cancer that is beyond the protective effect of their known nutrient content. In other words, their anticancer effects have little to do with their nutritional value in terms of vitamins and minerals. The anticancer compounds in cabbage-family vegetables include phenols, indoles, isothiocyanates, and various sulfur-containing compounds. These compounds exhibit no real nutritional activity and are therefore examples of anutrients. However, these cabbage-family compounds stimulate the body to detoxify and eliminate cancer-causing chemicals—a very profound and powerful weapon in the war against cancer.

Every year, scientists discover additional phytochemicals that produce remarkable health-promoting effects (see table 3.1 for example). These discoveries emphasize the importance of not relying on vitamin and mineral supplements for your nutritional needs that could otherwise be met with a healthful diet. Supplements are designed as additions to a healthful diet—that is why they are called supplements. A healthful diet must include not only adequate levels of known nutrients but also large quantities of fresh fruits and vegetables for their high content of unknown and known anutrients, phytochemicals, and accessory healing components.

table 3.1. health benefits of selected phytochemicals

PHYTOCHEMICAL	HEALTH BENEFITS	FOOD SOURCES
Allium compounds	Lower cholesterol levels, antitumor properties	Garlic and onions
Carotenes	Antioxidant, enhance immune system, anticancer properties	Dark-colored vegetables such as carrots, squash, spinach, kale, parsley; also cantaloupe, apricots, and citrus fruits
Coumarins	Antitumor properties, immune enhancement, stimulate antioxidant mechanisms	Carrots, celery, fennel, beets, citrus fruits
Dithiolthiones	Block the reaction of cancer-causing compounds within our cells	Cabbage-family vegetables
Flavonoids	Antioxidant, antiviral, and anti-inflammatory properties	Fruits, particularly darker fruits like cherries, blueberries; also vegetables, including tomatoes, peppers, and broccoli
Glucosinolates and indoles	Stimulate enzymes that detoxify cancer-causing compounds	Cabbage, Brussels sprouts, kale, radishes, mustard greens
Isothiocyanates and thiocyanates	Inhibit damage to genetic material (DNA)	Cabbage-family vegetables
Limonoids	Protect against cancer	Citrus fruits
Phthalides	Stimulate detoxification enzymes	Parsley, carrots, celery
Sterols	Block the production of cancer-causing compounds	Cucumbers, squash, cabbage-family vegetables

enzymes: necessary for life

One of the key reasons that fresh juice is referred to as a live food is because it contains active enzymes. As mentioned in chapter 2, enzymes are composed of vitamins and minerals. Their job is to speed up chemical reactions. Without enzymes, there would be no life in our cells. Enzymes are far more prevalent in raw foods such as fresh juice because they are extremely sensitive to heat and are destroyed during cooking and pasteurization.

There are two major types of enzymes: synthetases and hydrolases. The synthetases help build body structures by making or synthesizing larger molecules. The synthetases are also referred to as *metabolic enzymes*. The hydrolases or digestive enzymes work to break down large molecules into smaller more readily digestible ones by adding water to the larger molecule. This process is known as hydrolysis.

Digestion is the body process that utilizes the greatest level of energy. That is why one of the key energy-enhancing benefits of fresh juice is its highly digestible form. When we eat, our body works very hard at separating out the juice from the fiber in our food. (Remember, it is the juice that nourishes our cells.) The juice extractor does this for the body, but that is not the only benefit to digestion with fresh juice. Fresh juice and other live foods contain digestive enzymes that help break down the foods in the digestive tract, thereby sparing the body's valuable digestive enzymes.

This sparing action is referred to as the *law of adaptive secretion of digestive enzymes*.[1] That means if some of the food is digested by the enzymes contained in the food, the body will secrete fewer of its own enzymes. This allows vital energy in the body to be shifted from digestion to other body functions, such as repair and rejuvenation. Fresh juices require very little energy to digest, taking as few as 5 minutes to begin to be absorbed. In contrast, a big meal of steak and potatoes may sit in the stomach for hours. If a meal is composed entirely from cooked (no-enzyme) foods, most of the body's energy is directed at digestion. What happened to your energy levels after your last large meal of cooked foods? If you are like most people, your energy levels fell dramatically. What would your life be like if you directed less energy toward digestion and more energy to other body functions? It would be a life full of increased energy.

For maximum energy levels, it is often recommended that 50 to 75 percent of your diet (by volume) come from raw fruits, vegetables, nuts, and seeds. Juicing ensures that you can reach this percentage.

enzymes and human health

Perhaps the best example of the beneficial effects of plant enzymes is offered by bromelain, the enzyme found in the pineapple plant. Bromelain was introduced as a medicinal agent in 1957, and since that time over 200 scientific papers on its therapeutic applications have appeared in the medical literature.[2]

Bromelain has been reported in these scientific studies to exert a wide variety of beneficial effects, including:

- Assisting digestion
- Reducing inflammation in cases of arthritis, sports injury, or trauma
- Preventing swelling (edema) after trauma or surgery
- Inhibiting blood platelet aggregation; enhancing antibiotic absorption
- Relieving sinusitis
- Inhibiting appetite
- Enhancing wound healing

Although most studies have utilized commercially prepared bromelain, it is conceivable that drinking fresh pineapple juice exerts similar, if not superior, benefits. One question that often comes up when talking about enzymes like bromelain is whether the body actually absorbs enzymes in their active form. There is evidence that in both animals and humans up to 40 percent of bromelain consumed orally is absorbed intact.[3] This suggests that other plant enzymes may also be absorbed intact and exert beneficial effects.

carotenes

Carotenes or carotenoids represent the most widespread group of naturally occurring pigments in nature. They are a highly colored (red to yellow) group of fat-soluble compounds that function in plants to protect against damage produced during photosynthesis.[4] Carotenes are best known for their capacity for conversion into vitamin A, their antioxidant activity, and their correlation with the maximum life-span potential of humans, other primates, and mammals.

Over 400 carotenes have been characterized, but only 30 to 50 are believed to have vitamin A activity. These are referred to as *provitamin A carotenes*. The biological effects of carotenes have historically been based on their corresponding vitamin A activity. Beta-carotene was long thought of as the most active of the carotenes, because it has a higher provitamin A activity than other carotenes. However, considerable research shows that these vitamin A activities have been overblown, as there are other, non–vitamin A carotenes that exhibit far greater antioxidant and anticancer activities such as lutein, lycopene, and astaxanthin.[5] See table 3.2 for common carotenes, their vitamin A activity, and food sources.

The conversion of a provitamin A carotene into vitamin A depends on several factors: the level of vitamin A in the body, protein status, and adequate levels of thyroid hormones, zinc, and vitamin C. The conversion diminishes as carotene intake increases and when serum vitamin A levels are adequate; if vitamin A levels are sufficient, the carotene is not converted to vitamin A. Instead, it is delivered to body tissues for storage.

Unlike vitamin A, which is stored primarily in the liver,

table 3.2. carotenes, vitamin a activity, and food sources

CAROTENE	VITAMIN A ACTIVITY (%)	*FOOD SOURCES*
Beta-carotene	100	Green plants, carrots, sweet potatoes, squash, spinach, apricots, green peppers
Cryptoxanthin	50–60	Corn, green peppers, persimmons, papayas, lemons, oranges, prunes, apples, apricots, paprika, poultry
Alpha-carotene	50–54	Green plants, carrots, squash, corn, watermelons, green peppers, potatoes, apples, peaches
Gamma-carotene	42–50	Carrots, sweet potatoes, corn, tomatoes, watermelons, apricots
Beta-zeacarotene	20–40	Corn, tomatoes, yeast, cherries
Canthaxanthin	0	Mushrooms, trout, crustaceans
Capsanthin	0	Red peppers, paprika
Crocetin	0	Saffron
Lutein	0	Green plants, corn, potatoes, spinach, carrots, tomatoes, fruits
Lycopene	0	Tomatoes, carrots, green peppers, apricots, pink grapefruit
Zeaxanthin	0	Spinach, paprika, corn, fruits

unconverted carotenes are stored in fat cells, epithelial cells, and other organs (the adrenals, testes, and ovaries have the highest concentrations). Epithelial cells are found in the skin and the linings of the internal organs (including the respiratory tract, gastrointestinal tract, and genitourinary tract). A considerable number of population studies have demonstrated a strong correlation between carotene intake and a variety of cancers involving epithelial tissues (such as lung, skin, cervix, gastrointestinal tract). The higher the carotene intake, the lower the risk for cancer.

Cancer and aging share a number of common characteristics, including an association with oxidative damage, which has led to the idea that cancer prevention should also promote longevity. Likewise, foods and food compounds that protect against cancer also promote longevity. There is some evidence to support this claim, since it appears that tissue carotene content has a better correlation with maximal life-span potential (MLSP) of mammals, including humans, than any other factor that has been studied.[6] For example, the human MLSP of approximately 120 years correlates with serum carotene levels of 50 to 300 mcg/dl (micrograms per deciliter of blood), while other primates such as the rhesus monkey have an MLSP of approximately 34 years, correlating with serum carotene levels of 6 to 12 mcg/dl.

Since tissue carotenoids appear to be the most significant factor in determining a species' MLSP, a logical conclusion is that individuals within the species with higher carotene levels in their tissues would be the longest-lived. Tissue carotene contents can best be increased by eating and juicing a diet high in mixed carotenes.

The best sources of carotenes are dark green leafy vegetables (kale, collards, and spinach), and yellow-orange fruits and vegetables (apricots, cantaloupe, carrots, sweet potatoes, yams, and squash). See table 3.3 for carotene levels of raw fruits and vegetables. The carotenes present in green plants are found in the chloroplasts with chlorophyll, usually in complexes with a protein or lipid. Beta-carotene is the predominant form in most green leaves; the greater the intensity of the green, the greater the concentration of beta-carotene.

Orange fruits and vegetables (carrots, apricots, mangoes, yams, squash) typically have higher concentrations of provitamin A carotenes. Again, the provitamin A content parallels the intensity of the color.

In the orange and yellow fruits and vegetables, beta-carotene concentrations are high, but other carotenes are present as well, including many with more potent antioxidant and anticancer effects than beta-carotene. The red and purple vegetables and fruits (such as tomatoes, red cabbage, berries, and plums) contain a large portion of non–vitamin A active pigments, including flavonoids and carotenes. Legumes, grains, and seeds are also significant sources of carotenes.

table 3.3. carotene levels of raw fruits and vegetables

Approximate total carotene, micrograms per 100 g edible portion (100 g = 3.5 ounces)

Kale **75,000**	Apricots **3,500**
Spinach **37,000**	Peaches **2,700**
Collard greens **20,000**	Oranges **2,400–2,700**
Butternut squash **17,700**	Melons **2,100–6,200**
Carrots **11,100**	Yellow squash **1,400**
Beet greens **10,000**	Papayas **1,100–3,000**
Tomatoes **7,200**	Green bell pepper **900–1,100**
Brussels sprouts **7,000**	Zucchini **900**
Apples, unpeeled **5,500–12,600**	Blackberries **600**
Broccoli **5,200**	Grapes **200**
Acorn squash **3,900**	Apples, peeled **100–500**

Juicing provides greater benefit than beta-carotene supplements or intact carotene-rich foods because juicing ruptures cell membranes, thereby liberating important nutritional compounds like carotenes that can be locked within the plant's cell walls. Beta-carotene supplementation, though beneficial, provides only one particular type of carotene, whereas juicing a wide variety of carotene-rich foods will provide a broad range of carotenes, many of which have properties more advantageous than those of beta-carotene.

For example, lutein is a yellow-orange carotene that appears to offer significant protection against macular degeneration[7] while lycopene, a red carotene found in tomatoes, watermelon, and other red fruits and vegetables, has received attention for protecting against heart disease and the major cancers (i.e., breast, colon, lung, skin, and prostate cancer).[8] In one of the more detailed studies with lycopene, Harvard researchers discovered that men who consumed the highest levels of lycopene (6.5 mg per day) in their diet showed a 21 percent decreased risk of prostate cancer compared with those eating the lowest levels.[9] Men who ate two or more servings of tomato sauce each week were 23 percent less likely to develop prostate cancer during the 22 years of the study than were men who ate less than one serving of tomato sauce each month. Lycopene consumption has also been shown to lower the risk of heart disease, cataracts, and macular degeneration.

You cannot consume too much carotene. Studies done with beta-carotene have not shown it to possess any significant toxicity, even when used in very high doses in the treatment of numerous medical conditions.[10] However, increased carotene consumption can result in the appearance of slightly yellow- to orange-colored skin, because of the storage of carotenes in epithelial cells. This is known as carotenodermia and is probably a beneficial sign, simply indicating that the body has a good supply of carotenes.

juice, food, or pills?

Increasing your levels of lycopene, lutein, and zeaxanthin levels can play a central role in protecting against the development of macular degeneration. Although lycopene and lutein supplements are entering the marketplace, they are relatively expensive, especially when you compare them to food sources.

LYCOPENE SOURCE	TOTAL MILLIGRAMS OF LYCOPENE	COST
1 ounce tomato paste	16	$0.065
Lycopene supplement (one 15 mg capsule)	15	$0.44
1 (12-ounce) can tomato paste	192	$0.69
Lycopene supplement (one bottle of 60 capsules, each containing 15 mg)	900	$26.99

In short, it looks like the most economical and healthiest way to boost lycopene, lutein, and zeaxanthin levels is through diet. The top 20 foods rich in these important carotenes are as follows:

Apple
Bell peppers (red, orange, green, yellow)
Broccoli
Brussels sprouts
Celery
Corn
Cucumber
Green beans
Green grapes
Greens (spinach, kale, chard)
Honeydew melon
Kiwifruit
Mango
Orange
Peach
Peas
Red grapes
Scallions
Squash (zucchini, pumpkin, butternut, etc.)
Tomato paste or juice

flavonoids: nature's biological response modifiers

Flavonoids are plant pigments that exert antioxidant activity that is generally more potent and effective against a broader range of oxidants than the traditional antioxidant nutrients vitamins C and E, beta-carotene, selenium, and zinc. Flavonoids lend color to fruits and flowers, and are responsible for many of the medicinal properties of foods, juices, herbs, and bee pollen. More than 8,000 flavonoid compounds have been characterized and classified according to their chemical structure. Flavonoids are sometimes called "nature's

types of flavonoids

- The anthocyanidins and PCOs (short for proanthocyanidin oligomers) are the blue or purple pigments found in grapes, blueberries, and other foods. They can also be extracted from pine bark. These substances help prevent destruction of collagen, an important protein for healthy skin and connective tissue. Extracts of grape seeds and pine bark are popular supplements that provide PCOs.

- Quercetin is found in many foods. One of the best dietary sources is onions. Quercetin is often used in the treatment of allergies.

- Citrus bioflavonoids are found in fruits such as oranges, limes, lemons, and grapefruit. They appear to improve blood circulation and increase the integrity of tiny blood vessels (capillaries). Citrus bioflavonoids are often included in vitamin C supplements because they enhance the activity of vitamin C.

- Polyphenols are complex flavonoids contained in such foods as green tea, red wine, and even chocolate. They protect against heart disease and various cancers, especially in the gastrointestinal tract. They work by blocking the formation of cancer-causing chemicals such as nitrosamines.

biological response modifiers" because of their anti-inflammatory, antiallergic, antiviral, and anticancer properties.[11]

Flavonoids are sometimes considered "semi-essential" nutrients, but in my view they are as important to human nutrition as the so-called essential nutrients. Because they have a broader range of antioxidant activity as well as other important anticancer effects, include as many different types of flavonoids as possible in your diet.

Recent research suggests that flavonoids may be useful in the prevention and treatment of a very long list of health conditions, including cardiovascular disease, cancer, and allergies. In fact, many of the medicinal actions of foods, juices, herbs, and bee products (such as pollens and propolis) are now known to be directly related to their flavonoid content. Different flavonoids will provide different benefits. For example, the flavonoids responsible for the red to blue colors of blueberries, blackberries, cherries, grapes, hawthorn berries, and many flowers are termed anthocyanidins and proanthocyanidins. These flavonoids are found in the flesh of the fruit as well as the skin and possess very strong "vitamin P" activity. Among their effects is an ability to increase vitamin C levels within our cells, decrease the leakiness and breakage of small blood vessels, protect against free radical damage, and support our joint structures.

Flavonoids also have a very beneficial effect on collagen. Collagen is the most abundant protein of the body. It is responsible for maintaining the integrity of the ground substance responsible for holding together the tissues of the body. Collagen is also found in tendons, ligaments, and cartilage. Collagen is destroyed during inflammatory processes that occur in rheumatoid arthritis, periodontal disease, gout, and other inflammatory conditions involving bones, joints, cartilage, and other connective tissue. Anthocyanidins and other flavonoids affect collagen metabolism in many ways:

- **They have the unique ability to actually cross-link collagen fibers resulting in reinforcement of the natural cross-linking of collagen**

table 3.4. flavonoid content of selected foods

Milligrams per 100 g edible portion (100 g = 3.5 ounces)

FOODS	4-OXO-FLAVONOIDS*	ANTHOCYANINS	CATECHINS⁺	BIFLAVANS
FRUITS				
Apples	3–16	1–2	20–75	50–90
Apple juice				15
Apricots	10–18		25	
Blueberries		130–250	10–20	
Cherries, sour		45		25
Cherries, sweet			6–7	15
Cranberries	5	60–200	20	100
Currants, black	20–400	130–400	15	50
Currant juice		75–100		
Grapes, red		65–140	5–30	50
Grapefruit	50			
Grapefruit juice	20			
Hawthorn berries			200–800	
Oranges, Valencia	50–100			
Orange juice	20–40			

Peaches		1–12	10–20	90–120
Pears	1–5		5–20	1–3
Plums, blue		10–25	200	
Plums, yellow		2–10		
Raspberries, black		300–400		
Raspberries, red		30–35		
Strawberries	20–100	15–35	30–40	
Tomatoes	85–130			
VEGETABLES				
Cabbage, red		25		
Onions	100–2,000	0–25		
Parsley	1,400			
Rhubarb		200		
MISCELLANEOUS				
Beans, dry		10–1,000		
Chocolate, dark semisweet				170
Sage	1,000–1,500			
Tea	5–50		10–500	100–200
Wine, red	2–4	50–120	100–150	100–250

* 4-Oxo-flavonoids: the sum of flavanones, flavones, and flavanols (including quercetin).
+ Catechins include proanthocyanins.

that forms the so-called collagen matrix of connective tissue (ground substance, cartilage, tendon, etc.).
- They prevent free-radical damage with their potent antioxidant and free-radical scavenging action.
- They inhibit destruction to collagen structures by enzymes secreted by our own white blood cells during inflammation.
- They prevent the release and synthesis of compounds that promote inflammation, such as histamine.

Flavonoid components of berries are extremely beneficial in cases of arthritis and hardening of the arteries. Foods rich in anthocyanidins and proanthocyanidins appear to offer significant prevention as well as a potential reversal of the often lethal atherosclerotic processes.

Several studies have shown that people who have a high intake of plant flavonoids are less likely to die from heart disease or develop some cancers or other chronic diseases. In one of the largest studies, when researchers looked at the diets of nearly 100,000 men and women, they found that those who ate fruits and vegetables rich in different flavonoids had a lower risk of overall mortality owing to heart attack and strokes.[12] Other studies have shown a lower risk for other chronic diseases including lung and prostate cancer, type 2 diabetes, and asthma. See table 3.4 for the flavonoid content of common foods.

Still other flavonoids are remarkable anti-allergic compounds, modifying and reducing all phases of the allergic response by inhibiting the formation and secretion of potent inflammatory compounds. Several prescription medications developed for allergic conditions (asthma, eczema, hives, etc.) were actually patterned after flavonoid molecules. An example of an anti-allergy flavonoid is quercetin, which is available in many fruits and vegetables. Quercetin is a potent antioxidant that inhibits the release of histamine and other allergic compounds.

chlorophyll: nature's cleansing agent

Chlorophyll is the green pigment of plants found in the chloroplast compartment of plant cells. It is in the chloroplast that electromagnetic energy (light) is converted to chemical energy in the process known as photosynthesis. The chlorophyll molecule is essential for this reaction to occur.

The natural chlorophyll in green plants and their fresh juice is fat soluble. Most of the chlorophyll products found in health food stores, however, contain water-soluble chlorophyll. Because water-soluble chlorophyll is not absorbed from the gastrointestinal tract, its use is limited to ulcerative conditions of the skin and gastrointestinal tract.[13] Its beneficial effect is largely due to its astringent qualities, coupled with an ability to stimulate wound healing. These healing properties have also been noted with the topical administration of water-soluble chlorophyll in the treatment of skin wounds. Water-soluble chlorophyll is also used medically to help control body, fecal, and urinary odor.[14]

To produce a water-soluble chlorophyll, the natural chlorophyll molecule must be altered chemically. The fat-soluble form, the natural form of chlorophyll as found in fresh juice, offers several advantages over water-soluble chlorophyll. This is particularly true regarding chlorophyll's ability to stimulate hemoglobin and the production of red blood cells and to relieve excessive menstrual blood flow.[15] In fact, the chlorophyll molecule is very similar to the heme portion of the hemoglobin molecule of our red blood cells.

Unlike water-soluble chlorophyll, fat-soluble chlorophyll is absorbed well by the rest of the body and contains other components of the chloroplast complex (including beta-carotene and vitamin K_1) that possess significant health benefits not provided by water-soluble chlorophyll.

Like the other plant pigments, chlorophyll also possesses significant antioxidant and anticancer effects.[16] It has been suggested by some public health experts that chlorophyll be added to certain beverages, foods, chewing tobacco, and tobacco snuff to reduce cancer risk. A better recommendation would be to include fresh green vegetable juices regularly in the diet. Greens such as parsley, spinach, kale, and beet tops are rich not only in chlorophyll but also in minerals like calcium and carotenes. Parsley or some other green should be consumed whenever fried, roasted, or grilled foods are eaten, as parsley has been shown to reduce the cancer-causing risk of fried foods in human studies.[17] Presumably other greens would offer similar protection.

terpenes

The term *terpene* probably conjures up images of cleaning solvents, but while naturally occurring terpenes are used as an alternative to synthetic terpenes in many natural cleaning products, the primary health benefits of terpenes revolve around some impressive anticancer effects—both in prevention and possibly treatment.

D-limonene and perillyl alcohol are the most widely tested terpenes, having shown considerable benefits in animal studies against a wide number of cancers. Both of these terpenes are being investigated in humans with advanced cancers with encouraging preliminary results. For example, six individuals with advanced cancers were able to halt the progression of their cancer for periods of time ranging from 6 to 12 months while taking d-limonene.[18]

The best dietary sources of terpenes are citrus fruits, berries, cherries, and volatile herbs such as peppermint, basil, thyme, and rosemary. Citrus peels, especially lemons, are a particularly rich source of the beneficial terpene d-limonene so be sure to juice lemons with their peels.

summary

Fresh juice contains a wide range of substances once collectively referred to as anutrients but now most often simply called phytochemicals. Included in this category are enzymes; pigments like carotenes, chlorophyll, and flavonoids; and accessory food components. Although these substances possess little or no real "nutritional" value, they do exert profound health benefits.

Increasingly, experts are realizing that it is not just the essential nutrients that are significant. A healthful diet must include not only adequate levels of known nutrients but also large quantities of fresh fruits and vegetables for their high content of unknown and known anutrients, phytochemicals, and accessory healing components. Drinking fresh fruit and vegetable juice is a phenomenal way to increase your intake of these healing agents.

4

how to juice: getting started

To reap the rewards of juicing, you obviously need to choose a juicer from the wide variety available. Before discussing some of the features of juicers, it is important to differentiate a juicer from a blender.

A juicer separates the liquid from the pulp. Remember, fiber is very important, but it is the juice that nourishes our cells. It is the juice that we absorb. A blender is designed to liquefy all that is placed in it by chopping it up at high speeds. It may liquefy, but the nutrients are still not liberated. That said, a blender can be quite useful in conjunction with a juicer to create delicious smoothies.

Juicers were once found only in health food stores; now they are everywhere. Most department stores usually offer only a selection of low-power juicers; however, if you are serious about your health, get a serious juicer.

different types of juice extractors

Juice extractors use rapidly whirling blades or disks to cut fruit or vegetables into tiny pieces that are then spun to separate juice from pulp. Most can juice a variety of fruits and vegetables, including the skins, seeds, and stems of many fruits and vegetables. Some can even make sorbet, pâté, and nut butters. There are three main types of juice extractors currently on the marketplace, each with pros and cons:

- **Centrifugal juicers**
- **Masticating juicers**
- **Triturating juicers**

centrifugal juicers

Centrifugal juicers are typically the least expensive type of juice extractors and the most popular. When you push the produce through the feeding tube, it comes in contact with the bottom of the spinning basket where it is grated up into very fine pieces or pulp. Then, through centrifugal force, the tiny grated pieces are thrown against the sides of the basket to allow the juice to be extracted. Depending on the design, the pulp will either be expelled or contained within the inside of the unit.

Centrifugal juicers are easy to use and affordable (typically $40 to $200). However, because the extractor is spinning at a pretty high revolution per minute (RPM), the juice can get foamy and thus it oxidizes rapidly. When the juice oxidizes, it can taste bitter and may lose some of the phytochemicals because of the heat generated in the process. The units may also be difficult to clean.

masticating juicers

Masticating juicers (also known as single gear juicers) don't use centrifugal force. Instead, the food item is fed through a tube and comes into contact with an auger (a shaft with blades) that grinds up, or "masticates," the fruit or vegetable into a pulp just like when we chew our food. The pulp is squeezed up against a mesh strainer so the juice is extracted while the pulp gets ejected. Masticating juicers are more efficient than centrifugal juicers, yielding more juice from the same amount of raw food. They also run at a much lower rpm, especially slow juicers (see below), so the foam and oxidation is decreased. Most models do well with a variety of fruits and vegetables and some can even make sorbets, nut butters, pâtés, baby food, and

what is a slow juicer?

Slow juicers are masticating juicers that operate at only 80 rpm instead of the 1,000–24,000 rpm that a typical centrifugal high-speed juicer spins. The Hurom juicer is the lead machine in this category and the holder of unique patented technology. It is the juicer I currently own. A slow juicer is a little different than a typical masticating juicer as it uses the screwlike auger as a mortar and pestle to both crush and press the juice out of the fruit or vegetable. A slow juicer typically expels significantly more juice from the same foods, with much drier pulp. The key benefit of a slow juicer is the fact that the slow rpm preserves the precious enzymes, nutrients, and phytochemicals because there is no heat and less friction or damage during the juicing process. At higher rpm these compounds are more likely to become damaged and as a result taste a little bitter. A slow juicer generally produces better-tasting and higher-quality juice. That is the chief reason why I use it.

more. They are also durable but have smaller feeding tubes requiring smaller pieces of fruits and vegetables to be pushed through. On the downside, they are a significant piece of machinery so they tend to be heavy and clunky, and expensive (from $1,500 to $3,000).

triturating juicers

Triturating juicers are twin-gear juicers; the two interlocking gears grind up raw food. They are the most efficient juicers and run at the lowest rpm, so the effects of foam and oxidation are very low. They can also juice wheatgrass and leafy greens more efficiently than other models. Like masticating juicers, they can also be used to create sorbet, pâté, baby food, and more. Unfortunately, they are expensive ($300 to $900), and slower (it takes more time to juice the same amount of produce compared to centrifugal or masticating juicers). Cleanup is more involved as well, as these juicers are typically more cumbersome to take apart and put back together.

overall recommendations

There are great juicers within each category that would satisfy the classification of a good juice extractor. So it is difficult to give you a strong recommendation of one type over another. That said, here are some general guidelines:

- If you are only going to use a juicer occasionally or have no interest in nut butters, sorbets, or other uses, then definitely go with a centrifugal juicer. Just be sure to get a higher-quality version. There is a big difference between the higher-end models and the lower-end models. The small appliance maker Breville currently dominates the centrifugal juicer category and offers products at different price points. Their Juice Fountain Duo and Elite are by far the most popular.
- A masticating juicer, especially a slow juicer, is a great choice if you plan to juice frequently and want more than a juicer at a great price that will likely last you a lifetime. They are

a great combination of ease of use and a higher quality of juice.

- A triturating juicer is ideal for people who adopt a "raw" lifestyle, want greater functionality, and plan on regular juicing. It's expensive but generally worth the investment if you plan on making fresh wheatgrass juice on a frequent basis.

Although "how to juice" may seem pretty obvious, take the time to read through the manual or watch the instructional video if that is included with your juicer. Guidelines for individual fruits and vegetables will be discussed in chapters 5 and 6.

buy local organic produce

I strongly urge you to buy organic and local fruits and vegetables. The only way we are going to see significant reduction in pesticide and herbicide use is to stop buying foods that are sprayed. In the United States, the EPA estimates that more than 1.2 billion pounds of pesticides and herbicides are sprayed or added to food crops each year. That's roughly 5 pounds of pesticides for each man, woman, and child. There is a growing concern that in addition to these pesticides directly causing a significant number of cancers, exposure to these chemicals damages your body's detoxification mechanisms, thereby increasing your risk of getting cancer and other diseases.

We are all exposed to pesticides and other toxins in the air that we breathe, the environment, and the food that we eat. To illustrate just how problematic pesticides can be, let's take a quick look at the health problems of the farmer. The lifestyle of farmers is generally healthful: Compared to city dwellers, they have access to lots of fresh food; they breathe clean air, engage in extensive physical activity, and have a lower rate of cigarette smoking and alcohol use. Yet studies show that farmers have a higher risk of developing lymphomas, leukemias, and cancers of the stomach, prostate, brain, and skin.[1]

Perhaps the most problematic pesticides are the halogenated hydrocarbon family—DDE (dichlorodiphenyltrichloroethylene), PCB, PCP (pentachlorophenol), dieldrin, and chlordane. These chemicals persist almost indefinitely in the environment similar to DDT (dichlorodiphenyltrichloroethane), a pesticide that has been banned since 1972. DDT can still be found in the soil and root vegetables such as carrots and potatoes. Like the environment, our bodies also have a tough time detoxifying and eliminating these compounds. Instead, they end up being stored in our fat cells. What's more, inside the body these chemicals can act like the hormone estrogen and are thus suspected as a major cause of the growing epidemic of estrogen-related health problems, including breast cancer. Strong evidence also suggests that these chemicals increase the risk of lymphomas, leukemia, and pancreatic cancer, as well as play a role in low sperm counts and reduced fertility in men.

Avoiding pesticides is especially important in pre-school-aged children, who are at greater risk for two reasons: They eat more food relative to body mass, and they consume more foods higher in pesticide residues—such as juices, fresh fruits, and vegetables. A 2006 University of Washington study analyzed levels of breakdown products of organophosphorus pesticides (a class of insecticides that disrupt the nervous system) in the urine of 39 urban and suburban children aged 2 to 4 years. Concentrations of pesticide metabolites were six times lower in the children who ate organic fruits and vegetables compared to those eating conventional produce.[2]

After conducting an analysis of U.S. Department of Agriculture residue data for all pesticides for 1999 and 2000, the Consumers Union, the policy and action arm of *Consumer Reports*, warns parents of small children to limit or avoid conventionally grown foods known to have high pesticide residues, such as apples, cantaloupes, green beans (canned or frozen), pears, strawberries, tomatoes (Mexican grown), and winter squash.

Here are my recommendations for avoiding pesticides in your diet.

- Do not overconsume foods that have a tendency to concentrate pesticides, such as animal fat, meat, eggs, cheese, and milk.
- Try to buy local in-season produce.
- Buy organic produce, which is grown without the aid of synthetic pesticides and fertilizers.
- Develop a good relationship with your local grocery store produce manager. Explain your desire to reduce the exposure to pesticides and waxes and ask what measures the store takes to assure pesticide residues are within approved limits. Ask where the store gets its produce; make sure the store is aware that foreign produce is much more likely to contain not only excessive levels of pesticides but also pesticides that have been banned in the United States.
- Peel the skin or remove the outer layer of leaves of some produce; that may be all you need to do to reduce pesticide levels. The downside of this is that many of the nutritional benefits are concentrated in the skin and outer layers. An alternative measure is to remove surface pesticide residues, waxes, fungicides, and fertilizers by soaking the item in a mild solution of additive-free soap such as Ivory or pure Castile soap. All-natural, biodegradable cleansers are also available at most health food stores. To use, spray the food with the cleanser, gently scrub, and rinse.

Last, some fruit and vegetables are more likely to contain pesticides than others. Appendix C provides information from the Environmental Working Group, a nonprofit consumer advocate group, that evaluated pesticide contamination for 48 popular fruits and vegetables based on an analysis of over 100,000 tests for pesticides on these foods, conducted by the U.S. Department of Agriculture and the U.S. Food and Drug Administration.

summary

To prepare fresh fruit and vegetable juices, you will need a good juice extractor. Each type of juice extractor has pros and cons. As for produce, it is best to buy local and organic. Evidence is accumulating on the dangerous health effects of pesticides. If you purchase nonorganic produce, it is important to take precautions to reduce exposure to toxins.

5

a juicer's guide to fruits

Strictly speaking, a fruit is the ripened ovary of a female flower, but for our purposes we will recognize fruits as those plant foods typically eaten as an appetizer, dessert, or out of hand. The more popular and readily available fruits will be discussed here in terms of origin, types, nutritional benefits, selection, and preparation for juicing. A general rule when juicing fruits in recipes is to juice the softer fruits first, followed by the harder fruits, such as apples and pears. Be sure to prepare the fruits according to the guidelines that follow and the recommendations from the owner's manual of your juice extractor.

Since fruits contain a fair amount of natural fruit sugar, it is generally recommended to limit your intake to no more than 8 ounces of fruit juice once or twice daily. The sugars in the fruit will be absorbed quite rapidly, which is great if you need some quick energy, but if you suffer from hypoglycemia, diabetes, candidiasis, or gout, anything more than very small portions of fruit or fruit juice may aggravate your condition. If you have one of these conditions, I would recommend limiting your fruit juice consumption to 4 ounces at a time, no more than twice daily.

apples

Often referred to as the king of fruits, the apple originated in the Caucasus Mountains of western Asia and eastern Europe. In the United States, more than 25 varieties of apple are available; the most popular variety is the Delicious (both red and golden yellow). All apples are excellent for juicing. Try different varieties to find the one that you prefer. I like hard, crisp Granny Smith apples the best both for eating and juicing.

key benefits

According to the latest research, the old saying "An apple a day keeps the doctor away" is not just folklore. A comprehensive review of the scientific literature documents a broad range of health benefits.[1] Consumption of a fresh apple or drinking its equivalent as juice has shown an ability to increase the antioxidant activity in the blood within 30 minutes and last for 90 minutes. This antioxidant effect may explain why apple consumption was found to reduce the risk for cancer, cardiovascular disease, asthma, and Alzheimer's disease. Apples were also associated with improved outcomes related to cognitive decline of normal aging, diabetes, weight management, bone health, lung function, and peptic ulcers. Fresh apple juice has also been shown to be antiviral as described in chapter 1.

In one study, researchers in Finland followed more than 5,000 Finnish men and women for over 20 years. Those who ate the most apples and other flavonoid-rich foods (such as onions and tea) were found to have a 20 percent lower risk of heart disease compared to those who ate the least of these foods.[2] Apples lower cholesterol as well as reduce the oxidative damage to cholesterol that promotes hardening of the arteries.[3]

Apple consumption may also lower the risk for asthma. When British researchers surveyed nearly 1,500 adults in the United Kingdom about their eating habits during the previous year, the investigators found that people who ate at least two apples each week had a 22 to 32 percent lower risk for asthma compared to those who ate less of this fruit.[4] Other studies have shown that when apple consumption averages five apples per week it is associated with significantly improved lung function in adults and offsets the typical decline in lung function associated with aging.[5]

Apples are a good—but not great—source of many vitamins and minerals, particularly if they are unpeeled. It is the phytochemicals that really provide the health benefits, many of which are found in highest concentration in the peel. Unpeeled apples are particularly high in non–provitamin A carotenes and pectin. Pectin is a remarkable, beneficial fiber. Because it is a gel-forming fiber, pectin can improve the intestinal muscle's ability to push waste through the gastrointestinal tract. Pectin can also bind to and eliminate toxins in the gut as well as help reduce cholesterol levels. Since pectin is a water-soluble fiber, fresh juice still retains a portion of this beneficial fiber.

Apples contain high levels of flavonoid compounds with significant anticancer actions.[6] Fresh whole apples and fresh apple juice contain 100 to 130 mg per hundred grams (roughly 3.5 ounces) of these valuable compounds. The content of these compounds in canned, bottled, or frozen apple juice is at or near zero—another strong case for drinking your apple juice fresh.

As described in chapter 1, a lot of anticancer research has been done on ellagic acid. Much of the recent research has focused on pomegranate as the source because it contains flavonoid compounds that are broken down to ellagic acid in the body.[7] One of the prime actions of ellagic acid is to protect against damage to chromosomes and block the cancer-causing actions of many pollutants. For example, ellagic acid has been shown to block the cancer-causing effects of several compounds in cigarette smoke known collectively as polycyclic aromatic hydrocarbons. Ellagic acid is also a potent antioxidant and has also shown an ability to increase many of the body's antioxidant compounds, including glutathione.[8]

From this discussion it is obvious fresh apple juice has benefits of its own, but one of the key uses of apples is to mix them with other fruits as well as vegetables because of their sweet but not overpowering flavor.

nutritional analysis

1 medium raw apple with skin (138 g)		
NUTRIENTS & UNITS	**VITAMINS**	**MINERALS**
Water 115.83 g	Vitamin A 7 RE*	Potassium 159 mg
Calories 81 kcal	Vitamin C 7.8 mg	Calcium 10 mg
Protein 0.27 g	Thiamine 0.023 mg	Iron 0.25 mg
Fat 0.49 g	Riboflavin 0.019 mg	Magnesium 6 mg
Carbohydrate 21.05 g	Niacin 0.1 mg	Phosphorus 10 mg
		Sodium 1 mg

*RE = retinol equivalents

selection

You should definitely buy organic apples if you can. A few years ago publicity about the dangerous chemical known as ALAR that is sprayed on apples has curtailed its use, but apples are still treated with many other chemicals. In addition, conventionally grown apples are often waxed to keep them fresher longer. Organic apples may appear "waxy," but that's because these apples have a natural coating of a waxlike substance.

Fresh apples should be firm, crisp, and well colored. If an apple lacks color, it was likely picked before it was fully mature and has been ripened artificially. Apples picked when mature will have more color and better flavor and will store longer than apples picked too early. Check the hardness of the apple. A fresh apple will produce a characteristic snap when you apply pressure to the skin with a finger. Overripe apples will not give you a crisp snap; they will feel softer.

preparation for juicing

Wash organic apples; soak or spray nonorganic ones with a biodegradable wash, then rinse. Since the seeds of apples contain very small amounts of cyanide, many people recommend that you core the apples to remove the seeds. Cut the apples into wedges that the juicer will accommodate.

apple juice recipes

Apple juice is delicious on its own, or it can be mixed with both fruits and vegetables, especially to add a little sweetness to offset bitter vegetable juices. Try the recipes below and also Apple Spice (page 190), Apple Wonder (page 191), Basic Carrot-Apple (page 191), Better Red Than Dead—Fruity Version (page 192), Bone Builder's Cocktail (page 193), Bowel Regulator (page 193), Cherry Pop (page 193), Cholesterol-Lowering Tonic (page 193), Cruciferous Surprise (page 195), Everything but the Kitchen Sink (page 199), Femme Fatale (page 199), Ginger Ale (page 200), Ginger Hopper (page 201), Go Green Drink (page 202), Green Drink for Kids (page 202), High C (page 202), Iron Plus (page 204), Jicama-Carrot-Apple (page 204), Liver Mover (page 205), Liver Tonic (page 205), Liver Tonic Plus (page 205), Mint Foam (page 206), Purple Cow (page 208), Tummy Tonic (page 209), Waldorf Salad (page 210), and Zesty Cran-Apple (page 210).

APPLE-APRICOT
2 apples, cut into wedges
2 apricots, pitted

APPLE-APRICOT-PEACH
1 apple, cut into wedges
1 apricot, pitted
1 peach, pitted

APPLE-BERRY
1 cup berries (such as strawberries, blueberries, raspberries)
2 apples, cut into wedges

APPLE-CHERRY
1 cup pitted cherries
2 apples, cut into wedges

APPLE-GRAPE-LEMON
2 apples, cut into wedges
1 cup grapes
¼ lemon with skin

APPLE-GRAPEFRUIT
1 apple, cut into wedges
1 grapefruit, peeled

APPLE-KIWI
2 Golden Delicious apples, cut into wedges
4 kiwifruits

APPLE-MINT
4 apples, cut into wedges
½ handful of fresh mint

APPLE-ORANGE
2 apples, cut into wedges
2 oranges, peeled

APPLE-PAPAYA
2 apples, cut into wedges
½ papaya, seeded and sliced

APPLE-PEACH
2 apples, cut into wedges
2 peaches, pitted and sliced

APPLE-PEAR-GINGER
3 apples, cut into wedges
1 pear, sliced
½-inch slice of fresh ginger

apricots

The apricot is technically classified as a drupe: a fleshy, one-seeded fruit with the seed enclosed in a stony pit. The apricot is in the same family as the almond, cherry, peach, and plum, all of which originated in China. Alexander the Great is believed to have brought the apricot to Greece and ultimately the rest of Western civilization.

key benefits

Apricots are a good source of carotenes like lycopene and lutein, which give red, orange, and yellow colors to fruits and vegetables. These carotenes are particularly beneficial for preventing macular degeneration, heart disease, and cancer.

Apricots are also a good source of potassium, magnesium, and iron. Dried apricots are quite popular, but most contain high levels of sulfur dioxide (a preservative that is a common allergen), which is added during the drying process to inactivate enzymes that would cause the fruit to spoil. Alternative preservation methods, such as blanching, do not necessitate the use of sulfur.

nutritional analysis

3 raw apricots, pitted (107 mg)		
NUTRIENTS & UNITS	**VITAMINS**	**MINERALS**
Water 88 g	Vitamin A 90 RE	Potassium 115 mg
Calories 55 kcal	Vitamin C 10 mg	Calcium 20 mg
Protein 2 g	Thiamine 0.03 mg	Iron 0.6 mg
Fat trace	Riboflavin 0.04 mg	Magnesium 7 mg
Carbohydrate 12.8 g	Niacin 0.6 mg	Phosphorus 23 mg
		Sodium 1 mg

selection

Fresh, ripe apricots should be a uniform golden-orange color, round, and about 2 inches in diameter. Ripe apricots yield to a gentle pressure on the skin. If the fruit is quite hard or more yellow in appearance, it is unripe; if it is quite soft or mushy, it is overmature. Fresh apricots are in season June through August.

preparation for juicing

Wash organic apricots; soak or spray nonorganic ones with a biodegradable wash, then rinse. Slice them in half and remove the pit.

apricot juice recipes

Apricots are drier (85 percent water) than most other fleshy fruits and therefore do not work well as the sole component of a juice. Apricots mix quite deliciously with other fruits, especially apples, oranges, and peaches. In addition to the recipes below, see Apricot-Mango Ambrosia (page 191).

APRICOT-ORANGE
4 apricots, pitted
2 oranges, peeled

APRICOT-PEAR
4 apricots, pitted
1 pear, sliced

---

bananas

Although it looks like a tree, bananas actually grow on a plant. The difference between a tree and a plant is that in order to be a tree, there must be wood in the stem above the ground. Bananas are thought to have originated in Malaysia and spread to India, the Philippines, and New Guinea. The most popular type of banana is the large, yellow, smooth-skinned variety familiar to most Americans known as the

Manque or Gros Michel (Big Mike). Other varieties familiar to many are the smaller red-skinned type known as the Red Jamaican and the larger green bananas known as plaintains. Plaintains are used like a vegetable in that they are usually fried or cooked. Bananas are the second-leading fruit crop in the world, after grapes.

key benefits

Bananas are packed full of nutrition, especially potassium. An average-size banana contains a whopping 440 mg potassium and only 1 mg sodium. The effectiveness of potassium-rich foods such as bananas in lowering blood pressure and protecting against heart disease and strokes has been demonstrated by a number of studies. For example, in one study researchers tracked over 40,000 American male health professionals over 4 years to determine the effects of diet on blood pressure. Men who ate diets higher in potassium-rich foods, as well as foods high in magnesium, had a substantially reduced risk of stroke.[9] Bananas are a good source of pectin, a soluble fiber that lowers cholesterol as well as normalizes bowel function. In general, bananas are soothing to the gastrointestinal tract. Plaintain bananas have shown some promise in the treatment of peptic ulcers.

nutritional analysis

1 banana (114 g)		
NUTRIENTS & UNITS	**VITAMINS**	**MINERALS**
Water 85 g	Vitamin A 9 RE	Potassium 451 mg
Calories 105 kcal	Vitamin C 10.3 mg	Calcium 7 mg
Protein 1.18 g	Thiamine 0.051 mg	Iron 0.35 mg
Fat 0.55 g	Riboflavin 0.014 mg	Magnesium 33 mg
Carbohydrate 26.71 g	Niacin 0.616 mg	Phosphorus 22 mg
		Sodium 1 mg

selection

Bananas are best when they are yellow with no green showing and speckled with brown. Bananas with green tips are not quite ripe, but they will continue to ripen if stored at room temperature. After ripening, bananas can be stored in the refrigerator, and though the skin will turn dark brown, they will remain fresh for 3 to 5 days. Bananas that are bruised, discolored, or soft have deteriorated and should not be used.

preparation for juicing

Bananas do not lend themselves to juicing, but you can make fresh juice from other fruits and mix it with a banana in a blender. In the summer, try freezing a banana and blending it with fresh apple-strawberry juice to make a delicious smoothie.

banana smoothie recipes

A banana can be added to the following recipes to make a delicious smoothie: Enzymes Galore (page 199), Immune Power Fruit (page 203), Mike's Favorite (page 206), Monkey Shake (page 206), and Potassium Punch (page 207). Here is another great smoothie:

BANANA-CANTALOUPE SMOOTHIE

½ cantaloupe with skin, sliced

1 banana, peeled

Juice cantaloupe, pour juice into blender, add banana, and liquefy.

---

berries

Blackberries, blueberries, raspberries, strawberries, currants, and other berries will be discussed as a group. Berries flourish in many parts of the world, especially in the Northern Hemisphere. Hundreds of varieties of berries now exist as a result of accidental and intentional crossbreeding (hybridization).

key benefits

Berries are rich in vital nutrients yet low in calories. Hence berries are excellent foods for those who have a sweet tooth and are attempting to improve their quality of nutrition without increasing the caloric content of their diet. Juices prepared from fresh berries typically contain fewer than 100 calories per 8 ounces and provide a rich source of potassium, pure water, water-soluble fibers, and flavonoids. It is the flavonoids—mainly a group known as anthocyanidins—that are responsible for berries' color. For example, the purplish black of blackberries comes from the anthocyanidin known as cyanidin, while the red of strawberries is due to pelargonidin. The beneficial effects of flavonoids are discussed in chapter 3.

When researchers at Tufts University analyzed 60 fruits and vegetables for their antioxidant capability, blueberries came out on top, rating highest in their capacity to destroy free radicals. Other berries don't get as much press as blueberries, but they too possess significant antioxidant activity.

Most of the research has focused on blueberries and strawberries, but the research probably applies to other berries as well. Much of the research on blueberries has focused on its effects in protecting the brain and eyes from oxidative stress. For example, researchers found that feeding rats the human equivalent of a cup of blueberries a day significantly improved both the learning capacity and motor skills of aging rats, making them mentally equivalent to much younger rats. When the rats' brains were examined, the brain cells of the rats given blueberries were found to communicate more effectively with other brain cells than those of the other rats.[10] Strawberries have shown similar effects, indicating that all berries probably share this effect.[11] The practical interpretation of these studies is that berry consumption may help humans fight off brain disorders linked to oxidative stress like Alzheimer's and Parkinson's disease.

Berries have long been used for a wide range of medicinal effects; now research is supporting many of the folk uses of berries. During World War II, British Royal Air Force pilots consumed bilberry (a variety of blueberry) preserves before their night missions, believing the folk wisdom that bilberries improve night vision. After the war, numerous studies demonstrated that blueberry extracts do in fact improve nighttime visual acuity and lead to quicker adjustment to darkness and faster restoration of visual acuity after exposure to glare.

Bilberry extracts have been used by physicians for medical purposes in Europe since 1945. Most of the therapeutic applications have involved eye complaints. Results have been most impressive in individuals with retinitis pigmentosa, sensitivity to bright lights, diabetic retinopathy, and macular degeneration. Additional research also points out that bilberries may protect against cataracts and glaucoma and can be quite therapeutic in the treatment of varicose veins, hemorrhoids, and peptic ulcers.[12]

Most of the clinical studies have utilized a variety of berry extracts but primarily bilberry and black currants, concentrated for anthocyanoside content. To achieve a similar concentration using fresh fruit would require a daily intake of 12 to 16 ounces of fresh juice daily.

Berries, especially strawberries, are good sources of the anticancer compound ellagic acid. In one study, strawberries topped a list of eight foods most linked to lower rates of cancer deaths among a group of 1,271 elderly people in New Jersey. Those eating the most strawberries were three times less likely to develop cancer than those eating few or no strawberries.[13]

A human clinical study showed that a dosage of 60 g freeze-dried strawberry powder reduced the histologic grade of precancerous lesions of the esophagus in 80 percent of 36 patients indicating the potential of strawberry ingestion in preventing cancer. Given the higher concentration of active compounds in fresh, raw strawberries, the fresh juice would probably produce even better results.[14]

nutritional analysis

1 cup berries (144 g)		
NUTRIENTS & UNITS	**VITAMINS**	**MINERALS**
Water 123 g	Vitamin A 24 RE	Potassium 282 mg
Calories 74 kcal	Vitamin C 30.2 mg	Calcium 46 mg
Protein 1.04 g	Thiamine 0.043 mg	Iron 0.83 mg
Fat 0.65 g	Riboflavin 0.058 mg	Magnesium 29 mg
Carbohydrate 18.38 g	Niacin 0.576 mg	Phosphorus 30 mg
		Sodium 0 mg

selection

Buy the freshest berries possible. When berries are not in season, you can purchase unsweetened frozen berries and use them to make smoothies in the blender with fresh juice.

preparation for juicing

Wash organic berries; soak or spray nonorganic ones with a biodegradable wash, then rise.

berry juice recipes

Mixing 1 cup of berries with 2 apples is a good way to dilute some of the strong berry flavor if desired (as in Apple-Berry, page 71). Try the recipes below and also Better Red Than Dead—Fruity Version (page 192), Color Me Pink (page 195), Immune Power Fruit (page 203), Kids' Favorite (page 204), and Mike's Favorite (page 206).

BERRY-ORANGE
1 cup strawberries or other berries
2 oranges, peeled

BERRY-PINEAPPLE
1 cup berries
½ pineapple with skin, sliced

BERRY-PEAR
1 cup berries
2 pears, sliced

TRIPLE-BERRY
½ cup blackberries
½ cup strawberries
½ cup other berry
1 apple or pear, sliced

cantaloupes or muskmelons

In the United States, what we commonly refer to as a cantaloupe is actually a muskmelon; true cantaloupes don't have the netlike skin covering of the North American cantaloupe. Cantaloupes and muskmelons are thought to have originated in either Africa or the Middle East and are now grown all over the world.

key benefits

Cantaloupes are extremely nutrient dense, as defined by quality of nutrition per calorie. An entire one-pound cantaloupe is seldom over 150 calories, yet provides excellent levels of carotenes, potassium, and other valuable nutrients, especially if the skin is also juiced. One cup of cantaloupe is just 56 calories but provides 129 percent of the daily value for vitamin A and 90 percent of the daily value for vitamin C. It is also a good source of dietary fiber, folate, niacin (vitamin

B_3), pantothenic acid (vitamin B_5), and thiamin (vitamin B_1). Cantaloupe has been shown to contain the compound adenosine, which is currently being used in patients with heart disease to keep the blood thin and relieve angina attacks.[15]

nutritional analysis

½ cantaloupe without skin (267 g)		
NUTRIENTS & UNITS	**VITAMINS**	**MINERALS**
Water 240 g	Vitamin A 861 RE	Potassium 825 mg
Calories 94 kcal	Vitamin C 112.7 mg	Calcium 28 mg
Protein 2.34 g	Thiamine 0.096 mg	Iron 0.57 mg
Fat 0.74 g	Riboflavin 0.056 mg	Magnesium 28 mg
Carbohydrate 22.33 g	Niacin 1.53 mg	Phosphorus 45 mg
		Sodium 23 mg

selection

The three principal signs of a ripe cantaloupe are (1) no stem, but a smooth, shallow basin where the stem was once attached; (2) thick, coarse, and corky netting or veining over the surface; and (3) a yellowish buff skin color under the netting. Overripeness is characterized by a pronounced yellowing with a soft, watery, and insipid flesh. Avoid overly bruised melons. Examine the stem scar to make sure that no mold is growing. Keep cantaloupes at room temperature if a little hard, in the refrigerator if fully ripe.

preparation for juicing

Wash organic cantaloupes; soak or spray nonorganic ones with a biodegradable wash, then rinse. Slice the cantaloupe in half, remove the seeds, cut away any large bruises, and then cut it into strips that will feed through the juicer. There is no need to remove the skin if your juicer can handle it. Don't worry—the skin will not impact the taste, as there is not much juice in it.

cantaloupe juice recipes

Cantaloupe juice is fantastic on its own. See Banana-Cantaloupe Smoothie (page 75) and Kids' Favorite (page 204). Here is another great-tasting cantaloupe recipe:

CANTALOUPE-WATERMELON

½ cantaloupe with skin, sliced

As much watermelon as desired

---

cherries

Cherries are grown in every state and throughout most parts of the world. Where the cherry originally came from is not known. There are two main types of cherries: sweet and sour. The 500 varieties of sweet cherries include Bing, black, Windsor, and Napoleon. There are over 270 varieties of sour cherries, also referred to as tart, pie, or red cherries. The sweet cherries are best for juicing. In general, the darker the cherry, the better it is for you.

key benefits

Cherries, both sweet and tart, are high in vitamin C, beta-carotene, potassium, and pectin. Cherries also contain significant levels of boron, favorably affecting bone health. One of the most popular medicinal uses of cherry juice has been in the treatment and prevention of gout—a painful form of arthritis characterized by increased blood levels of uric acid and the formation of uric acid crystals in joints.[16] In one study, 10 healthy women were asked to eat a bowl of

Bing cherries for breakfast. For 2 days prior, they were not allowed to drink tea or red wine or eat strawberries or any other antioxidant-rich fruits or vegetables that could have interfered with the evaluation of the specific effects of Bing cherry. Results indicated that the cherry intake not only lowered blood levels of uric acid but also increased the urinary excretion of uric acid and lowered markers of inflammation such as C-reactive protein (a chemical produced by the liver that increases rapidly during inflammation, such as in a gout attack) and nitric oxide (a chemical that is also involved in damaging arthritic joints).[17]

A follow-up study on healthy men and women had them consume the equivalent of 45 cherries per day for 28 days. Again, significant reductions in C-reactive protein and nitric oxide were observed.[18]

In the most recent study in 633 patients with gout conducted at the Boston University School of Medicine in Massachusetts, cherry intake (defined as 1/2 cup or 10 to 12 cherries or the equivalent in extract form) during a 2-day period was associated with a 35 percent lower risk for gout attacks and cherry extract intake was associated with a 45 percent lower risk. The risk for gout attacks was reduced by 75 percent when cherry intake was combined with allopurinol, the standard drug used in the prevention of gout attacks.[19]

The beneficial effects are primarily due to flavonoids known as anthocyanins. These compounds are known to inhibit inflammation and have been associated with many health benefits, including protection against coronary artery disease and some types of cancer. In research conducted at Michigan State University, two of the anthocyanidins found in cherries—isoquercitrin and quercitrin—have been found to inhibit the growth of colon cancer. Cherries also contain perillyl alcohol, a natural compound that appears to be extremely powerful in reducing the incidence of all types of cancer. Recent research suggests that POH shuts down the growth of cancer cells by depriving them of the proteins they need to grow. In studies, POH has performed favorably in the treatment of advanced carcinomas of the breast, prostate, and ovary and has also exhibited cancer-fighting activity in preclinical breast cancer tests. In animal studies, POH has been shown to induce the regression of 81 percent of small breast cancers and up to 75 percent of advanced breast cancers.[20]

nutritional analysis

1 cup pitted cherries (145 g)		
NUTRIENTS & UNITS	**VITAMINS**	**MINERALS**
Water 117.09 g	Vitamin A 31 RE	Potassium 325 mg
Calories 104 kcal	Vitamin C 10.2 mg	Calcium 21 mg
Protein 1.74 g	Thiamine 0.073 mg	Iron 0.56 mg
Fat 1.39 g	Riboflavin 0.087 mg	Magnesium 16 mg
Carbohydrate 24 g	Niacin 0.58 mg	Phosphorus 28 mg
		Sodium 1 mg

selection

Good cherries have bright, glossy, plump-looking surfaces and fresh-looking stems. They should be firm but not hard. Overmature cherries are usually easy to spot. Soft, leaking flesh, brown discoloration, and mold growth are all indications of decay.

preparation for juicing

Wash organic cherries; soak or spray nonorganic ones with a biodegradable wash, then rinse. Remove the stems and use a cherry pitter or cut the cherries in half to remove the pit.

cherry juice recipes

Fresh cherry juice is delicious on its own but can also be mixed with apples and other fruits. See Apple-Cherry (page 71), Better Red Than Dead—Fruity Version (page 192), and Cherry Pop (page 193). Also try these combinations:

CHERRY-PEACH
1 cup pitted cherries
1 peach, pitted
1 apple or pear, sliced

CHERRY-PEAR
1 cup pitted cherries
2 pears, sliced

CHERRY-PINEAPPLE
1 cup pitted cherries
½ pineapple with skin, sliced

---

cranberries

Cranberries grow wild in Europe, North America, and Asia. Almost all of the world cranberry crop is produced in the United States, however. Most Americans associate cranberries with Thanksgiving and Christmas dinner, but more and more individuals are eating and drinking these berries throughout the year.

key benefits

Cranberries are quite bitter and have been used more for their medicinal rather than nutritional benefits. Cranberries and cranberry juice have been used to treat bladder infections and have been shown to be quite effective in several clinical studies. Cranberries have long been valued for their ability to reduce the risk of urinary tract infections. A 1994 placebo-controlled study of 153 elderly women that was published in the *Journal of the American Medical Association* (*JAMA*) showed that cranberries do help prevent urinary tract infection.[21]

In the *JAMA* study, the women given the cranberry juice had fewer than half as many urinary infections—42 percent to be precise—as the control group, who received a placebo drink that contained no real cranberry juice. In this groundbreaking study, the dose of cranberry juice was 300 ml (about 1¼ cups), while in most of the later studies, subjects have downed about 16 ounces (2 cups) of cranberry juice each day. A number of other studies have now further confirmed anecdotal tales of cranberry's effectiveness in both treating and preventing urinary tract infections.

Cranberry juice not only acidifies the urine and contains an antibacterial agent called hippuric acid but it has also been shown to reduce the ability of *E. coli* bacteria to adhere to the walls of the urinary tract. (For infection to occur, a pathogen must first adhere to and penetrate the mucosal surface of the urinary tract walls. If *E. coli* cannot adhere, it's washed away and voided with the flow of urine.) Since 80 to 90 percent of urinary tract infections are caused by *E. coli*, cranberries provide significant protection against this common problem.[22]

Cranberries may also help prevent kidney stones. Cranberries contain quinic acid, which, because it is not broken down in the body but is excreted unchanged in the urine, renders the urine mildly acid. This mild acidity prevents calcium and phosphate ions from forming insoluble stones. In patients with recurrent kidney stones, cranberry juice has also been shown to reduce the amount of ionized calcium by more than 50 percent. Since in the United States, 75 to 85 percent of kidney stones are composed of calcium salts, cranberry's effects on calcium may provide significant protective benefit.[23]

Like other berries, cranberries have also shown considerable effects in preliminary studies in protecting against heart disease and cancer owing primarily to their flavonoid components.[24]

nutritional analysis

1 cup cranberries (145 g)		
NUTRIENTS & UNITS	**VITAMINS**	**MINERALS**
Water 122.68 g	Vitamin A 15 RE	Potassium 129 mg
Calories 82 kcal	Vitamin C 18.9 mg	Calcium 9 mg
Protein 1 g	Thiamine 0.070 mg	Iron 0.24 mg
Fat 0.55 g	Riboflavin 0.073 mg	Magnesium 7 mg
Carbohydrate 20.49 g	Niacin 0.521 mg	Phosphorus 15 mg
		Sodium 9 mg

selection

Cranberries that are ripe are plump, red, shiny, and firm. Poor quality is indicated by shriveling, dull appearance, and softness. Fresh cranberries can be stored in the refrigerator for several months with only minimal loss of moisture and nutritional value.

preparation for juicing

Wash organic cranberries; soak or spray nonorganic ones with a biodegradable wash, then rinse.

cranberry juice recipes

Again, since cranberries are quite bitter, it is best to mix them with a sweeter fruit, such as apple or grapes. Try Cranberry Crush (page 195) and Zesty Cran-Apple (page 210) as well as this one:

CRANBERRY-PEAR
    1 cup cranberries
    2 pears, sliced

grapefruit

The grapefruit was first noticed on Barbados in 1750; by 1880 it had become an important commercial crop in Florida. The best grape-fruits are grown in Florida and Texas. For juicing purposes, grape-fruits with a red-pink meat, such as the Ruby Red and Star Ruby, are best.

key benefits

Grapefruit contains many active flavonoids, terpenes, and other health-promoting and cancer-fighting compounds. Therapeutically, grapefruit consumption has also been shown to normalize hemat-ocrit levels.[25] The hematocrit refers to the percentage of red blood cells per volume of blood. The normal hematocrit level is 40 to 54 percent for men and 37 to 47 percent for women. When hematocrit levels are low, it usually reflects anemia. When hematocrit levels are high, it may reflect severe dehydration or an increased number of red blood cells. A high hematocrit reading is associated with an in-creased risk for heart disease because it means that the blood is too viscous (thick).

Naringin, a flavonoid isolated from grapefruit, has been shown to promote the elimination of old red blood cells by the body. This prompted researchers to evaluate the effect of eating 1/2 to 1 grape-fruit per day on hematocrit levels. As expected, the grapefruit was able to lower high hematocrit levels. However, researchers were sur-prised to find that it had no effect on normal hematocrit levels and actually increased low hematocrit levels.

This balancing action is totally baffling to most drug scientists but not to experienced herbalists who have used terms such as al-terative, amphiteric, adaptogenic, or tonic to describe this effect. For example, many natural compounds in herbs and foods appear to impact body control mechanisms to aid in the normalization of many of the body's processes. When there is an elevation in a certain body function, the herb or food will have a lowering effect, and when there is decrease in a certain body function, it will have a heightening effect. Grapefruit appears to have this effect on hematocrit levels.

Grapefruit, especially those with deep red or pink flesh, are an excellent source of the carotene lycopene, an important carotene that battles heart disease, cancer, and macular degeneration.

Grapefruit is also rich in other cancer-fighting chemicals, such as d-limonene, which inhibits tumor formation by promoting the formation of a detoxifying enzyme (glutathione-S-transferase) in the liver. This enzyme sparks a reaction in the liver that helps to make toxic compounds more water soluble for excretion from the body. Pulp of citrus fruits like grapefruit also contains glucarates, compounds that may help prevent breast cancer by helping the body get rid of excess estrogen.

Grapefruit and grapefruit juice have the potential to interact with numerous drugs, especially some cholesterol-lowering drugs including statins such as atorvastatin (Lipitor), lovastatin (Mevacor), and simvastatin (Zocor, Simlup, SIMCOR, Simvacor), but not pravastatin (Pravachol), fluvastatin (Lescol), or rosuvastatin (CRESTOR). In general, if you are taking any medication, it is important to check for any interactions with any food, especially grapefruit.

nutritional analysis

1 grapefruit, peeled (230 g)		
NUTRIENTS & UNITS	**VITAMINS**	**MINERALS**
Water 209 g	Vitamin A 29 RE	Potassium 321 mg
Calories 74 kcal	Vitamin C 79 mg	Calcium 27 mg
Protein 1.5 g	Thiamine 0.083 mg	Iron 0.2 mg
Fat 0.24 g	Riboflavin 0.046 mg	Magnesium 19 mg
Carbohydrate 18.58 g	Niacin 0.575 mg	Phosphorus 20 mg
		Sodium 1 mg

selection

Ruby Red and Star Ruby grapefruits are the best for juicing. Good-quality grapefruits are firm but springy to the touch, well shaped, and heavy for their size. Grapefruits that are soft, wilted, flabby, or have green on the skin should not be consumed.

preparation for juicing

Grapefruits should always be peeled. Citrus peels have some beneficial oils but contain a compound known as citral that antagonizes some of the effects of vitamin A. After the fruit is peeled, it should be cut into wedges small enough to feed through the juicer.

grapefruit juice recipes

Try the recipes below and also Apple-Grapefruit (page 71), and Grape-Grapefruit (page 91), Color Me Pink (page 195), and Color Me Red (page 195).

GRAPEFRUIT-ORANGE
  ½ grapefruit, peeled
  2 oranges, peeled

GRAPEFRUIT-PAPAYA
  1 grapefruit, peeled
  ½ papaya, seeded and sliced

GRAPEFRUIT-PINEAPPLE
  1 grapefruit, peeled
  ½ pineapple with skin, sliced

grapes

Grapes have been eaten since prehistoric times, cultivated as far back as 5000 BC, and continue to be the leading fruit crop in the world. There are three main types: Old World, North American, and hybrids. The versatile Old World variety accounts for over 95 percent of the grapes grown in the world and is used for table grapes, raisins, and wine. North American grapes, including the Concord and Niagara, are available in seedless varieties and are well suited for juice and as table grapes but not for raisins. The hybrid, a cross between Old World and North American grapes, is used primarily in the production of wine.

key benefits

Grapes provide similar nutritional benefits to other berries. The nutritional quality can be enhanced by also eating the seeds. Grapes are an excellent source of health-promoting flavonoids. Typically, the stronger the color, the higher the concentration of flavonoids. Grape seed extracts, rich in flavonoids known as procyanolic oligomers, are widely used as a general antioxidant and in treating varicose veins and other venous disorders.[26] These flavonoids are extremely powerful antioxidants and have also been shown to reverse atherosclerosis. In fact, grapes and products made from grapes, such as wine and grape juice, are thought to explain the "French paradox"; the French eat a diet high in saturated fats and cholesterol yet have a lower risk for heart disease than Americans. One clue that may help explain this paradox is their frequent consumption of grapes and red wines. Grape juice consumption has been shown to increase the antioxidant capacity in the blood and reduce oxidative damage to cholesterol.[27]

Both red wine and grape juice have been shown to increase the antioxidant capacity in the blood, protect against vascular damage, and prevent blood platelets from clumping together to form potentially serious blood clots.[28]

nutritional analysis

1 cup North American type grapes (92 g)		
NUTRIENTS & UNITS	**VITAMINS**	**MINERALS**
Water 75 g	Vitamin A 9 RE	Potassium 176 mg
Calories 58 kcal	Vitamin C 3.7 mg	Calcium 13 mg
Protein 0.58 g	Thiamine 0.085 mg	Iron 0.27 mg
Fat 0.32 g	Riboflavin 0.052 mg	Magnesium 5 mg
Carbohydrate 15.78 g	Niacin 0.276 mg	Phosphorus 9 mg
		Sodium 2 mg

selection

Grapes do not continue to ripen after harvesting, so look for grapes that are well colored, firmly attached to the stem, firm, and wrinkle-free. Green grapes are usually the sweetest. After purchase, the grapes should be stored in the refrigerator, where they will maintain their freshness for several days.

preparation for juicing

Wash organic grapes; soak or spray nonorganic ones with a biodegradable wash, then rinse.

grape juice recipes

Pure grape juice is pretty sweet; you may want to dilute it with water or use it as a base for lemonade or cranberry juice. Try the recipes below and also Apple-Grape-Lemon (page 71), Gina's Sweet Sunshine (page 200), and Zesty Cran-Apple (page 210).

GRAPE-GRAPEFRUIT
　　1 cup grapes
　　1 grapefruit, peeled

GRAPE-LEMON-PINEAPPLE

1 cup grapes

¼ lemon with skin

½ pineapple with skin, sliced

---

kiwifruits

The kiwifruit was developed in New Zealand from a smaller, less-tasty fruit, the Chinese gooseberry. It is now grown in California and becoming more and more popular in America. The kiwifruit is a small oval that is brown and fuzzy on the outside; inside, it contains a sherbet green meat surrounding small jet black edible seeds.

key benefits

Kiwifruits are rich in enzymes if juiced unpeeled and with the seeds. They are also rich in antioxidants including lutein and zeaxanthin that support eye health.[29] In a study with 6- and 7-year-old children in northern and central Italy, the more kiwi or citrus fruit these children consumed, the less likely they were to have respiratory-related health problems including wheezing, shortness of breath, or night coughing.[30]

nutritional analysis

1 large kiwifruit (91 g)		
NUTRIENTS & UNITS	**VITAMINS**	**MINERALS**
Water 75.58 g	Vitamin A 16 RE	Potassium 302 mg
Calories 55 kcal	Vitamin C 89 mg	Calcium 24 mg
Protein 0.9 g	Thiamine 0.018 mg	Iron 0.37 mg
Fat 0.4 g	Riboflavin 0.046 mg	Magnesium 27 mg
Carbohydrate 13.54 g	Niacin 0.455 mg	Phosphorus 37 mg
		Sodium 4 mg

selection

Kiwifruits should feel firm but not rock hard. They should give slightly when pressed.

preparation for juicing

Simply cut them up unpeeled or peeled. Kiwifruit mixes deliciously with most other fruits, especially grapes and oranges.

kiwi juice recipes

See Apple-Kiwi (page 71), Digestive Delight (page 197), and Mint Foam (page 206). And give these recipes a try, too:

KIWI-ORANGE
  3 kiwifruits
  2 oranges, peeled

KIWI-PAPAYA
  3 kiwifruits
  ½ papaya, seeded and sliced

---

lemons

The lemon originated somewhere in Southeast Asia. Since the lemon tree is more sensitive to freezing temperatures than other citrus trees, it has been the most difficult to cultivate. But, unlike other citrus trees, the lemon tree bears fruit continuously. California and Florida lead the United States in the production of lemons.

key benefits

Lemons are rich in vitamin C and potassium. The vitamin C content and storage capacity of lemons made them useful for sailors in the battle against scurvy during long voyages. Lemons also contain a substance known as d-limonene (see chapter 3), which is being used to dissolve gallstones and is showing extremely promising anticancer properties.[31] The highest content of limonene is found in the peel and white spongy inner parts.

nutritional analysis

1 medium lemon, peeled (58 g)		
NUTRIENTS & UNITS	**VITAMINS**	**MINERALS**
Water 51.61 g	Vitamin A 2 RE	Potassium 80 mg
Calories 17 kcal	Vitamin C 30.7 mg	Calcium 15 mg
Protein 0.64 g	Thiamine 0.023 mg	Iron 0.35 mg
Fat 0.17 g	Riboflavin 0.012 mg	Magnesium 4 mg
Carbohydrate 5.41 g	Niacin 0.058 mg	Phosphorus 9 mg
		Sodium 1 mg

selection

A ripe lemon should have a fine-textured skin with a deep yellow color and be firm to the touch. Deep yellow lemons are usually less acidic than the lighter or greenish yellow varieties. They are also usually thinner-skinned and yield a larger proportion of juice. Avoid dried-out, shriveled, or hard-skinned fruit.

preparation for juicing

Wash organic lemons; soak or spray nonorganic ones with a biodegradable wash, then rinse. You can use the peel if you are juicing less than half a lemon; otherwise, it is a good idea to peel it (see Grapefruit, page 87).

lemon juice recipes

Lemon juice is usually too sour on its own; it must be mixed with other juices. Here is an easy recipe for lemonade that is outstanding: Juice 4 apples and 1/2 lemon with the skin and serve over crushed ice. See the Apple-Grape-Lemon (page 71), Grape-Lemon-Pineapple (page 92), Gina's Sweet Sunshine (page 200), Ginger Ale (page 200), Kill the Cold (page 204), and Zesty Cran-Apple (page 210).

---

limes

The lime is similar to the lemon, only smaller and greener. Like the lemon, the lime originated somewhere in Southeast Asia. Like lemons, limes were used by sailors to combat scurvy during long voyages, especially British sailors, hence the term *limeys*.

key benefits

Limes do not differ much in nutritional value from lemons (see opposite). They are an excellent source of vitamin C and provide good levels of vitamin B_6, potassium, and folate. They also supply flavonoids and limonene.

selection

Limes should be green in color and heavy for their size. If limes show purple to brown spots, this is a sign that they are decaying.

preparation for juicing

Wash organic limes; peel, then soak or spray nonorganic ones with a biodegradable wash, then rinse. You can use the peel if you are juicing less than half a lime; otherwise, it is a good idea to discard the peel (see Grapefruit, page 87). Lime juice is usually too sour on its own and must be mixed with other juices. The addition of lime seems to have a "cooling" effect.

lime juice recipes

Limes can be substituted for lemons in any recipe. See Apple Wonder (page 191).

---

mangoes

Mangoes originated in India and are now grown in many tropical locations, including California, Hawaii, and Florida. Mangoes are one of the leading fruit crops of the world. In fact, more mangoes are consumed by more people on a regular basis than are apples.

key benefits

Mangoes are a good source of potassium, vitamin C, carotenes, and flavonoids. Mangoes provide a rich assortment of antioxidants and have long been valued as a health-promoting fruit. Research conducted in 2002 by Dr. Sue Percival, an associate professor with the University of Florida's Institute of Food and Agricultural Sciences, has shown that mangoes can inhibit the formation and growth of cancer cells.[32] Interestingly, Dr. Percival compared an organic extract containing mango's carotenes to a water-soluble mango extraction in their effectiveness against cancer formation. According to her findings, mango's water-soluble portion was about 10 times more effective in preventing cancer cell formation than its carotenes. Compounds in the aqueous portion of the mango include not only water-soluble nutrients like vitamin C but also valuable flavonoid compounds.

Dr. Percival's research confirmed earlier research conducted at the University of Hawaii in 1997. In this study, white blood cells from mice were exposed to cancer-causing substances and then to mango extract. Lab tests showed the mango's ability to stop normal cells from turning into cancer cells.

Human evidence also demonstrates that mangoes can help fight cancer. A diet analysis of 64 patients with gallbladder cancer and 101 patients with gallstones showed that mango consumption was correlated with a 60 percent reduction in risk for gallbladder cancer—the highest reduction in risk for this cancer found for any fruit or vegetable.[33]

Mangoes also contain a number of enzymes including one similar to the papain in papayas, a well-known digestive aid. In tropical countries where the mango is grown, it is often used as a meat tenderizer since its powerful proteolytic enzymes help break down proteins. In addition to its papain-like enzyme, the mango also contains a number of other enzymatic compounds that help improve digestion including magneferin, katechol oxidase, and lactase.

Because of their high iron content, mangoes are used as blood builders in India and are suggested for the treatment of anemia and as a beneficial food for women, especially during pregnancy and menstruation. People who suffer from muscle cramps, stress, and heart problems can benefit from the high potassium and magnesium content, which also helps those with acidosis.

The mango may also offer some protection against infections. The Department of Epidemiology and International Health at the University of Alabama conducted a 4-month study of 176 Gambian children in which those who received dried mango were found to have higher blood levels of retinol (vitamin A) than those who were given placebo. Since vitamin A's nickname is the "anti-infective vitamin," the mango may literally be a lifesaving fruit in developing countries where there is a severe seasonal shortage of carotenoid-rich foods.[34]

Infants in Gambia and India were found to have the best gut integrity and thus the least intestinal disease and diarrhea during the 3 months when mangoes are in season in each country.[35] Not surprisingly, the mango was also shown in a study conducted in Mexico to afford some protection against giardia, an organism responsible for severe diarrhea.[36]

One of the most delicious tropical fruits, the mango is sweet but can be safely enjoyed by persons with diabetes. When plasma glucose and insulin responses to various tropical fruits were compared, the glucose response curve to mango was the lowest of all.[37]

nutritional analysis

One mango, edible portion (no peel or pit), cup 100 g		
NUTRIENTS & UNITS	**VITAMINS**	**MINERALS**
Water 84 g	Vitamin A 54 RE	Potassium 168 mg
Energy 60 kcal	Vitamin C 36 mg	Calcium 11 mg
Protein 0.82 g	Thiamin 0.03 mg	Iron 0.16 mg
Fat 0.38 g	Riboflavin 0.04 mg	Magnesium 10 mg
Carbohydrate 15 g	Niacin 0.7 mg	Phosphorus 14 mg
	Vitamin B$_6$ 0.119 mg	Sodium 1 mg
	Folic acid 43 mcg	

selection

A ripe mango will yield slightly to pressure. Mangoes should be yellowish green with a smooth skin and emit a sweet fragrance. Avoid fruit that is too hard or soft, bruised, and smells of fermentation. Although they come in all sizes, the larger ones are the easiest to use for juicing.

preparation for juicing

Wash organic mangoes; soak or spray nonorganic ones with a bio-degradable wash, then rinse. Mangoes have a pit at the center, so you will need to cut this away and then cut the fruit into strips or wedges.

mango juice recipes

Mangoes yield a thicker juice, so you'll want to juice them with fruits like apples, pears, and oranges that have a high water content. See Apricot-Mango Ambrosia (page 191). Also try these combinations:

MANGO-ORANGE
1 mango, pitted and sliced
2 oranges, peeled

MANGO-PEAR
1 mango, pitted and sliced
2 pears, sliced

MANGO-PAPAYA
1 mango, pitted and sliced
½ papaya, seeded and sliced

MANGO-PINEAPPLE
1 mango, pitted and sliced
½ pineapple with skin, sliced

---

nectarines (see PEACHES AND NECTARINES)

---

oranges

The modern-day orange evolved from varieties native to southern China and Southeast Asia. Oranges are by far the leading fruit crop of the United States. Personally, I prefer the California orange (the Valencia) to the Florida variety, although the latter will typically generate more juice. Mandarin oranges, tangerines, tangelos, and citron provide benefits similar to those of the orange.

key benefits

Everyone knows that oranges are an excellent source of vitamin C. Equally important to the nutritional value of oranges is its supply of flavonoids. The combination of vitamin C and flavonoids makes oranges a very valuable aid in strengthening the immune system, supporting connective tissues of our body like the joints, gums, and ground substance, and promoting overall good health. One of the most important flavonoids in oranges is hesperidin. Hesperidin has been shown to lower high blood pressure as well as cholesterol in animal studies and to have strong anti-inflammatory properties. Most of the hesperidin is found in the peel and inner white pulp of the orange rather than in its liquid orange center.[38]

The consumption of oranges and orange juice has been shown to protect against cancer, support the immune system, and help fight viral infections. In addition to vitamin C and flavonoids, oranges also contain good amounts of carotenes, pectin, potassium, and folic acid.

nutritional analysis

1 raw California orange (121 g)		
NUTRIENTS & UNITS	**VITAMINS**	**MINERALS**
Water 104.5 g	Vitamin A 28 RE	Potassium 217 mg
Calories 59 kcal	Vitamin C 58.7 mg	Calcium 48 mg
Protein 1.26 g	Thiamine 0.205 mg	Iron 0.11 mg
Fat 0.36 g	Riboflavin 0.048 mg	Magnesium 12 mg
Carbohydrate 14.49 g	Niacin 0.332 mg	Phosphorus 21 mg
		Sodium 0 mg

selection

Fresh oranges are of the best quality when they are well colored, heavy, firm, and have a fine-textured skin. Look out for moldy; severely bruised; and soft, puffy oranges. Oranges keep well in the refrigerator for more than a week.

preparation for juicing

Peel the oranges, trying to retain as much of the white spongy portion as possible. Cut into wedges and feed into the juicer.

orange juice recipes

Orange juice is delicious on its own. Three oranges will usually yield more than 8 ounces of juice. See Apple-Orange (page 71), Apricot-Orange (page 73), Berry-Orange (page 79), Kiwi-Orange (page 93), Mango-Orange (page 99), Apricot-Mango Ambrosia (page 191), Cranberry Crush (page 195), Enzymes Galore (page 199), Gina's Sweet Sunshine (page 200), Immune Power Fruit (page 203), Monkey Shake (page 206), Orange Aid, (page 206) and Potassium Punch (207). Try these recipes, too:

ORANGE-PAPAYA
2 oranges, peeled
½ papaya, seeded and sliced

ORANGE-PEACH
2 oranges, peeled
1 peach, pitted

papayas

The papaya originated in Central America. The green unripe papaya is the source of papain, a protein-digesting enzyme similar to bromelain. Papain is used commercially in many meat tenderizers.

key benefits

Papayas are rich in antioxidant nutrients like carotenes, vitamin C, and flavonoids. They are also a very good source of folate, vitamin E, vitamin A, and potassium. In addition to providing protective benefits against cancer, heart disease, and other disease associated with free-radical damage, papayas are valued for their content of papain—an enzyme often used as a digestive aid. Although the ripe fruit does not contain as much papain as the unripe fruit, it does contain some papain. Papain has been used for a number of medicinal properties including use in such conditions as indigestion, chronic diarrhea, hay fever, sports injuries and other causes of trauma, and allergies. Basically, papain is used in a similar manner as bromelain from pineapple.

nutritional analysis

1 papaya, peeled (304 g)		
NUTRIENTS & UNITS	**VITAMINS**	**MINERALS**
Water 270 g	Vitamin A 612 RE	Potassium 780 mg
Calories 117 kcal	Vitamin C 187.8 mg	Calcium 72 mg
Protein 1.86 g	Thiamine 0.082 mg	Iron 0.3 mg
Fat 0.43 g	Riboflavin 0.097 mg	Magnesium 31 mg
Carbohydrate 29.82 g	Niacin 1.028 mg	Phosphorus 16 mg
		Sodium 8 mg

selection

Papayas should be yellow-green in color and firm, but not rock hard, to the touch. Overmature papayas will be soft and will usually show signs of decay.

preparation for juicing

Wash organic papayas; soak or spray nonorganic ones with a biode-gradable wash, then rinse. Papayas contain small black seeds, which are edible but quite bitter. I recommend that you cut the papaya in half, remove the seeds, and then cut it into slices.

papaya juice recipes

Papaya juice is good on its own. See Apple-Papaya (page 71), Grapefruit-Papaya (page 89), Kiwi-Papaya (page 93), Mango-Papaya (page 99), Orange-Papaya (page 101), Enzymes Galore (page 199), Monkey Shake (page 206), and Potassium Punch (page 207). Also try the following recipes:

PAPAYA-PEAR

½ papaya, seeded and sliced

2 pears, sliced

PAPAYA-PINEAPPLE

½ papaya, seeded and sliced

½ pineapple with skin, sliced

peaches and nectarines

The peach is native to China. There are numerous varieties of peaches, but there are two main types: freestone and clingstone. This refers to how easy it is to remove the pit from the fruit. Popular freestone varieties include Elberta, Hale, and Golden Jubilee. Popular clingstone varieties are the Fortuna, Johnson, and Sims. Nectarines are essentially peaches without the fuzz.

key benefits

Eight ounces of pure peach or nectarine juice contain fewer than 100 calories yet provide some important nutrients like potassium, carotenes, flavonoids, and natural sugars. Peaches provide a good source of carotenes particularly beneficial for preventing macular degeneration, heart disease, and cancer.

nutritional analysis

1 peach (87 g)		
NUTRIENTS & UNITS	**VITAMINS**	**MINERALS**
Water 76.26 g	Vitamin A 47 RE	Potassium 171 mg
Calories 37 kcal	Vitamin C 5.7 mg	Calcium 5 mg
Protein 0.61 g	Thiamine 0.025 mg	Iron 0.1 mg
Fat 0.08 g	Riboflavin 0.036 mg	Magnesium 6 mg
Carbohydrate 9.65 g	Niacin 0.861 mg	Phosphorus 11 mg
		Sodium 0

selection

Fresh peaches and nectarines should be fairly firm. They will ripen at home at room temperature if they are not fully ripe when purchased. The color indicates the variety of the peach rather than ripeness; hence color should not be used as a gauge for ripeness. Be on the lookout for bruises and signs of spoilage. Once they are ripe, store peaches in the refrigerator.

preparation for juicing

Wash organic peaches; soak or spray nonorganic ones with a biodegradable wash, then rinse. Cut in half, remove the stone being careful to get all of it, then slice into wedges.

peach juice recipes

Peaches yield a thicker juice, so you'll want to juice them with apples or pears. See the Apple-Apricot-Peach (page 71), Cherry-Peach (page 84), Orange-Peach (page 101), and Potassium Punch (page 207). And try this one, too:

PEACH-PEAR

1 peach, pitted and sliced   2 pears, sliced

---

pears

The pear originated in western Asia but is now cultivated throughout much of the world. There are numerous varieties of pears. The best varieties for juicing include the Bosc, D'Anjou, Bartlett, and Comice.

key benefits

Pears are an excellent source of water-soluble fibers including pectin. In fact, pears are actually higher in pectin that apples. This makes them quite useful in helping to lower cholesterol levels as well as in toning the intestines.

Pears are often recommended by health care practitioners as a hypoallergenic fruit that is less likely to produce an adverse response than other fruits. Particularly in the introduction of first fruits to infants, pear is often recommended as a safe way to start.

Pears, like apples, can be added to vegetable-based juices to improve their flavor.

nutritional analysis

1 pear (166 g)		
NUTRIENTS & UNITS	**VITAMINS**	**MINERALS**
Water 139 g	Vitamin A 3 RE	Potassium 208 mg
Calories 98 kcal	Vitamin C 6.6 mg	Calcium 19 mg
Protein 0.65 g	Thiamine 0.033 mg	Iron 0.41 mg
Fat 0.66 g	Riboflavin 0.066 mg	Magnesium 9 mg
Carbohydrate 25 g	Niacin 0.166 mg	Phosphorus 18 mg
		Sodium 1 mg

selection

As pears ripen, their skin color changes from green to the color characteristic for the variety. Bosc pears turn brown, D'Anjou and Bartlett pears turn yellow, and Comice pears have a green mottled skin. Fresh pears are best when they yield to pressure like an avocado does. Unripe pears will ripen at home if stored at room temperature. Once ripe, they should be refrigerated. Firm pears are much easier to juice than soft pears.

preparation for juicing

Wash organic pears; soak or spray nonorganic ones with a biodegradable wash, then rinse before cutting the pear into slices or wedges.

pear juice recipes

Pear juice is delicious on its own, and it also mixes quite well with many fruits and vegetables. Try the recipe below and also Apple-Pear-Ginger (page 71), Apricot-Pear (page 73), Berry Happy (page 191), Berry-Pear (page 79), Bowel Regulator (page 193), Cherry-Pear (page 84), Cranberry-Pear (page 86), Green Drink for Kids (page

202), Mango-Pear (page 99), Papaya-Pear (page 103), and Peach-Pear (page 105).

PEAR-PLUM

2 plums, pitted   2 pears, sliced

---

pineapples

The pineapple is native to South America. The United States ranks as one of the world's leading suppliers of pineapples, although the only state that produces them is Hawaii. The edible flesh of the pineapple has a characteristic flavor often described as a mixture of apple, strawberry, and peach.

key benefits

Fresh pineapple is rich in bromelain, a group of sulfur-containing proteolytic (protein-digesting) enzymes that not only aid digestion but can also effectively reduce inflammation and swelling and have even been used experimentally as an anticancer agent. A variety of inflammatory agents are inhibited by the action of bromelain. In clinical human trials, bromelain has demonstrated significant anti-inflammatory effects, reducing swelling in inflammatory conditions such as acute sinusitis, sore throat, arthritis, and gout, and speeding recovery from injuries and surgery. To maximize bromelain's anti-inflammatory effects, pineapple should be eaten alone between meals to prevent its enzymes being used up in digesting food.[39]

Pineapple is an excellent source of the trace mineral manganese, which is an essential cofactor in a number of enzymes important in energy production and antioxidant defenses. For example, the key oxidative enzyme superoxide dismutase, which disarms free radicals produced within the mitochondria (the energy production factories within our cells), requires manganese. Just 1 cup of fresh pineapple juice supplies more than 50 percent of the daily value for this very important trace mineral.

nutritional analysis

1 cup diced peeled pineapple (155 g)		
NUTRIENTS & UNITS	**VITAMINS**	**MINERALS**
Water 135 g	Vitamin A 4 RE	Potassium 175 mg
Calories 77 kcal	Vitamin C 23.9 mg	Calcium 11 mg
Protein 0.6 g	Thiamine 0.143 mg	Iron 0.57 mg
Fat 0.66 g	Riboflavin 0.056 mg	Magnesium 21 mg
Carbohydrate 19.21 g	Niacin 0.651 mg	Phosphorus 11 mg
		Sodium 1 mg

selection

The main thing to be concerned about is the presence of decayed or moldy spots. Check the bottom stem scar. Ripe pineapples have a fruity, fragrant aroma, are more yellow than green in color, and are heavier for their size.

preparation for juicing

Twist or cut off the top. Wash and scrub organic pineapples; soak or spray nonorganic ones with a biodegradable wash, then scrub and rinse. If your juicer will handle it, simply cut up the pineapple, skin and all, into pieces that can be fed into the juicer.

pineapple juice recipes

Pineapple is low in calories and makes a fantastic base for fruit drinks, especially when mixed with berries. See Berry-Pineapple (page 79), Cherry-Pineapple (page 84), Grape-Lemon-Pineapple (page 92), Grapefruit-Pineapple (page 89), Mango-Pineapple (page 99), Papaya-Pineapple (page 103), Digestive Delight (page 197), Don Juan (page 198), Enzymes Galore (page 199), Immune Power Fruit (page 203), Mike's Favorite (page 206), Orange Aid (page 206), and Pineapple-Ginger Ale (page 207).

---

plums and prunes

Like peaches and apricots, plums are classified as a drupe because of their hard pit or stone surrounded by soft, pulpy flesh with a thin skin. Plums originated in Europe and Asia. There are five main types: European, Japanese, American, damson, and ornamental. A prune is a dried plum, just like a raisin is a dried grape.

key benefits

Plums and prunes are often used for their laxative effects. Prunes are more effective than plums in this capacity. Plums are good sources of carotenes, flavonoids, potassium, and iron. They contain neochlorogenic and chlorogenic acid, two related compounds that have well-documented antioxidant effects.

In a 2001 study, prunes were shown to help offset women's significantly increased risk for accelerated bone loss during the first 3 to 5 years after menopause. When 58 postmenopausal women ate about 12 prunes each day for 3 months, they were found to have higher blood levels of enzymes and growth factors that indicate bone formation than women who did not consume prunes.

Presumably consumption of plums or plum juice may offer similar benefit.[40]

nutritional analysis

1 plum (66 g)		
NUTRIENTS & UNITS	**VITAMINS**	**MINERALS**
Water 56.23 g	Vitamin A 21 RE	Potassium 113 mg
Calories 36 kcal	Vitamin C 6.3 mg	Calcium 2 mg
Protein 0.52 g	Thiamine 0.028 mg	Iron 0.07 mg
Fat 0.41 g	Riboflavin 0.063 mg	Magnesium 4 mg
Carbohydrate 8.6 g	Niacin 0.33 mg	Phosphorus 7 mg
		Sodium 0

selection

Plums vary in color and size. They can be as small as a cherry or as large as a peach, and their skin can be green, yellow, blue, or purple. Select fresh plums based on the color characteristic to the variety. Ripe plums are firm to slightly soft. Avoid plums that have skin breaks or brownish discolorations or that are overly soft.

preparation for juicing

Wash organic plums; soak or spray nonorganic ones with a biodegradable wash, then rinse. Prunes can be rehydrated by soaking them in water (2 to 4 prunes per 1 cup water) for 24 hours and then added, along with the soaking water, to the blender.

plum juice recipes

See Pear-Plum (page 107) and Bowel Regulator (page 193).

pomegranate

The pomegranate is one of the oldest fruits as well as richest in history and folklore. Native to the area of modern-day Iran and Iraq, the pomegranate has been cultivated since ancient times and has spread through the world. The fruit is about the size of an orange. The rind color can range from yellow-orange to deep reddish purple. Inside the fruit, there are a multitude of seed pips yielding a tangy, sweet, rich and flavorful juice.

key benefits

Pomegranate juice appears to be particularly useful in improving heart and vascular health. It is remarkably rich in antioxidants, such as soluble polyphenols, tannins, and anthocyanins. Animal research has indicated that components of pomegranate juice can retard atherosclerosis, reduce plaque formation, and improve arterial health. Human clinical studies have supported the role of pomegranate juice (240 ml/day) in benefiting heart health.[41] In one study of patients with high blood pressure, consumption of pomegranate juice for 2 weeks was shown to reduce systolic blood pressure by inhibiting an enzyme (serum angiotensin-converting enzyme) that causes vascular contraction.[42] Juice consumption may also inhibit viral infections. Metabolites of pomegranate juice flavonoids localize specifically in the prostate gland, colon, and intestinal tissues, and clinical studies indicate that pomegranate juice supports the health of these tissues and fights cancer.[43]

Pomegranate contains a group of flavonoid components known as ellagitannins that are broken down into ellagic acid when ingested. This compound has been discussed previously under Apples and Berries. It exerts significant anticancer effects. Pomegranate is able to raise blood levels of ellagic acid, indicating that many of the ellagitannins are rapidly converted to ellagic acid. Many commercially available pomegranate extracts are being standardized to contain 40 percent (or more) ellagic acid; however, there is a synergistic action of several pomegranate constituents with ellagic acid, indicating that consumption of the full range of phytochemicals produces a greater effect beyond a high ellagic acid content.

nutritional analysis

Per 100 g (3.5 ounces) seed pips		
NUTRIENTS & UNITS	**VITAMINS**	**MINERALS**
Water 82 g	Vitamin A 0 RE	Potassium 113 mg
Calories 83 kcal	Vitamin C 10 mg	Calcium 10 mg
Protein 1.7 g	Thiamine 0.07 mg	Iron 0.3 mg
Fat 1.2 g	Riboflavin 0.05 mg	Magnesium 12 mg
Carbohydrate 18.7 g	Niacin 0.29 mg	Phosphorus 36 mg
		Sodium 0

selection

Pomegranates should be plump and round and heavy for their size, with a rich, fresh color; they should be free of cuts and blemishes. Larger fruits promise more seeds and more juice. Whole fruits can be stored for a month in a cool, dry area or refrigerated up to 2 months.

preparation for juicing

The first step involves cutting off the crown of the pomegranate. This is the part with the stem at the top. Once the crown is removed, cut the pomegranate into four sections. Place the sections into a bowl of water and, using your fingers, gently roll the arils out from the membrane. Once the seed pips have been separated, drain out the water and you are ready to place them in the juice extractor.

pomegranate juice recipes

Try the recipe below and also Berry Happy (page 191) and Better Red Than Dead—Fruity Version (page 192).

POMEGRANATE-BLUEBERRY JUICE

1 cup pomegranate seeds	2 cups blueberries

raspberries (see BERRIES)

strawberries (see BERRIES)

tangerines (see ORANGES)

watermelon

Watermelons originated in Africa but have been cultivated since ancient times in Europe and Asia. Today watermelons are grown worldwide in tropical, semitropical, and temperate climates. The most common watermelon consumed in the United States is light to dark green with stripes or mottling on the outside covering a bright red flesh with dark brown or black seeds. The flesh can also be pink, orange, yellow, or white.

key benefits

Watermelon, as its name would imply, is an excellent source of pure water. It is very low in calories. If watermelon juice is prepared using the rind and all, the nutritional quality improves dramatically, as the nutrients are highly concentrated in the rind and seeds. Watermelon is an excellent diuretic.

nutritional analysis

1 cup diced rindless, seedless watermelon (160 g)		
NUTRIENTS & UNITS	**VITAMINS**	**MINERALS**
Water 146.42 g	Vitamin A 58 RE	Potassium 186 mg
Calories 50 kcal	Vitamin C 15.4 mg	Calcium 13 mg
Protein 0.99 g	Thiamine 0.128 mg	Iron 0.28 mg
Fat 0.68 g	Riboflavin 0.032 mg	Magnesium 17 mg
Carbohydrate 11.5 g	Niacin 0.32 mg	Phosphorus 14 mg
		Sodium 3 mg

selection

People tap on watermelons to determine if they sound hollow and are therefore ripe; however, this practice does not mean success. Look for watermelons that have a smooth surface and a cream-colored underbelly. Despite the best precautions, it is difficult to judge the quality of a watermelon without cutting it in half. When cut, indicators of a good watermelon include firm, juicy red flesh with dark brown to black seeds. The presence of white streaks in the flesh or white seeds usually indicates immaturity.

preparation for juicing

Wash, scrub, and rinse organic watermelon; soak or spray nonorganic watermelon with a biodegradable wash, then scrub and rinse.

Cut the watermelon (rind and all) into long strips that will feed into the juicer.

watermelon juice recipes

Watermelon juice is best consumed alone or in combination with other melon juices. See Cantaloupe-Watermelon (page 81).

summary

Fruits are delicious and extremely important to a healthful diet. They are packed full of a wide array of beneficial phytochemicals, especially flavonoids. Since fruits contain a fair amount of natural fruit sugar, it is generally recommended to limit your intake to no more than 8 ounces of fruit juice taken once or twice daily. The sugars in the fruit will be absorbed quite rapidly, which is great if you need some quick energy, but if you suffer from hypoglycemia, diabetes, candidiasis, or gout, more than 2 servings of fruit or fruit juice may aggravate your condition. If you have one of these conditions, I would recommend limiting your fruit juice consumption to 8 ounces at a time and no more than twice daily.

6

a juicer's guide to vegetables

In Latin, the word *vegetable* means "to enliven or animate." The name is appropriate, as vegetables do truly give us life. More and more evidence is accumulating that shows vegetables can prevent as well as treat many diseases, especially the chronic degenerative diseases like heart disease, cancer, diabetes, and arthritis. Vegetables provide the broadest range of nutrients and phytochemicals of any food class. They are rich sources of vitamins, minerals, carbohydrates, and

table 6.1. the origins of our modern vegetables

NORTHERN EUROPE	MIDDLE EAST	NORTH AMERICA
Beet	Fava bean	Jerusalem artichoke
Broccoli	Cabbage	
Brussels sprouts	Carrot	**CENTRAL AMERICA**
Cabbage	Cauliflower	Common bean
Chives	Cucumber	Corn
Collards	Lentil	Jicama
Fennel	Lettuce	Peppers
Horseradish	Mustard	Pumpkin
Mustard	Radish	Squash
Peas	Spinach	Sweet potato
Rutabaga	Watercress	Tomato
Turnip	Yam	
Watercress		**SOUTH AMERICA**
	INDIA AND ASIA	Corn
MEDITERRANEAN	Beet	Lima beans
Artichoke	Bok choy	Pepper
Asparagus	Chives	Potato
Celery	Carrot	Sweet potato
Chard	Eggplant	Tomato
Chickpea	Garlic	
Endive	Leek	**AFRICA**
Kale	Mung bean	Fava bean
Kohlrabi	Onion	Cowpea
Olive	Pea	Okra
Parsley	Shallot	Yam
Parsnip	Turnip	
	Waterchestnut	

protein. The little fat they contain is in the form of essential fatty acids. Vegetables provide high quantities of valuable phytochemicals, especially fiber and carotenes.

The best way to consume many vegetables is in their fresh, raw form, which provides many important phytochemicals in much higher concentrations. One exception is that it may not be wise to consume more than four servings per week of raw cabbage-family vegetables (including broccoli, cauliflower, and kale) because these foods in their raw state contain compounds that can interfere with thyroid hormone production.

When cooking vegetables, it is very important that they not be overcooked, as this will not only result in loss of important nutrients but it will also alter the flavor of the vegetable. Light steaming, baking, and quick stir-frying are the best ways to cook vegetables. Do not boil or overcook vegetables unless you are making soup, as much of the nutrients will be left in the water. If fresh vegetables are not available, frozen vegetables are preferred over their canned counterparts. Frozen vegetables retain higher nutrient and phytochemical levels than canned vegtables.

---

asparagus

The asparagus is a member of the lily family native to the Mediterranean. It has been used as a medicinal plant in the treatment of arthritis and rheumatism and as a diuretic. Asparagus is now grown all over the world.

key benefits

Asparagus is low in calories and carbohydrates but very rich in protein. In fact, a 4-ounce glass of asparagus juice contains more protein than 1 cup cooked rice or corn. Asparagus is also a good source for many vitamins and minerals, including vitamin C, riboflavin, and folic acid. Asparagus contains the amino acid asparagine, which when excreted in the urine can give off a strong odor. Don't be alarmed; this is short-lived.

nutritional analysis

6 raw asparagus spears (100 g)		
NUTRIENTS & UNITS	**VITAMINS**	**MINERALS**
Water 92 g	Vitamin A 16 RE	Potassium 278 mg
Calories 32 kcal	Vitamin C 33 mg	Calcium 22 mg
Protein 2.5 g	Thiamine 0.18 mg	Iron 1 mg
Fat 0.2 g	Riboflavin 0.5 mg	Magnesium 18 mg
Carbohydrate 5 g	Niacin 1.5 mg	Phosphorus 62 mg
	Vitamin B$_6$ 0.18 mg	Sodium 2 mg
	Folic acid 104 mcg	

selection

The best-quality asparagus will be firm and fresh, and the tips will be closed. The greener the stalk, the higher the concentration of nutrients and phytochemicals.

preparation for juicing

Wash organic asparagus; soak or spray nonorganic asparagus with a biodegradable wash, then rinse. Feed the asparagus into the juicer with the head end going in first.

asparagus juice recipes

Asparagus is pretty strong on its own. Add it to Basic Carrot-Apple (page 191), or try the following recipes:

ASPARAGUS-CARROT-CELERY
    4 asparagus spears
    3 carrots
    2 celery ribs

ASPARAGUS-CELERY
    6 asparagus spears
    4 celery ribs

beans, string or snap

The string or snap bean originated in Mexico and Peru. Native Americans cultivated the plant northward and southward, and Spanish explorers took it to Europe.

key benefits

String beans are an excellent source of protein and water-soluble fiber compounds, including gums and pectins. Legumes, in general, provide exceptional nutritional benefit to the diabetic. Numerous studies have shown a diet high in legumes will lead to better blood sugar control in diabetics. Presumably a great deal of the beneficial effects would exist in the juice.

nutritional analysis

1 cup raw string beans (135 g)		
NUTRIENTS & UNITS	**VITAMINS**	**MINERALS**
Water 124 g	Vitamin A 71 RE	Potassium 151 mg
Calories 36 kcal	Vitamin C 11 mg	Calcium 61 mg
Protein 1.84 g	Thiamine 0.065 mg	Iron 1.11 mg
Fat 0.18 g	Riboflavin 0.1 mg	Magnesium 29 mg
Carbohydrate 8.26 g	Niacin 0.5 mg	Phosphorus 33 mg
	Vitamin B$_6$ 0.28 mg	Sodium 17 mg
	Folic acid 63.2 mcg	

selection

The beans should be fresh-looking and green in color, and they should audibly snap when broken. Avoid string beans that are dry and wrinkled in appearance.

preparation for juicing

Wash organic beans; soak or spray nonorganic ones with a biodegradable wash, then rinse.

bean juice recipes

String bean juice on its own is quite thick and not very tasty; a cup of beans can be juiced and added to Basic Carrot-Apple (page 191).

---

beets

Beets belong to the same family as spinach and chard, the Chenopodiaceae family. Both the root and the leaves are eaten. Beets were originally cultivated in Europe and Asia but are now grown worldwide, both for food and as a source for sugar production.

key benefits

The beet greens are higher in nutritional value than the roots, especially in calcium, iron, vitamin A, and vitamin C. Beet roots have long been used for medicinal purposes, primarily focusing on disorders of the liver. Beets have also gained recognition for their anticancer and heart health–promoting properties.

The pigment that gives beets their rich purple-crimson color—*betacyanin*—is a powerful cancer-fighting agent. The combination of their betacyanin and fiber content is probably the factor responsible for the protective role of beets against colon cancer noted in experimental studies.[1] Beet fiber has also been shown to have a favorable effect on bowel function and cholesterol levels.[2] In animal studies, beet fiber has been shown to increase the level of the antioxidant enzymes (specifically glutathione peroxidase and glutathione-S-transferase) as well as increase the number of special white blood cells responsible for detecting and eliminating abnormal cells. In a study in patients with stomach cancer, beet juice was found to be a potent inhibitor of the formation of nitrosamines and of the cell mutations caused by these compounds.[3]

The effects of beet juice on the heart and vascular system have actually been studied in several clinical evaluations with extremely beneficial results. In one of the first studies, researchers at Barts and the London School of Medicine discovered that drinking just 16 ounces of fresh beet juice a day significantly reduced systolic pressure (top number) and diastolic pressure (bottom number) up to 10 mm Hg in healthy subjects.[4] Beet juice lowered blood pressure within just an hour with a peak drop occurring 3 to 4 hours after ingestion. These researchers showed that the decrease in blood pressure was due to the chemical formation of nitrite from the dietary nitrates in the juice. The dietary nitrate in the juice is converted in saliva into nitrite by bacteria on the tongue. The peak time of reduction in blood pressure correlated with the appearance and peak levels of nitrite in the blood. Once in the general circulation, nitrite can be converted to nitric oxide by the cells that line blood vessels. Nitric oxide is a powerful dilator of blood vessels. With the dilation of blood vessels there is less resistance to the blood being pumped resulting in lower blood pressure.

Since this initial study in 2008, several other studies have looked at the effect of drinking beet juice and its effects on raising blood nitrite levels.[5] Although there are other dietary sources of nitrates, what is particularly interesting is that drinking beet juice is considerably more effective in raising blood nitrite levels than eating a very high intake of nitrate-rich foods. In fact, the level of nitrate in the diet has minimal impact on plasma nitrate and nitrite, but drinking a glass of beet juice at breakfast can significantly increase plasma nitrate and nitrite throughout the day. It should also be pointed out that eating cooked beets won't give you the same quantity of nitrates as beet juice because the cooking process deteriorates some of the nitrates.

The most recent study on the blood-pressure-lowering effects of beet juice was conducted at the Baker IDI Heart and Diabetes Institute in Melbourne, Australia.[6] In the study, 15 men and 15 women drank either 17.6 ounces of a beet juice beverage containing 500 g beet and apple juice (72 percent beet, 28 percent apple) or a placebo juice. The participants had their blood pressure measured at baseline and at least hourly for 24 hours following juice consumption using an ambulatory blood pressure monitor. This same procedure was repeated 2 weeks later, with those who drank the placebo on the first round receiving beet juice on the second and vice versa. The results were that drinking beet juice showed lowered systolic blood pressure by an average of 4 to 5 points after only 6 hours. Here is the significance of this effect: It would cut the rate of strokes and heart attacks by about 10 percent. In terms of lives, that would mean about 60,000 lives saved each year.

Beet juice can also have a positive effect on the body during exercise. Several studies have shown that six days of drinking a glass of beet juice enhanced overall physical performance and heart functioning during exercise.[7] In a 2009 study, 12 male cyclists ingested 140 ml/day of a concentrated beet juice or a placebo (nitrate-depleted beet juice) for 6 days and were then crossed over to the other drink after a 14-day washout period.[8] After supplementation on Day 6, subjects performed 60 minutes of submaximal cycling, followed by a 10 km time trial. Time-trial performance (953 versus 965 seconds) and power output (294 versus 288 watts) improved after the real beet juice compared with the placebo. In the submaximal cycling,

WARNING: Drinking a lot of beet juice can cause your urine and stools to look like they contain blood. Do not be alarmed—it is simply the red pigments in the beet juice.

the use of oxygen (VO_{2MAX}) was lower with the real beet juice ingestion as well. What do all of these data mean? In short, beet juice promotes increased physical stamina and performance.

nutritional analysis

2 beets without tops (163 g)		
NUTRIENTS & UNITS	**VITAMINS**	**MINERALS**
Water 142.22 g	Vitamin A 3 RE	Potassium 528 mg
Calories 77 kcal	Vitamin C 17.9 mg	Calcium 25 mg
Protein 2.41 g	Thiamine 0.082 mg	Iron 1.5 mg
Fat 0.23 g	Riboflavin 0.033 mg	Magnesium 34 mg
Carbohydrate 16.3 g	Niacin 0.652 mg	Phosphorus 78 mg
	Vitamin B_6 0.08 mg	Sodium 118 mg
	Folic acid 151 mcg	

selection

Good-quality beets should have their greens intact. The greens should be fresh-looking, with no signs of spoilage. Slightly flabby greens can be restored to freshness if stored in the refrigerator in water. If it is too late, simply cut off the greens. The beet root should be firm, smooth, and vibrant red-purple, not soft, wrinkled, and dull-colored. The smaller beets are generally better for juicing.

preparation for juicing

Wash organic beet roots or greens; soak or spray nonorganic ones with a biodegradable wash, then rinse.

beet juice recipes

Beet juice tends to be irritating to the throat and esophagus if consumed alone. Try the recipes below and also Better Red Than Dead (page 192), Better Red Than Dead—Fruity Version (page 192),

Cleansing Cocktail (page 194), Color Me Red (page 195), Iron Plus (page 204), Liver Mover (page 205), and Liver Tonic (page 205).

BEET-CARROT
½ beet with top
4 carrots

BEET-CARROT-CELERY
½ beet with top
3 carrots
2 celery ribs

BEET-CARROT-PARSLEY
½ beet with top
4 carrots
½ handful of parsley

BEET-CARROT-PEPPER
½ beet with top
3 carrots
½ green or red bell pepper

BEET-CARROT-SPINACH
½ beet with top
3 carrots
½ cup spinach

BEET–SWEET POTATO
½ beet with top
1 sweet potato
1 apple, cut into wedges (optional)

---

bitter melon

Bitter melon, also known as balsam pear, is a tropical fruit widely cultivated in Asia, Africa, and South America. Usually the bitter-flavored unripe fruit is used as a vegetable. In addition to being part of the diet, unripe bitter melon has been used extensively in folk medicine as a remedy for diabetes. The ripe fruit is showing promise in the treatment of leukemia, but the ripe fruit is not readily available in the United States. Both unripe and ripe bitter melon are available primarily at Asian grocery stores.

key benefits

The blood-sugar-lowering action of the fresh juice of the unripe bitter melon has been confirmed in scientific studies in animals and humans.

Bitter melon contains a compound known as charantin that is more potent than the drug tolbutamide, which is often used in the treatment of type 2 diabetes to lower blood sugar levels. Bitter melon also contains an insulin-like compound referred to as polypeptide-P or vegetable insulin. Since polypeptide-P and bitter melon appear to have fewer side effects than insulin, they have been suggested as replacements for insulin in some patients. However, it may not be necessary to inject the material, as the oral administration of as little as 2 ounces of the juice has shown good results in clinical trials in patients with diabetes.[9]

Bitter melon has also been found to contain antiviral proteins.[10] Two of these proteins, which are present in the seeds, fruit, and leaves of bitter melon, have been shown to inhibit the AIDS virus in vitro (in test tube studies). In 1996, the scientists conducting this research filed a U.S. patent on a novel protein they found and extracted from the fruit and seeds of bitter melon, which they named MAP 30. In addition to being "useful for treating tumors and HIV infections" (according to the patent), MAP 30 has also demonstrated powerful antiviral activity against other viruses including the herpes simplex virus. The ripe fruit of bitter melon has been shown to exhibit some rather profound anticancer effects, especially in leukemia and prostate cancer.[11]

selection

The bitter melon is a green, cucumber-shaped fruit with gourdlike bumps all over it. It looks like an ugly cucumber. Choose smaller fruit, as you will not need, or want, much of the juice. The fruit should be firm, like a cucumber.

preparation for juicing

Wash organic bitter melon; soak or spray nonorganic bitter melon with a biodegradable wash, then rinse. Slice it into strips that can be fed into the juicer.

WARNING: Diabetics taking hypoglycemic drugs (such as glucophage, chlorpropamide, glyburide, or phenformin) may need to alter the dosage of these drugs if consuming bitter melon on a daily basis.

Bitter melon should not be eaten by pregnant women. Active constituents (the alpha and beta monorcharins) in bitter melon have been shown to stimulate the uterus and may cause preterm labor if used in pregnancy. Bitter melon may also produce a hypoglycemic effect. In pregnancy, hypoglycemia can result in untoward effects for both the mother and the fetus.

bitter melon juice recipes

It is called bitter melon with good reason. But remember, in the clinical studies the dose was only 2 ounces. I would recommend just taking it on its own, because its flavor is extremely difficult to mask. However, you can try combining it with 8 ounces Basic Carrot-Apple (page 191).

---

broccoli

A member of the cruciferous, or cabbage, family of vegetables, broccoli developed from wild cabbage native to Europe, was improved by the Romans and later-day Italians, and is now cultivated throughout the world.

key benefits

Broccoli is one of the most nutrient-dense foods. A 1-cup serving provides about the same amount of protein as a cup of corn or rice, but less than one-third the calories. Broccoli is one of the richest sources of vitamin C. Like the other members of the cabbage family, broccoli is demonstrating remarkable anticancer effects (see Cabbage), particularly in breast cancer.

One of the key cancer-fighting compounds in broccoli is sulforaphane. This compound was first identified in broccoli sprouts grown in plastic laboratory dishes by scientists at the Johns Hopkins University School of Medicine in Baltimore. These researchers were investigating the anticancer compounds present in broccoli when they discovered that broccoli sprouts contain anywhere from 30 to 50 times the concentration of protective chemicals that are found in mature broccoli plants.[12] Feeding sulforaphane-rich broccoli sprout extracts dramatically reduced the frequency, size, and number of tumors in laboratory rats exposed to a standard carcinogen. Human studies with sulforaphane and other broccoli components have shown that these compounds stimulate the body's production of detoxification enzymes and exert antioxidant effects.[13]

Preliminary studies suggest that to cut the risk of cancer in half, the average person would need to eat about 2 pounds of broccoli or similar vegetables per week. Because the concentration of sulforaphane is much higher in broccoli sprouts than in mature broccoli, the same reduction in risk theoretically might be had with a weekly intake of just a little over an ounce of sprouts.

Sulforaphane may also be proven to be effective for helping the body get rid of *Helicobacter pylori*.[14] These bacteria are responsible for most peptic ulcers and also increase a person's risk of getting gastric cancer threefold to sixfold; they are also a causative factor in a wide range of other stomach disorders including gastritis, esophagitis, and acid indigestion.

nutritional analysis

⅔ cup raw broccoli (100 g)		
NUTRIENTS & UNITS	**VITAMINS**	**MINERALS**
Water 91.46 g	Vitamin A 207 RE	Potassium 212 mg
Calories 26 kcal	Vitamin C 56.4 mg	Calcium 56 mg
Protein 2.81 g	Thiamine 0.053 mg	Iron 0.81 mg
Fat 0.29 g	Riboflavin 0.096 mg	Magnesium 18 mg
Carbohydrate 4.76 g	Niacin 0.47 mg	Phosphorus 50 mg
	Vitamin B$_6$ 0.13 mg	Sodium 24 mg
	Folic acid 67 mcg	

selection

Broccoli should be dark green, deep sage green, or purplish green, depending on the variety. The stalks and stems should be tender and firm. Yellowed or wilted leaves indicate loss of much of the nutritional value. Avoid wilted, soft, and noticeably aged broccoli.

preparation for juicing

Wash organic broccoli; soak or spray nonorganic broccoli with a biodegradable wash, then rinse. Slice the broccoli into strips. Feed the broccoli into the juicer headfirst.

broccoli juice recipes

Broccoli juice needs to be mixed with other juices to make it more palatable. Juice ½ cup broccoli and add it to Basic Carrot-Apple (page 191). In addition to the recipes below try Cruciferous Surprise (page 195), Everything but the Kitchen Sink (page 199), High C (page 202), and Iron Plus (page 204).

BROCCOLI-CARROT
1 broccoli spear
3 carrots

BROCCOLI-CARROT-CELERY
1 broccoli spear
3 carrots

1 celery rib

BROCCOLI-CARROT-PARSLEY
1 broccoli spear
3 carrots
½ cup parsley

---

brussels sprouts

Like broccoli, Brussels sprouts evolved from the wild cabbage. They were developed to its present form near Brussels (hence the name). They are cultivated throughout the world. In the United States, almost all Brussels sprouts come from California.

key benefits

Brussels sprouts are similar in nutritional quality to broccoli. As a member of the cabbage family, Brussels sprouts are being investigated for their anticancer properties (see Cabbage).

nutritional analysis

1 cup raw Brussels sprouts (150 g)		
NUTRIENTS & UNITS	**VITAMINS**	**MINERALS**
Water 136 g	Vitamin A 112 RE	Potassium 494 mg
Calories 60 kcal	Vitamin C 96 mg	Calcium 56 mg
Protein 4 g	Thiamine 0.16 mg	Iron 1.88 mg
Fat 0.8 g	Riboflavin 0.124 mg	Magnesium 32 mg
Carbohydrate 13.5 g	Niacin 0.92 mg	Phosphorus 88 mg
	Vitamin B$_6$ 0.28 mg	Sodium 34 mg
	Folic acid 94 mcg	

selection

Brussels sprouts should be firm and fresh in appearance, with a good green color. Avoid ones with dull, wilted, or yellow leaves.

preparation for juicing

Wash organic Brussels sprouts; soak or spray nonorganic ones with a biodegradable wash, then rinse.

brussels sprouts juice recipes

The phosphorus content of Brussels sprouts is nearly twice as high as their calcium content, and high phosphorus consumption has been linked to osteoporosis, because it will reduce the utilization and promote the excretion of calcium. Therefore, it is wise to juice Brussels sprouts with foods higher in calcium, like kale, spinach, and parsley. Brussels sprouts are pretty strong on their own; add 1/2 cup or 4 sprouts to Basic Carrot-Apple (page 191).

BRUSSELS SPROUTS–CARROT–SPINACH
 4 Brussels sprouts   1/2 cup spinach
 3 carrots

---

cabbage

The cruciferous family of vegetables includes cabbage, broccoli, cauliflower, Brussels sprouts, kale, collard, mustard, radishes, rutabagas, turnips, and other common vegetables. This family of vegetables is receiving much attention for its impressive anticancer properties (discussed below).

The modern-day cabbage developed from wild cabbage that was brought to Europe from Asia by roving bands of Celtic people around

600 BC. Cabbage spread as a food crop throughout northern Europe (Germany, Poland, Russia, Austria) because it was well adapted to cooler climates, had high yields per acre, and could be stored over the winter in cold cellars.

There are numerous types of cabbage, including different varieties of red and green cabbage. Varieties of cabbage are now cultivated throughout much of the northern latitudes of the Northern Hemisphere.

key benefits

The cabbage family of vegetables offers numerous health benefits. From a nutrient standpoint, cabbage provides excellent levels of many known nutrients, including vitamin C, potassium, iron, and calcium. But perhaps more important than the nutrient content of cabbage is the phytochemical level. The cabbage family contains more phytochemicals with demonstrable anticancer properties than any other vegetable family. In fact, one of the American Cancer

table 6.2. phytochemicals in cabbage with anticancer properties

COMPOUND	METHOD OF ACTION
Dithioltiones	Induce antioxidant and detoxification mechanisms
Glucosinolates	Induce antioxidant and detoxification mechanisms
Indoles	Induce antioxidant and detoxification mechanisms; improve metabolism of estrogen
Isothiocyanates	Inhibit cancer development and tumor growth
Coumarins	Block reaction of cancer-causing compounds at key sites
Phenols	Induce detoxification enzymes and prevent the formation of carcinogens

Society's key dietary recommendations to reduce the risk of cancer is to include in the diet on a regular basis cruciferous vegetables.

As is evident in table 6.2, the phytochemicals in cabbage work primarily by increasing antioxidant defense mechanisms as well as improving the body's ability to detoxify and eliminate harmful chemicals and hormones. The anticancer effects of cabbage-family vegetables have been noted in population studies. Consistently, the higher the intake of cabbage-family vegetables, the lower the rates of cancer, particularly breast cancer.[15]

Cabbage-family vegetables' chief anticancer phytochemicals are known as glucosinolates. The chief glucosinolate is indole-3-carbinol (I3C)—a compound formed from parent compounds whenever cruciferous vegetables are crushed or cut. Juicing is a fantastic way to dramatically form I3C in cabbage-family vegetables. The breaking of the cruciferous vegetable cells in juicing causes activation of the enzymes that make the I3C. Cooking deactivates this enzyme. IC3 and other glucosinolates are antioxidants and potent stimulators of natural detoxifying enzymes in the body. I3C is converted in the stomach to several compounds, including diindolymethane (DIM). Studies have shown that increasing the intake of cabbage-family vegetables or taking I3C or DIM as a dietary supplement significantly increased the conversion of estrogen from cancer-producing forms to nontoxic breakdown products.[16]

Fresh cabbage juice has also been shown to be extremely effective in the treatment of peptic ulcers, usually in less than 7 days (discussed fully in chapter 8).[17]

Cabbage-family vegetables contain goitrogens, compounds that can interfere with thyroid hormone action in certain situations (low iodine levels, primarily). The goitrogens are largely isothiocyanates that block the utilization of iodine; however, there is no evidence that these compounds in cruciferous vegetables interfere with thyroid function to any significant degree when dietary iodine levels are adequate. Therefore, it is a good idea if large quantities of cruciferous vegetables (more than four servings a day) are being consumed that the diet also contain adequate amounts of iodine. Iodine is found in kelp and other seaweeds, vegetables grown near the sea, seafood, iodized salt, and food supplements. Rutabagas and turnips contain the highest concentration of the goitrogens, so do not consume these raw very often.

nutritional analysis

½ head raw cabbage (500 g)		
NUTRIENTS & UNITS	**VITAMINS**	**MINERALS**
Water 420 g	Vitamin A 57 RE	Potassium 1,116 mg
Calories 108 kcal	Vitamin C 215 mg	Calcium 212 mg
Protein 5.5 g	Thiamine 0.23 mg	Iron 2.5 mg
Fat 0.82 g	Riboflavin 0.14 mg	Magnesium 67 mg
Carbohydrate 24.4 g	Niacin 1.4 mg	Phosphorus 110 mg
	Vitamin B$_6$ 0.43 mg	Sodium 82 mg
	Folic acid 207 mcg	

selection

Cabbage should appear fresh and crisp with no evidence of decay or worm injury.

preparation for juicing

Wash organic cabbage; soak or spray nonorganic cabbage with a biodegradable wash, then rinse. Cut the cabbage into slender wedges that can be fed into the juicer.

cabbage juice recipes

Cabbage juice is pretty strong on its own. See the recipes below and also Cruciferous Surprise (page 195), Purple Cow (page 208), and Vitamin U for Ulcer (page 210).

CABBAGE-CARROT

½ head of cabbage, cut into wedges

3 carrots

CABBAGE-CARROT-CELERY

½ head of cabbage, cut into wedges

3 carrots

2 celery ribs

CABBAGE-CARROT-PARSLEY

½ head of cabbage, cut into wedges

3 carrots

½ cup parsley

---

carrots

Carrots are believed to have originated in the Middle East and Asia. The earlier varieties were mostly purple and black. Apparently the modern-day carrot was originally a mutant variety lacking certain purple or black pigments. Carrots are now cultivated worldwide.

key benefits

The carrot is the king of vegetables. Of the commonly consumed vegetables, it is the highest source of pro–vitamin A carotenes. In fact, as shown below, two carrots provide roughly 4,050 retinol equivalents, or roughly four times the RDA for vitamin A. But, unlike vitamin A, beta-carotene and other carotenes in carrots do not cause toxicity. Carrots are full of many other nutrients and anutrients, but it is their carotene content that is most talked about.

Carrots are an excellent source of antioxidant compounds that help protect against cardiovascular disease and cancer and also promote good vision, especially night vision. In one study that examined the diets of 1,300 older adults in Massachusetts, those who had at least one serving of carrots and/or squash each day had a 60 percent reduction in their risk of heart attacks compared to those who ate less than one serving of these carotenoid-rich foods per day.[18]

High carotene intake has been linked with a 20 percent decrease in postmenopausal breast cancer and an up to 50 percent decrease in the incidence of cancers of the bladder, cervix, prostate, colon, larynx, and esophagus. Extensive human studies suggest that a diet including as little as one carrot per day could conceivably cut the rate of lung cancer in half.[19]

carrots, yellow skin, and safety

Eating a lot of carrots or carrot juice can lead to excess carotenes being stored in adipose tissue, the liver, other organs (the adrenals, testes, and ovaries have the highest concentrations), and the skin. Carotenes from carrots deposited in the skin can result in a yellowing of the skin known as carotenodermia. This occurrence is not serious. Carotenodermia is not directly attributable to dietary intake or supplementation; however, it may be indicative of a deficiency in a necessary factor that converts beta-carotene into vitamin A such as zinc, thyroid hormone, vitamin C, or protein.

The ingestion of large amounts of carrots or carrot juice (0.45 to 1.0 kg of fresh carrots per day for several years) has, however, been shown to cause a decrease in the number of white blood cells as well as menstrual disorders.[20] Although the blood carotene levels of these patients did reach levels (221 to 1,007 mcg/dl) similar to those of patients taking high doses of beta-carotene supplements for medical reasons (typically 800 mcg/dl), the disturbances are due to some other factor in carrots, as neither of these effects nor any others have been observed in subjects consuming very high doses of pure beta-carotene equivalent to 4 to 8 pounds of raw carrots over long periods of time.[21]

Since carrots are among the 20 foods on which pesticide residues have been most frequently found, choose carrots grown organically.

nutritional analysis

2 raw carrots (144 g)		
NUTRIENTS & UNITS	**VITAMINS**	**MINERALS**
Water 126 g	Vitamin A 4,050 RE	Potassium 466 mg
Calories 62 kcal	Vitamin C 13.4 mg	Calcium 38 mg
Protein 1.5 g	Thiamine 0.14 mg	Iron 0.72 mg
Fat 0.28 g	Riboflavin 0.84 mg	Magnesium 22 mg
Carbohydrate 14.6 g	Niacin 1.3 mg	Phosphorus 64 mg
	Vitamin B$_6$ 0.2 mg	Sodium 50 mg
	Folic acid 20 mcg	

selection

Carrots should be fresh-looking, firm, smooth, and vibrantly colored. Avoid carrots that have cracks, are bruised, or have mold growing on them. The deeper the orange, the more beta-carotene present in the carrot. Avoid carrots that are excessively cracked as well as those that are limp or rubbery (a sign of age). In addition, if the carrots do not have their tops attached, look at the stem end and ensure that it is not darkly colored as this is also a sign of age. If the green tops are attached, they should be brightly colored and feathery, not wilted. Since the sugars are concentrated in the carrots' core, generally those with larger diameters will have a larger core and therefore be sweeter.

Carrots are hardy vegetables that will keep longer than many others if stored properly. The trick to preserving the freshness of carrot roots is to minimize the amount of moisture they lose. To do this, make sure to store them in the coolest part of the refrigerator in a perforated plastic bag or wrapped in a paper towel, which will reduce the amount of condensation that is able to form. They should be able to keep fresh for about 2 weeks. Carrots should also be stored away from apples, pears, potatoes, and other fruits and vegetables that produce ethylene gas since it will cause them to become bitter.

If you purchase carrot roots with attached green tops, the tops should be cut off before storing in the refrigerator since they will cause the carrots to wilt prematurely as they pull moisture from the roots. While the tops can be stored in the refrigerator, kept moist by being wrapped in a damp paper, they should really be used soon after purchase since they are fragile and will quickly begin to wilt.

preparation for juicing

Wash organic carrots; soak or spray nonorganic ones with a biodegradable wash, then scrub and rinse. It is recommended that you cut off the carrot tops. At the very least, do not juice more than a few carrot greens, as they are a rich source of compounds that once absorbed into the body can react with sunlight to produce a severe sunburn or rash. Feed the carrots into the juicer fat end first to avoid getting the carrot stuck.

carrot juice recipes

Carrot juice is one of the most popular juices because it is delicious on its own. Its sweet flavor makes it a valuable addition to many bitter-tasting vegetable juices. Try the recipes below and also Asparagus-Carrot-Celery (page 119), Beet-Carrot (page 125), Beet-Carrot-Celery (page 125), Beet-Carrot-Parsley (page 125), Beet-Carrot-Pepper (page 125), Beet-Carrot-Spinach (page 125), Broccoli-Carrot (page 130), Broccoli-Carrot-Celery (page 130), Broccoli-Carrot-Parsley (page 130), Brussels Sprouts–Carrot–Spinach (page 131), Cabbage-Carrot (page 135), Cabbage-Carrot-Celery (page 135), Cabbage-Carrot-Parsley (page 135), Basic Carrot-Apple (page 191), Better Red Than Dead (page 192), Bone Builder's Cocktail (page 193), Cholesterol-Lowering Tonic (page 193), Cleansing Cocktail (page 194), Cruciferous Surprise (page 195), Diuretic Formula (page 197), Energizer (page 198), Everything but the Kitchen Sink (page 199), Ginger Hopper (page 201), Immune Power Veggie (page 203), Iron Plus (page 204), Jicama-Carrot-Apple (page

204), Liver Tonic (page 205), Popeye's Power Drink (page 207), Potassium Power (page 207), Super V-7 (page 209), and Vitamin U for Ulcer (page 210).

CARROT-CAULIFLOWER
4 carrots
1 cup cauliflower

CARROT-CELERY
4 carrots
4 celery ribs

CARROT-CELERY-PARSLEY
4 carrots
3 celery ribs
½ cup parsley

CARROT-CUCUMBER-PARSLEY
4 carrots
½ cucumber
½ cup parsley

CARROT–DANDELION GREENS
5 carrots
½ cup dandelion greens

CARROT–DANDELION ROOT
4 carrots
1 dandelion root

CARROT-DANDELIONS-SPINACH
4 carrots
1 dandelion root
½ cup spinach

CARROT-FENNEL
4 carrots
½ fennel bulb

CARROT–JERUSALEM ARTICHOKE
4 carrots
1 cup Jerusalem artichoke

CARROT-JICAMA
5 carrots
½ cup jicama

CARROT-KALE
5 carrots
3 kale leaves

CARROT-LEEK-PARSLEY
4 carrots
1 leek
1 cup parsley

CARROT-LETTUCE
4 carrots
1 head of lettuce, cut into wedges

CARROT-ONION-PARSLEY
4 carrots
½ onion
1 cup parsley

CARROT-PEPPER
   5 carrots
   ½ green or red bell pepper

CARROT-TURNIP
   4 carrots
   1 turnip with greens

CARROT-RADISH
   4 carrots
   ¼ Daikon radish or
   2 radishes with greens

CARROT-WHEATGRASS
   5 carrots
   ½ cup wheatgrass

CARROT-SPINACH
   5 carrots
   1 cup spinach

CARROT–SWEET POTATO
   4 carrots
   ½ sweet potato

---

cauliflower

Like broccoli and Brussels sprouts, cauliflower also evolved from the wild cabbage. It is thought that the original variety may have come from Asia, but it was in Italy that it was developed to its present form. Because cauliflower is susceptible to both frost and hot weather, over 80 percent of the U.S. crop is produced in California.

key benefits

Cauliflower is not as nutrient dense as many of the other cabbage-family vegetables. Cauliflower is white because of the ribbed, coarse green leaves that protect the curd from sunlight, thereby impeding the development of chlorophyll. While this process contributes to the white coloring of most of the varieties, cauliflower can also be found in light green and purple colors. Its white color is a sign that it has much less of the beneficial carotenes and chlorophyll. Cauliflower is a good source of boron (see page 35), as it will not grow well in boron-deficient soil. For the anticancer properties of cauliflower, see Cabbage.

nutritional analysis

1 cup raw cauliflower, cut into 1-inch pieces (100 g)		
NUTRIENTS & UNITS	**VITAMINS**	**MINERALS**
Water 92.26 g	Vitamin A 2 RE	Potassium 355 mg
Calories 24 kcal	Vitamin C 71.5 mg	Calcium 29 mg
Protein 2 g	Thiamine 0.76 mg	Iron 0.58 mg
Fat 0.18 g	Riboflavin 0.057 mg	Magnesium 14 mg
Carbohydrate 4.9 g	Niacin 0.63 mg	Phosphorus 46 mg
	Vitamin B_6 0.231 mg	Sodium 15 mg
	Folic acid 66 mcg	

selection

Cauliflower should be fresh-looking, with clean, white-colored flower heads and crisp fresh leaves. Avoid cauliflower with wilted leaves, dirty flower heads, or obvious signs of decay.

preparation for juicing

Wash organic cauliflower; soak or spray nonorganic cauliflower with a biodegradable wash, then scrub and rinse. Cut the cauliflower into pieces that will easily fit into the juicer.

cauliflower juice recipes

Straight cauliflower juice is pretty strong; mix 1/2 cup with Basic Carrot-Apple (page 191) or Energizer (page 198).

---

celery

Celery is a member of the umbelliferous family along with carrots, parsley, and fennel. Modern celery evolved from wild celery native to the Mediterranean, where its seeds were once widely used as a medicine, particularly as a diuretic.

key benefits

Celery is an excellent source of vitamin C and fiber. It is a very good source of potassium, folate, vitamin B_6, and vitamin B_1. Celery is a good source of calcium and vitamin B_2. While it is true that celery contains higher amounts of sodium than most other vegetables, the sodium levels are offset by relatively very high levels of potassium. Furthermore, the amount is not significant even for the most salt-sensitive individuals. One celery rib contains approximately 35 mg sodium. Because celery juice is rich in potassium and sodium, it makes a great electrolyte replacement drink.

Celery contains phytochemicals known as coumarins that are being shown to tone the vascular system and lower blood pressure; they may also be useful in cases of migraines. Two researchers at the University of Chicago Medical Center have performed studies on a coumarin compound found in celery, 3-n-butylphthalide (3nB), and found that it can indeed lower blood pressure.[22] In animal studies, a very small amount of 3nB lowered blood pressure by 12 to 14 percent and also lowered cholesterol by about 7 percent. The equivalent dose in humans can be supplied in about 4 celery ribs. The research was prompted by the father of one of the researchers, who after eating 1/4 pound celery every day for 1 week observed his blood pressure dropped from 158/96 to a normal reading of 118/82.

Clinical research indicates that celery may be particularly helpful for sufferers of gout as 3nB appears to significantly lower the production of uric acid.[23] Celery may also help lower cholesterol, prevent cancer by improving detoxification, and extend lifespan.[24] In the animal model of Alzheimer's disease, 3nB treatment significantly improved learning deficits as well as long-term spatial memory.[25]

3nB treatment also significantly reduced total cerebral beta-amyloid plaque deposition that is the hallmark brain lesion of Alzheimer's. The researchers concluded "3nB shows promising preclinical potential as a multitarget drug for the prevention and/or treatment of Alzheimer's disease."

nutritional analysis

3 raw celery ribs (120 g)

NUTRIENTS & UNITS	VITAMINS	MINERALS
Water 114 g	Vitamin A 16 RE	Potassium 340 mg
Calories 18 kcal	Vitamin C 7.6 mg	Calcium 44 mg
Protein 0.8 g	Thiamine 0.04 mg	Iron 0.6 mg
Fat 1.4 g	Riboflavin 0.04 mg	Magnesium 14 mg
Carbohydrate 4.4 g	Niacin 0.36 mg	Phosphorus 32 mg
	Vitamin B_6 0.036 mg	Sodium 106 mg
	Folic acid 10.6 mcg	

selection

The best celery is light green, fresh-looking, and crisp. The ribs should snap, not bend. Limp, pliable celery should be avoided.

preparation for juicing

Cut the bottom portion to separate the ribs and allow for complete cleaning. Wash organic celery; soak or spray nonorganic celery with a biodegradable wash, then rinse.

celery juice recipes

Celery juice can be quite satisfying on its own, but it is usually mixed with other juices. See the recipes below and also Asparagus-Carrot-Celery (page 119), Asparagus-Celery (page 119), Beet-Carrot-Celery (page 125), Broccoli-Carrot-Celery (page 130), Cabbage-Carrot-Celery (page 135), Carrot-Celery (page 139), Apple Wonder (page 191), Cleansing Cocktail (page 194), Cucumber-Celery Cooler (page 196), Cucumber-Celery Mojito Cooler (page 196), Diuretic Formula (page 197), Everything but the Kitchen Sink (page 199), Femme Fatale (page 199), Go Away Gout (page 201), Go Away Pain (page 201), Go Green Drink (page 202), Go-Go Green Drink (page 202), Potassium Power (page 207), Super V-7 (page 209), Vitamin U for Ulcer (page 210), and Waldorf Salad (page 210).

CELERY-CABBAGE
4 celery ribs

½ head of cabbage, cut into wedges

CELERY-CUCUMBER
4 celery ribs

½ cucumber

CELERY-CUCUMBER-KALE
4 celery ribs

½ cucumber

3 kale leaves

CELERY-CUCUMBER-PARSLEY
4 celery ribs

½ cucumber

½ cup parsley

CELERY-CUCUMBER-PARSLEY-SPINACH
4 celery ribs

½ cucumber

½ cup parsley

½ cup spinach

CELERY–DANDELION GREENS
4 celery ribs

1 cup dandelion greens

CELERY-FENNEL
4 celery ribs

½ fennel bulb

CELERY-FENNEL-PARSLEY
4 celery ribs

½ fennel bulb

½ cup parsley

CELERY-LETTUCE-SPINACH
4 celery ribs

1 head of lettuce, cut into wedges

½ cup spinach

chard, swiss (see KALE)

collards (see KALE)

cucumbers

The cucumber is a tropical plant that originated in Southeast Asia. Cucumbers are refreshing vegetables in their fresh form; unfortunately, over 70 percent of the U.S. cucumber crop is used to make pickles. This fact means that most cucumbers are consumed as pickles, a less nutritious form.

key benefits

Fresh cucumbers are composed primarily of water. The hard skin of the cucumber is an excellent source of some important minerals like silica, which contributes to the strength of connective tissue, which includes the intracellular cement, muscles, tendons, ligaments, cartilage, and bone. Without silica, connective tissue would not be properly constructed. Cucumber juice is often recommended as a source of silica and as a way to improve the complexion and the health of the skin.

nutritional analysis

1 raw cucumber (301 g)		
NUTRIENTS & UNITS	**VITAMINS**	**MINERALS**
Water 289 g	Vitamin A 14 RE	Potassium 448 mg
Calories 39 kcal	Vitamin C 0.09 mg	Calcium 42 mg
Protein 1.63 g	Thiamine 0.06 mg	Iron 0.84 mg
Fat 0.39 g	Riboflavin 0.9 mg	Magnesium 33 mg
Carbohydrate 8.76 g	Niacin 0.752 mg	Phosphorus 51 mg
	Vitamin B₆ 0.156 mg	Sodium 6 mg
	Folic acid 42 mcg	

selection

Cucumbers should be well shaped and medium to dark green in color. Avoid withered, shriveled, and yellow ones. Try to buy cucumbers that have not been waxed.

preparation for juicing

Wash organic cucumbers; soak or spray nonorganic ones with a biodegradable wash, then rinse. Waxed cucumbers should be peeled.

cucumber juice recipes

Cucumber juice on its own is not that satisfying; it's best mixed with other juices. See the recipes below and also Carrot-Cucumber-Parsley (page 139), Celery-Cucumber (page 144), Celery-Cucumber-Parsley (page 144), Celery-Cucumber-Parsley-Spinach (page 144), Celery-Cucumber-Kale (page 144), Cucumber Celery Cooler (page 196), Cucumber-Celery Mojito Cooler (page 196), Everything but the Kitchen Sink (page 199), Salad in a Glass (page 208), and Super V-7 (page 209).

CUCUMBER-TOMATO-PARSLEY

½ cucumber

2 tomatoes, quartered

½ cup parsley

CUCUMBER-TOMATO-WATERCRESS

½ cucumber

2 tomatoes, quartered

1 bunch of watercress

---

daikon radish

Radishes are discussed at length below. The daikon radish deserves its own section because it is an ideal root vegetable for juicing—it's large, has a high water content, and is packed full of health benefits.

Daikon in Japanese translates to "large root." The daikon radish is used in a variety of forms in Japanese cuisine. For example, daikon is also frequently grated and mixed into ponzu (a soy sauce and citrus juice condiment) as a dip. Daikon radish sprouts are used for salad or garnishing of sashimi. Daikon is also central to the cuisines of China, Korea, India, and in food throughout the rest of Asia.

key benefits

Raw daikon is used throughout Asia not only to complement the taste of foods but also to aid in their digestion. Raw daikon is abundant in digestive enzymes. In Japan, restaurants serve grated daikon in tempura dip to help digest oils and shredded daikon with sushi to help digest the protein. It is important, however, to drink daikon juice immediately because in just 30 minutes nearly 50 percent of its enzymes are lost.

Since the daikon radish belongs to the cabbage family, it has many anticancer properties (see discussion of cabbage on page 131). It helps prevent the formation of cancer-causing compounds in the body, such as nitrosamines, as well as aids in their elimination. All radish varieties are highly valued for their effects in improving processes within the liver that enhance the detoxification of harmful compounds.

Daikon exerts diuretic activity helping the body get rid of excess fluid. It is also very useful in upper respiratory infections, exerting a decongesting effect to help thin respiratory mucus.

All varieties of radishes and their greens are very low in calories and an excellent source of vitamin C.

nutritional analysis

1 cup, diced, 100 g		
NUTRIENTS & UNITS	**VITAMINS**	**MINERALS**
Water 63 g	Vitamin A 2 RE	Potassium 233 mg
Calories 16 kcal	Vitamin C 15 mg	Calcium 25 mg
Protein 0.68 g	Thiamin 0.02 mg	Iron 0.34 mg
Fat 0.7 g	Riboflavin 0.02 mg	Magnesium 10 mg
Carbohydrate 1.9 g	Niacin 0.25 mg	Phosphorus 20 mg
	Vitamin B_6 0.07 mg	Sodium 14 mg
	Folic acid 25 mcg	

selection

Daikon radishes should be firm with no visible signs of mold or spoilage. Avoid soft, withered, shriveled, or discolored ones. Daikons can be stored for up to 2 weeks.

preparation for juicing

Daikon radishes should be washed thoroughly and cut lengthwise for preparation to feed into the juicer.

daikon radish juice recipes

Daikon radish juice can have a strong taste, so it is often mixed with carrot, celery, or apple juices. But, of course, if you like things a bit pungent and spicy, it's a great addition to any juice recipe. See

Cruciferous Surprise Extreme (page 196), Digestive Fire (page 197), Diuretic Formula Plus (page 197), Enzymes Galore Plus (page 199), Ginger Hopper Plus (page 201), Immune Power Veggie Extreme (page 203), Liver Mover (page 205), Liver Tonic (page 205), Liver Tonic Plus (page 205), Some Like It Hot (page 208), Spicy Jicama Fiesta (page 209), and Tomato Zest (page 209).

---

dandelions

The dandelion is a perennial plant with an almost worldwide distribution. While many individuals consider the dandelion an unwanted weed, herbalists all over the world have revered this valuable herb. Its name is a corruption of the French for "tooth-of-the-lion" (*dent-de-lion*), which describes the herb's leaves with their several large, pointed teeth. Its scientific name, *Taraxacum*, is from the Greek *taraxos* (disorder) and *akos* (remedy). This alludes to dandelions' ability to correct a multitude of disorders. Dandelions have a long history of folk use throughout the world. In Europe, dandelions were used in the treatment of fevers, boils, eye problems, diarrhea, fluid retention, liver congestion, heartburn, and various skin problems. In China, dandelions have been used in the treatment of breast problems (cancer, inflammation, lack of milk flow), liver diseases, appendicitis, and digestive ailments. Their use in India, Russia, and other parts of the world revolved primarily around their action on the liver.

key benefits

Dandelions are a rich source of nutrients and other compounds that may improve liver functions, promote weight loss, and possess diuretic effects. The dandelion is particularly high in vitamins and minerals, protein, choline, inulin, and pectins. Its carotenoid content is extremely high as reflected by its higher vitamin A content than carrots: Dandelions have 14,000 IU (international units) vitamin A per 100 g compared to 11,000 IU for carrots. Dandelions should be thought of as an extremely nutritious food and rich source of medicinal compounds that have a toning effect on the body. Both the greens and the roots can be used for this purpose.

Dandelion root supports the liver, both as food and medicine. Studies in humans and laboratory animals have shown that dandelion root enhances the flow of bile, improving such conditions as liver congestion, bile duct inflammation, hepatitis, gallstones, and jaundice. Dandelions' action on increasing bile flow is twofold: They have a direct effect on the liver, causing an increase in bile production and flow to the gallblandder (choleretic effect), and a direct effect on the gallbladder, causing contraction and release of stored bile (cholagogue effect). Dandelions' historical use in such a wide variety of conditions is probably closely related to their ability to improve liver function.[26]

Dandelions have also been used historically in the treatment of obesity. This fact prompted researchers to investigate dandelions' effect on the body weight of experimental animals. When these animals were administered a fluid extract of dandelion greens for one month, they lost as much as 30 percent of their initial weight. Much of the weight loss appeared to be a result of significant diuretic activity.[27]

selection

Wild dandelions are plentiful in most parts of the United States. Dandelion greens are often available commercially as well, especially at open markets and health food stores. The fresher the dandelions, the better.

preparation for juicing

Dandelion greens and roots should be washed thoroughly. For some juicers the whole dandelion may be able to be pushed through; otherwise, slice the roots and bunch up the greens.

dandelion juice recipes

You will want to mix dandelions with other vegetables. See these recipes: Carrot–Dandelion Greens (page 139), Carrot–Dandelion Root (page 139), Carrot-Dandelions-Spinach (page 139), Celery–Dandelion Greens (page 144), Diuretic Formula (page 197), and Liver Tonic recipes (page 205).

---

fennel

Fennel is a member of the umbelliferous family along with celery, carrots, and parsley. Like many vegetables, modern-day fennel was developed in Italy. It has a long history as a medicinal plant in the Mediterranean region. Fennel has a licorice flavor.

key benefits

Fennel does offer some good nutrition, but it is largely used for its more medicinal effects. Among herbalists, fennel is referred to as (1) an intestinal antispasmodic; (2) a carminative, or compound that relieves or expels gas; (3) a stomachic, or compound that tones and strengthens the stomach; and (4) an anodyne, or compound that relieves or soothes pain. Fennel also contains substances known as phytoestrogens, making it useful in many conditions specific to women, especially menopause. Fennel is even higher in coumarin compounds than celery or carrots.

nutritional analysis

1 cup, diced, 70 g		
NUTRIENTS & UNITS	**VITAMINS**	**MINERALS**
Water 63 g	Vitamin A 0 RE	Potassium 143 mg
Calories 22 kcal	Vitamin C 0 mg	Calcium 1 mg
Protein 1.36 g	Thiamin 0.1 mg	Iron 0.21 mg
Fat 0.13 g	Riboflavin 0.17 mg	Magnesium 7 mg
Carbohydrate 2.5 g	Niacin 4.6 mg	Phosphorus 52 mg
	Vitamin B$_6$ 0.039 mg	Sodium 1 mg
	Folic acid 15 mcg	

selection

Fennel should be bought with the stems and fronds attached, which indicate freshness. Like celery, its branches should snap with pressure as opposed to bending.

preparation for juicing

Wash organic fennel; soak or spray nonorganic fennel with a biodegradable wash, then rinse. Cut up the bulb and branches so that they can be fed into the juicer.

fennel juice recipes

Fennel is pretty strong-tasting on its own, so unless you really love licorice, mix it with carrots, apples, pears, or celery. See Carrot-Fennel (page 139), Celery-Fennel (page 144), Celery-Fennel-Parsley (page 144), Femme Fatale (page 199), and Tummy Tonic (page 209).

---

garlic

Garlic is a member of the lily family. It is cultivated worldwide. The garlic bulb is composed of individual cloves enclosed in a papery skin. Garlic has been used throughout history to treat a variety of conditions. Sanskrit records document garlic remedies approximately 5,000 years ago; the Chinese have been using it for at least 3,000 years. The Codex Ebers, an Egyptian medical papyrus dating to about 1550 BC, mentions garlic as an effective remedy for a variety of ailments. Hippocrates, Aristotle, and Pliny cited numerous therapeutic applications for garlic. In general, garlic has been used throughout the world to treat coughs, toothache, earache, dandruff, hypertension, atherosclerosis, hysteria, diarrhea, dysentery, diphtheria, vaginitis, and many other conditions.

Stories, verse, and folklore (such as its alleged ability to ward off vampires) give historical documentation to garlic's power. Sir John Harrington in *The Englishman's Doctor*, written in 1609, summarized garlic's virtues and faults:

> *Garlic then have power to save from death*
> *Bear with it though it maketh unsavory breath,*
> *And scorn not garlic like some that think*
> *It only maketh men wink and drink and stink.*

key benefits

The therapeutic uses of garlic are quite extensive. Its consumption should be encouraged, despite its odor, especially in individuals with elevated cholesterol levels, heart disease, high blood pressure, diabetes, candidiasis, asthma, infections (particularly of the respiratory tract), and gastrointestinal complaints.

Many studies have found that garlic decreases total serum cholesterol levels while increasing serum HDL cholesterol levels. HDL cholesterol, often termed the "good" cholesterol, is a protective factor against heart disease.[28] Garlic has also demonstrated blood-pressure-lowering action in many studies. Garlic has been shown to decrease the systolic pressure by 20 to 30 mm Hg and the diastolic by 10 to 20 mm Hg in patients with high blood pressure.[29]

In a 1979 study of three populations of vegetarians in the Jain community in India who consumed differing amounts of garlic and onions, numerous favorable effects on blood lipids were observed in the group that consumed the largest amount (see table 6.3).[30] The study is quite significant because the subjects had nearly identical diets, except for garlic and onion ingestion.

table 6.3. effects of garlic and onion consumption on serum lipids under carefully matched diets

GARLIC CONSUMPTION	CHOLESTEROL LEVEL	TRIGLYCERIDE LEVEL
Garlic 50 g / wk	159 mg/dl	52 mg/dl onion 600 g / wk
Garlic 10 g / wk	172 mg/dl	75 mg/dl onion 200 g / wk
No garlic or onions	208 mg/dl	109 mg/dl

Source: G. S. Sainani, D. B. Desai, N. H. Gohre, et al., "Effect of Dietary Garlic and Onion on Serum Lipid Profile in Jain Community," *Indian Journal of Medical Research* 69 (1979): 776–80.

Garlic has also been found to do the following:

- **Lower blood sugar levels in diabetes.**
- **Help eliminate heavy metals like lead.**
- **Promote detoxification reactions.**
- **Enhance the immune system.**
- **Protect against cancer.**
- **Exert antimicrobial effects.**

It is beyond the scope of this book to detail all the wonderful properties of this truly remarkable medicinal plant. Its use as a food should be encouraged, despite its odor, especially in individuals with elevated cholesterol levels, heart disease, high blood pressure, diabetes, candida infections, asthma, infections (particularly respiratory tract infections), and gastrointestinal complaints.

Much of garlic's therapeutic effect is thought to result from its volatile factors, composed of sulfur-containing compounds: allicin, diallyl disulfide, diallyl trisulfide, and others. Other constituents of garlic include additional sulfur-containing compounds, high concentrations of trace minerals (particularly selenium and germanium), glucosinolates, and enzymes. The compound allicin is mainly responsible for the pungent odor of garlic.

Many of the therapeutic compounds in garlic have not been found in cooked, processed, and commercial forms, so the broad range of beneficial effects attributed to garlic are best obtained from fresh, raw garlic, although limited, specific effects can be obtained from the other forms. For medicinal purposes, at least 3 garlic cloves a day is recommended; for protective measures, at least 1 garlic clove a day is a good idea.

selection

Buy fresh garlic. Do not buy garlic that is soft, shows evidence of decay such as mildew or darkening, or is beginning to sprout.

preparation for juicing

Remove the garlic clove from the bulb and wrap it in a green vegetable, such as parsley. This accomplishes two things: (1) It prevents the garlic from popping out of the juicer and (2) the chlorophyll helps bind some of the odor. It is a good idea to juice the garlic first, as the other vegetables will remove the odor from the machine.

garlic juice recipes

You can add garlic to Energizer (page 198). Also see Cholesterol-Lowering Tonic (page 193) and Immune Power Veggie (page 203).

ginger

Ginger is an erect perennial herb that has thick tuberous rhizomes (underground stems and root). It originated in southern Asia, although it is now extensively cultivated throughout the tropics, including India, China, Jamaica, Haiti, and Nigeria. Exports from Jamaica to all parts of the world amount to more than 2 million pounds annually. Ginger has been used for thousands of years in China to treat numerous health conditions.

key benefits

Historically, the majority of complaints for which ginger was used concerned the gastrointestinal system. Ginger is generally regarded as an excellent carminative (a substance that promotes the elimination of intestinal gas) and intestinal spasmolytic (a substance that relaxes and soothes the intestinal tract).

A clue to ginger's success in eliminating gastrointestinal distress is offered by recent double-blind studies that showed ginger to be effective in preventing the symptoms of motion sickness, especially seasickness. In fact, in one study ginger was shown to be far superior to Dramamine (dimenhydrinate), a commonly used over-the-counter and prescription drug for motion sickness.[31] Ginger reduces all symptoms associated with motion sickness, including dizziness, nausea, vomiting, and cold sweating.

Ginger has also been used to treat the nausea and vomiting associated with pregnancy. Recently, the benefit of ginger was confirmed in hyperemesis gravidarum, the most severe form of morning sickness.[32] This condition usually requires hospitalization. Ginger-root powder at a dose of 250 mg four times a day brought about a significant reduction in both the severity of the nausea and the number of vomiting attacks.

Ginger has also been shown to be a very potent inhibitor of the formation of the inflammatory compounds prostaglandin and thromboxanes. This could explain some of ginger's historical use as an anti-inflammatory agent. However, fresh ginger also has strong antioxidant properties and contains a protease (a protein-digesting enzyme) that may have action similar to bromelain on inflammation.

In one clinical study, seven patients with rheumatoid arthritis, for whom conventional drugs had provided only temporary or partial relief, were treated with ginger. One patient took 50 g lightly cooked ginger per day, while the remaining six took either 5 g fresh or 0.1 to 1 g powdered ginger daily. All patients reported substantial improvement, including pain relief, joint mobility, and decrease in swelling and morning stiffness.[33] Ginger has also been shown to significantly reduce serum cholesterol and improve liver function.

Although most scientific studies have used powdered ginger, fresh ginger at an equivalent dosage is believed to yield even better results because it contains active enzymes and higher levels of other more active constituents as well. Most studies used 1 g powdered ginger. This would be equivalent to about 10 g or 1/3 ounce fresh ginger, roughly a 1/4-inch slice.

selection

Fresh ginger can now be purchased in the produce section at most supermarkets. The bronze root should be fresh-looking, with no signs of decay like soft spots, mildew, or a dry, wrinkled skin. Store fresh ginger in the refrigerator.

preparation for juicing

Slice the amount of ginger desired and feed into the juicer. It's best to feed the ginger in first, before whatever you are juicing it with in order to make sure it is juiced thoroughly.

ginger juice recipes

See Apple-Pear-Ginger (page 71), Apple Spice (page 190), Cholesterol-Lowering Tonic (page 193), Digestive Delight (page 197), Don Juan (page 198), Ginger Ale (page 200), Ginger Hopper (page 201), Immune Power Veggie (page 203), Kill the Cold (page 204), Pineapple-Ginger Ale (page 207), and Tummy Tonic (page 209).

---

jerusalem artichoke

The Jerusalem artichoke, often referred to as a sunchoke, is native to North America. It is not part of the artichoke family; in fact, it belongs to the daisy family (Compositae) and is closely related to the sunflower. *Jerusalem* is thought to be an English corruption of Ter Neusen, the place in the Netherlands from which the plant was introduced into England, although *Webster*'s says that *Jerusalem* is a corruption of *girasole*, "sunflower" in Italian. The plants were cultivated by the Native Americans.

key benefits

Jerusalem artichokes are full of a sugar known as inulin. Inulin is a polysaccharide, or starch, that is handled by the body differently than other sugars. In fact, inulin is not used by the body for energy metabolism. This makes Jerusalem artichokes extremely beneficial to diabetics. Inulin has actually been shown to improve blood sugar control. Since the body does not utilize the primary carbohydrate of the Jerusalem artichoke, the calorie content is virtually nil, only 7 per 100 g (roughly 3½ ounces).

Although inulin is not utilized by the human body, it does provide nutrition to health-promoting bacteria in the intestinal tract. Specifically, inulin promotes the growth of bifidobacteria, a cousin of *Lactobacillus acidophilus,* the primary organism in live yogurt cultures.[34] One caveat: Since the majority of carbohydrate in Jerusalem artichoke is indigestible inulin, these tubers may, like beans, cause flatulence in some people, so try them out in small amounts initially.

Jerusalem artichokes may also have some immune-enhancing activity, as inulin also has the ability to enhance the *complement system* of our immune system. The complement system is responsible for increasing host defense mechanisms such as neutralizing viruses, destroying harmful bacteria, and increasing the movement of white blood cells (neutrophils, monocytes, eosinophils, and lymphocytes) to areas of infection. Many medicinal plants, like echinacea and burdock, owe much of their immune-enhancing effects to inulin. Jerusalem artichokes are one of the richest sources of inulin available.

nutritional analysis

1 cup, diced, 75 g		
NUTRIENTS & UNITS	**VITAMINS**	**MINERALS**
Water 60 g	Vitamin A 0 RE	Potassium 152 mg
Calories 250 kcal	Vitamin C 15 mg	Calcium 18 mg
Protein 0.42 g	Thiamin 0.02 mg	Iron 0.28 mg
Fat 0.7 g	Riboflavin 0.02 mg	Magnesium 12 mg
Carbohydrate 2.8 g	Niacin 0.14 mg	Phosphorus 14 mg
	Vitamin B$_6$ 0.03 mg	Sodium 14 mg
	Folic acid 20 mcg	

selection

Fresh Jerusalem artichokes should be firm, with no visible signs of mold, discoloration, or spoilage.

preparation for juicing

Wash organic Jerusalem artichokes; soak or spray nonorganic ones with a biodegradable wash, then rinse.

jerusalem artichoke juice recipes

By itself, the juice is pretty harsh; it is best to mix it with carrot, apple, or pear. See also Carrot–Jerusalem Artichoke (page 139) and Immune Power Veggie (page 203).

---

jicama

Jicama, pronounced HEE-ka-ma, is a turnip-shaped root vegetable native to Mexico and Central America.

key benefits

Jicama's high water content (86 to 90 percent) makes it a fantastic vegetable to juice. Like most root vegetables, it is especially high in potassium. Its flavor is very similar to that of a water chestnut. In fact, many Asian restaurants substitute jicama for the more expensive water chestnut.

selection

High-quality jicama should be firm and heavy for its size. Jicama that is shriveled, soft, or particularly large is likely to be tough, woody, and contain less water.

preparation for juicing

Wash organic jicama; soak or spray nonorganic jicama with a biode-gradable wash, then scrub and rinse. Cut up the jicama into pieces that will feed into the juicer.

jicama juice recipes

Jicama is too potent to drink on its own. See Carrot-Jicama (page 139), Jicama-Carrot-Apple (page 204), and Spicy Jicama Fiesta (page 209).

---

kale and other greens

Kale is probably the closest relative of wild cabbage in the whole cabbage family. Kale and collards are essentially the same vegetable, but kale has leaves with curly edges and is less tolerant of heat. Kale is native to Europe, where it has been cultivated for many centuries as food for people as well as animals. In the United States, kale is grown primarily on the East Coast from Delaware to Florida. Other greens of the cabbage family such as mustard greens, turnip greens, kohlrabi, and watercress offer benefits like those of kale and collards and can be used similarly.

key benefits

Greens like kale are among the most highly nutritious vegetables. Kale is rich in essential vitamins and minerals, especially calcium, potassium, and iron. A cup of kale juice has more calcium than a cup of milk. Furthermore, it contains almost three times as much calcium as phosphorus. High phosphorus consumption has been linked to osteoporosis, as it will reduce the utilization and promote the excretion of calcium.

As a member of the cabbage family, kale exhibits the same sort of anticancer properties (see Cabbage). It is an excellent source of carotenes and chlorophyll.

nutritional analysis

1 cup raw kale (100 g)		
NUTRIENTS & UNITS	**VITAMINS**	**MINERALS**
Water 88 g	Vitamin A 1,066 RE	Potassium 243 mg
Calories 45 kcal	Vitamin C 102 mg	Calcium 206 mg
Protein 5 g	Thiamine 0.11 mg	Iron 1.8 mg
Fat 1 g	Riboflavin 0.2 mg	Magnesium 12 mg
Carbohydrate 7 g	Niacin 1.8 mg	Phosphorus 64 mg
	Vitamin B$_6$ 0.18 mg	Sodium 2 mg
	Folic acid 183 mcg	

selection

High-quality kale is fresh, tender, and dark green. Avoid greens that show dry or yellowing leaves, evidence of insect injury, or decay.

preparation for juicing

Rinse organic kale; soak or spray nonorganic kale with a biodegradable wash, then rinse. A salad spinner is a great way to dry the leaves and prepare them for juicing. Usually the leaves can be fed into the juicer intact; large leaves may need to be cut.

kale juice recipes

The juice of kale and other greens is difficult to drink on its own because the greens are so bitter but can be added to other juices for a delicious and healthful drink. See the Carrot-Kale (page 139), Celery-Cucumber-Kale (page 144), Bone Builder's Cocktail (page 193), Cruciferous Surprise (page 195), Go Green Drink (page 202),

Go-Go Green (page 202), Green Drink for Kids (page 202), Iron Plus (page 204), and Purple Cow (page 208).

leeks

Leeks are related to onions and garlic. While the bulbs of garlic and onions are typically the edible portion, the edible portion of the leek is above the roots and stem base (the white base of the leaves and the green leaves).

key benefits

Leeks share many of the qualities of onions and garlic, but they are less dense. This means that larger quantities of leeks would need to be consumed in order to produce effects similar to those of onions and garlic. Presumably, leeks can lower cholesterol levels, improve the immune system, and fight cancer in a way similar to onions and garlic.

nutritional analysis

½ cup raw leeks (100 g)		
NUTRIENTS & UNITS	**VITAMINS**	**MINERALS**
Water 82 g	Vitamin A 60 RE	Potassium 347 mg
Calories 90 kcal	Vitamin C 17 mg	Calcium 50 mg
Protein 2.2 g	Thiamine 0.11 mg	Iron 1.1 mg
Fat 0.3 g	Riboflavin 0.06 mg	Magnesium 6 mg
Carbohydrate 11.2 g	Niacin 0.5 mg	Phosphorus 50 mg
	Vitamin B$_6$ 0.05 mg	Sodium 5 mg
	Folic acid 20 mcg	

selection

Leeks should have broad, dark, solid leaves and a thick white neck with a base about 1 inch in diameter. Those with yellowing, wilted, or discolored leaves should be avoided.

preparation for juicing

Wash organic leeks; soak or spray nonorganic ones with a biodegradable wash, and then rinse. Slice lengthwise into pieces that can be fed into the juicer.

leek juice recipes

Leek juice is quite potent on its own, so it is best to mix it with more palatable bases. See Carrot-Leek-Parsley (page 139) and Basic Carrot-Apple (page 191).

---

lettuce

Lettuce varieties are members of the daisy or sunflower family (Compositae). Most varieties of lettuce exude small amounts of a white, milky liquid when their leaves are broken. This "milk" gives lettuce its slightly bitter flavor and its scientific name, *Lactuca sativa*, since *Lactuca* is derived from the Latin word for "milk." Lettuce can be classified into various categories. Here are the most common:

- Iceberg: With green leaves on the outside and whitish ones on the inside, this variety of head lettuce has a crisp texture and a watery, mild taste. The best known variety of crisphead lettuce is iceberg.
- Romaine: Also known as cos, this variety of head-forming lettuce has deep green, long leaves with a crisp texture and deep taste.
- Butterhead: This type of lettuce features tender large leaves that form a loosely arranged head that is easily separated from

the stem, a sweet flavor, and a soft texture. The best known varieties of butterhead lettuce include Boston and Bibb.
- Loose-leaf: Featuring broad, curly leaf varieties that are green and/or red, the leaf lettuces offer a delicate taste and a mildly crispy texture. Best known varieties of leaf lettuce include green leaf and red leaf.

Arugula, endive, and watercress are not considered lettuce, but these greens are often used interchangeably with lettuces in salads.

key benefits

In general, the darker the lettuce the greater the nutrient content. Hence, romaine has more nutritional value than loose-leaf, which has more than butterhead, which in turn has more than iceberg. Lettuce is a good source of chlorophyll and vitamin K. Romaine lettuce is an excellent source of vitamin A, folate, vitamin C, vitamin B_1, and vitamin B_2 as well as the minerals manganese and chromium.

nutritional analysis

1 head raw iceberg (700 g)		
NUTRIENTS & UNITS	**VITAMINS**	**MINERALS**
Water 517 g	Vitamin A 178 RE	Potassium 852 mg
Calories 70 kcal	Vitamin C 21 mg	Calcium 102 mg
Protein 5.4 g	Thiamine 0.25 mg	Iron 2.7 mg
Fat 1 g	Riboflavin 0.16 mg	Magnesium 48 mg
Carbohydrate 11.26 g	Niacin 1 mg	Phosphorus 108 mg
	Vitamin B_6 0.22 mg	Sodium 48 mg
	Folic acid 301 mcg	

selection

Good-quality lettuce will appear fresh, crisp, and free from any evidence of decay. Avoid lettuce that has a rusty appearance and signs of decay.

preparation for juicing

Rinse organic lettuce; soak or spray nonorganic lettuce with a biodegradable wash, then rinse. A salad spinner is a great way to dry the leaves and prepare them for juicing. Cut the lettuce into wedges or feed the leaves into the juicer intact, folding them if necessary. The darker lettuce varieties are the best to juice.

lettuce juice recipes

See the Carrot-Lettuce (page 139) and Celery-Lettuce-Spinach (page 144). Lettuce can be added to the following recipes: Basic Carrot-Apple (page 191), Energizer (page 198), and Salad in a Glass (page 208).

---

mustard greens

Mustard greens are the leaves of the mustard plant (*Brassica juncea*), which is a member of the cabbage, or cruciferous, family. In addition to producing these wondrously nutritious greens, this plant also produces the acrid-tasting brown seeds that are used to make Dijon mustard. For more information, see Kale, as mustard greens share the same benefits.

onions

Onions, like garlic, are members of the lily family. Onions originated in the central part of Asia, from Iran to Pakistan, and moved northward into the southern part of Russia. Numerous forms and varieties of onion are cultivated worldwide. Common varieties are white globe, yellow globe, red globe, and green (shallots or scallions). With the globe onions, the part used is the fleshy bulb, while with green onions, both the long slender bulb and the green leaves are used.

key benefits

Onions, like garlic, contain a variety of organic sulfur compounds. Onion also has the enzyme alliinase, which is released when the onion is cut or crushed, resulting in the so-called crying factor (propanethial S-oxide). Other constituents include flavonoids (primarily quercetin), phenolic acids, sterols, saponins, pectin, and volatile oils. Although not nearly as valued a medicinal agent as garlic, onion has been used almost as widely. Onions possess many of the same effects as garlic (see Garlic). There are, however, some subtle differences that make one more advantageous than the other in certain conditions.

Like garlic, onions and onion extracts have been shown to decrease blood lipid levels, prevent clot formation, and lower blood pressure in several clinical studies. Onions have significant blood-sugar-lowering action, comparable to that of the prescription drugs tolbutamide and phenformin often given to diabetics. The active blood-sugar-lowering principle in onions is believed to be allyl propyl disulphide (APDS), although other constituents, such as flavonoids, may play a significant role as well. Experimental and clinical evidence suggests that APDS lowers glucose by competing with insulin (also a disulfide molecule) for breakdown sites in the liver, thereby increasing the life span of insulin. Other mechanisms, such as increased liver metabolism of glucose or increased insulin secretion, have also been proposed.[35]

Onion has been used historically to treat asthma because it inhibits the production of compounds that cause the bronchial muscle to spasm, along with its ability to relax the bronchial muscle.[36]

The liberal use of the *Allium* species (garlic, onions, leeks, and so on) appears particularly indicated considering the major disease processes (such as atherosclerosis, diabetes, and cancer) of the twentieth century.

nutritional analysis

½ onion, raw (100 g)		
NUTRIENTS & UNITS	**VITAMINS**	**MINERALS**
Water 90 g	Vitamin A 0	Potassium 155 mg
Calories 34 kcal	Vitamin C 8.4 mg	Calcium 25 mg
Protein 1.18 g	Thiamine 0.06 mg	Iron 0.37 mg
Fat 0.26 g	Riboflavin 0.01 mg	Magnesium 10 mg
Carbohydrate 7.3 g	Niacin 0.1 mg	Phosphorus 29 mg
	Vitamin B_6 0.157 mg	Sodium 2 mg
	Folic acid 19.9 mcg	

selection

Globe onions should be clean and hard, with dry, smooth skins. Avoid onions in which the seed stem has developed, as well as those that are misshaped and show evidence of decay.

Green onions should have fresh-looking green tops and a white neck. Yellowing, wilted, or discolored tops should be avoided.

preparation for juicing

Peel and wash organic onions; peel, then soak or spray nonorganic ones with a biodegradable wash, then rinse.

onion juice recipes

Onion juice is too strong to be consumed straight. In many recipes, you can substitute onion for garlic. See Carrot-Onion-Parsley (page 139).

---

parsley

Parsley, like carrots and celery, is a member of the umbelliferous family. It is native to the Mediterranean. Unfortunately, most parsley is now used as a garnish instead of a food.

key benefits

Parsley is extremely rich in a wide number of nutrients, chlorophyll, and carotenes. The high chlorophyll content of parsley can help mask the odor and taste of many other foods, such as garlic. Ingesting parsley has been shown to inhibit the increase in urinary mutagenicity following the ingestion of fried foods.[37] This is most likely due to the chlorophyll (see chapter 3), but other compounds in parsley such as vitamin C, flavonoids, and carotenes have also been shown to inhibit the cancer-causing properties of fried foods.

Parsley has benefits well beyond its chlorophyll content. It has long been used for medicinal purposes and is regarded as an excellent "nerve stimulant." Empirical evidence seems to support and is probably responsible for so many juice enthusiasts labeling parsley-containing juices "energy drinks."

nutritional analysis

½ cup chopped parsley (30 g)		
NUTRIENTS & UNITS	**VITAMINS**	**MINERALS**
Water 26.5 g	Vitamin A 156 RE	Potassium 161 mg
Calories 10 kcal	Vitamin C 27 mg	Calcium 39 mg
Protein 0.66 g	Thiamine 0.02 mg	Iron 1.86 mg
Fat 0.09 g	Riboflavin 0.033 mg	Magnesium 13 mg
Carbohydrate 2 g	Niacin 0.2 mg	Phosphorus 12 mg
	Vitamin B$_6$ 0.05 mg	Sodium 12 mg
	Folic acid 55 mcg	

selection

Parsley can be grown at home or purchased fresh from the grocery store. Parsley should be bright, fresh, green, and free from yellowed leaves or dirt. Slightly wilted parsley can be revived to freshness in cold water.

preparation for juicing

Wash organic parsley; soak or spray nonorganic parsley with a biodegradable wash, then rinse. Use a salad spinner to dry. Ball up sprigs of parsley in your hand and then feed into the juicer.

parsley juice recipes

Parsley juice on its own is quite strong; it is wise to mix it with other juices. In addition to the recipes below, try Beet-Carrot-Parsley (page 125), Broccoli-Carrot-Parsley (page 130), Cabbage-Carrot-Parsley (page 135), Carrot-Celery-Parsley (page 139), Carrot-Cucumber-Parsley (page 139) Carrot-Leek-Parsley (page 139), Carrot-Onion-Parsley (page 139), Celery-Cucumber-Parsley (page 144), Celery-Cucumber-Parsley-Spinach (page 144), Celery-Fennel-Parsley (page

144), Cucumber-Tomato-Parsley (page 147), Bone Builder's Cocktail (page 193), Cholesterol-Lowering Tonic (page 193), Cleansing Cocktail (page 194), Cucumber Celery Cooler (page 196), Don Juan (page 198), Energizer (page 198), Go Green Drink (page 202), Go-Go Green (page 202), Immune Power Veggie (page 203), Popeye's Power Drink (page 207), Potassium Power (page 207), Salad in a Glass (page 208), and Super V-7 (page 209).

PARSLEY-SPINACH-TOMATO
½ cup parsley
½ cup spinach
4 tomatoes, quartered

PARSLEY-TOMATO
1 cup parsley
4 tomatoes, quartered

---

peppers, bell (sweet)

Peppers belong to the Solanaceae, or nightshade, family of vegetables, which also includes potatoes, eggplant, and tomatoes. Peppers are native to Central and South America. Sweet or bell peppers are available in red, green, yellow, and black. Red bell peppers are actually green peppers that have been allowed to ripen on the vine; hence, they are much sweeter. The hotter chili peppers are used in much smaller quantities.

key benefits

Bell peppers are one of the most nutrient-dense foods available and are good sources of a wide number of nutrients including vitamin C, beta-carotene, vitamin K, thiamin, folic acid, and vitamin B_6. Bell peppers are also a very good source of phytochemicals with exceptional antioxidant activity. The red variety will have significantly higher levels of nutrients than the green. Red peppers also contain lycopene, a carotene that offers protection against cancer and heart disease.

Bell peppers also contain substances that have been shown to prevent clot formation and reduce the risk for heart attacks and strokes. Although not as rich in these compounds as chili peppers, bell pepper consumption should be promoted in individuals with elevated cholesterol levels.

nutritional analysis

1 green bell pepper (74 g)		
NUTRIENTS & UNITS	**VITAMINS**	**MINERALS**
Water 68.65 g	Vitamin A 39 RE	Potassium 144 mg
Calories 18 kcal	Vitamin C 95 mg	Calcium 4 mg
Protein 0.63 g	Thiamine 0.063 mg	Iron 0.94 mg
Fat 0.33 g	Riboflavin 0.037 mg	Magnesium 10 mg
Carbohydrate 3.93 g	Niacin 0.407 mg	Phosphorus 16 mg
	Vitamin B_6 0.121 mg	Sodium 2 mg
	Folic acid 12.5 mcg	

selection

Peppers should be fresh, firm, and bright in appearance. Avoid peppers that appear dry or wrinkled, or show signs of decay.

preparation for juicing

Wash organic peppers; soak or spray nonorganic ones with a biodegradable wash, then rinse. Remove the seeds and cut into pieces that will fit into the juicer.

pepper juice recipes

Straight green bell pepper juice is pretty strong; you may want to use only a quarter to a half a pepper in a base of tomato or carrot juice.

Larger amounts of the sweet red variety can be used. Try the recipe below and also Beet-Carrot-Pepper (page 125), Carrot-Pepper (page 140), Bone Builder's Cocktail (page 193), Everything but the Kitchen Sink (page 199), High C (page 202), Purple Cow (page 208), Salad in a Glass (page 208), Some Like It Hot (page 208), and Super V-7 (page 209).

PEPPER-TOMATO
½ green or red bell pepper   4 tomatoes, quartered

potatoes

Potatoes are members of the Solanaceae, or nightshade, family and are native to the Andes Mountains of Bolivia and Peru, where they have been cultivated for 7,000 years. Potatoes were brought to Europe by Spanish explorers in the early part of the sixteenth century. Potatoes are a hardy crop and became a particular favorite in Ireland, largely as a result of the tremendous rise in population in the 1800s coupled with a declining economy. Because an acre and a half of land could produce enough potatoes to feed a family of five for a year, many Irish families came to depend on potatoes for sustenance, especially when times were tough. Several hundred varieties of potatoes are grown worldwide. For juicing, the red and russet varieties may be best.

key benefits

Potatoes are an excellent source of many nutrients, including potassium and vitamin C. Potatoes are actually low in calories: a medium-size potato contains only 115. Unfortunately, most Americans eat the potato in the form of French fries, hash browns, potato chips, or baked potatoes smothered with butter or sour cream, which counters their nutritional value. The protein quality of potatoes is actually quite high. Although it is about the same amount as in corn or rice, potatoes contain lysine, an essential amino acid often lacking in grains.

nutritional analysis

1 cup, diced (182 g)		
NUTRIENTS & UNITS	**VITAMINS**	**MINERALS**
Water 144 g	Vitamin A 4 RE	Potassium 630 mg
Calories 142 kcal	Vitamin C 25 mg	Calcium 15 mg
Protein 4.3 g	Thiamine 0.28 mg	Iron 1.84 mg
Fat 0.3 g	Riboflavin 0.056 mg	Magnesium 24 mg
Carbohydrate 31.8 g	Niacin 3 mg	Phosphorus 58 mg
	Vitamin B_6 0.47 mg	Sodium 46 mg
	Folic acid 24 mcg	

selection

Use only high-quality potatoes that are firm and display the characteristic features of the variety. Avoid wilted, leathery, or discolored potatoes, especially those with a green tint.

preparation for juicing

Wash organic potatoes; soak or spray nonorganic ones with a biodegradable wash, then scrub and rinse. Cut the potato into pieces that will fit into the juicer.

potato juice recipes

Potato juice on its own is quite stout and will turn black quickly if not consumed immediately. Try adding 1 potato to these recipes: Basic

Carrot-Apple (page 191), Energizer (page 198), and Ginger Hopper (page 201).

radishes

Radishes (*Raphanus sativus*) are root vegetables whose white flesh resembles turnips in its texture but whose sharp biting flavor is unique. Like other members of the cruciferous family, which includes such nutritional superstars as broccoli, cabbage, and Brussels sprouts, radishes contain beneficial cancer-fighting compounds known as isothiacyanates, which are also the source of their pungency.

Radishes have been developed in many varieties, each with its own distinctive color (mostly variations of reds, whites, and blacks), shape (as long as 3 feet), size (up to 100 pounds), and level of pungency (from mild to searingly sharp). Like many other root vegetables, the radish also produces green leafy tops that are edible and add a peppery zest to salads and fresh juice.

Some varieties of radish are quick-growing spring roots while others are slow-growing summer and winter vegetables. The most popular spring varieties are those that have bright red or red and white round roots, such as Red Globe, Cherry Belle, Early Scarlet Globe, Cherry Beauty, Red Boy, Champion, Comet, and Sparkler White Tip. These are small round or oval-shaped radishes with crisp, white flesh that range from 1 to 4 inches in diameter.

White Icicle, the most popular long-rooted spring type, is a tapered root that grows up to 6 inches long and whose flesh is less pungent than the round varieties. The winter varieties produce long large roots whose flavor is usually more biting and whose texture more fibrous and less crisp than the spring and summer varieties. The winter varieties—April Cross, Everest, Omny, Black Spanish Long, and Black Spanish Round—take twice as long to mature as the spring radishes and are usually grown as a fall crop for winter storage. One exception is a winter variety called California Mammoth White. The flesh of these 8-inch-long oblong-shaped roots is even milder than that of the White Icicle.

See also Daikon Radish, the favored variety in Asian cultures.

key benefits

In addition to being an excellent source of vitamin C and potassium, the radish, like the beet, has been used as a medicinal food for liver disorders. Radishes contain a variety of chemicals that increase the flow of bile, thus helping to maintain a healthy gallbladder and improving digestion.

As a member of the cruciferous vegetable family, the radish shares the beneficial cancer-protective actions of its cousins, broccoli, cabbage, kale, and Brussels sprouts.

In India, both radish root and greens are used not only to prevent vitamin C deficiency but also as a diuretic, expectorant, and laxative and to treat gastric discomfort, and as a laxative.

nutritional analysis

1 cup bulbs without greens (100 g)		
NUTRIENTS & UNITS	**VITAMINS**	**MINERALS**
Water 63 g	Vitamin A 2 RE	Potassium 233 mg
Calories 16 kcal	Vitamin C 15 mg	Calcium 25 mg
Protein 0.68 g	Thiamine 0.02 mg	Iron 0.34 mg
Fat 0.7 g	Riboflavin 0.02 mg	Magnesium 10 mg
Carbohydrate 1.9 g	Niacin 0.25 mg	Phosphorus 20 mg
	Vitamin B_6 0.07 mg	Sodium 14 mg
	Folic acid 25 mcg	

selection

Good-quality red radishes should have their greens intact. The greens should be fresh-looking with no signs of spoilage. Slightly flabby greens can be restored to freshness if stored in the refrigerator in water; if it is too late and the greens are spoiled, simply cut them off. The radish root should be firm, smooth and vibrant red versus soft, wrinkled, and dull-colored.

Red and white radishes are sold year-round, although supplies are best in spring. Black radishes have a longer shelf life and are at their peak in winter and early spring. Daikons are most flavorful in fall and winter.

Store radishes in perforated bags in the vegetable crisper of your refrigerator. Fresh radishes with the greens attached can be stored for 3 to 5 days, but the greens will draw moisture and nutrients from the roots. With their greens removed, the radish bulbs will keep much longer—about 2 to 4 weeks.

preparation for juicing

Radishes and their greens should be washed thoroughly. Larger varieties may need to be cut lengthwise for preparation to feed into the juicer.

radish juice recipes

Radish juice can have a strong taste, so it is often mixed with carrot, celery, or apple juices. Try Cruciferous Surprise Extreme (page 196), Digestive Fire (page 197), Diuretic Formula Plus (page 197), Enzymes Galore Plus (page 199), Ginger Hopper Plus (page 201), Immune Power Veggie Extreme (page 203), Liver Mover (page 205), Liver Tonic (page 205), Liver Tonic Plus (page 205), Some Like It Hot (page 208), Spicy Jicama Fiesta (page 209), and Tomato Zest (page 209).

spinach

Spinach is believed to have originated in southwestern Asia or Persia. It has been cultivated in many areas of the world for hundreds of years not only as a food but also as an important medicinal plant in many traditional systems of medicine.

key benefits

There is much lore regarding spinach. It was regarded historically as a plant with remarkable abilities to restore energy, increase vitality, and improve the quality of the blood. There are sound reasons why spinach would produce such results, primarily the fact that spinach contains twice as much iron as most other greens. Spinach, like other chlorophyll- and carotene-rich vegetables, is a strong protector against cancer. In addition to carotenes like lutein, researchers have identified at least 13 different flavonoid compounds in spinach that function as antioxidants and as anticancer agents.[38] The anticancer properties of these spinach flavonoids have been sufficiently impressive to prompt researchers to create specialized spinach extracts that could be used in controlled studies. These spinach extracts have been shown to slow down cell division in stomach cancer cells (gastric adenocarcinomas) and, in studies on mice, to reduce skin cancers (skin papillomas).[39] A study of adult women living in New England in the late 1980s also showed intake of spinach to be inversely related to incidence of breast cancer.[40] In other words, the more spinach was consumed the lower the risk of breast cancer.

nutritional analysis

1 cup raw spinach (55 g)		
NUTRIENTS & UNITS	**VITAMINS**	**MINERALS**
Water 51 g	Vitamin A 376 RE	Potassium 312 mg
Calories 12 kcal	Vitamin C 16 mg	Calcium 56 mg
Protein 1.6 g	Thiamine 0.04 mg	Iron 1.52 mg
Fat 0.2 g	Riboflavin 0.1 mg	Magnesium 44 mg
Carbohydrate 2 g	Niacin 0.4 mg	Phosphorus 28 mg
	Vitamin B$_6$ 0.11 mg	Sodium 22 mg
	Folic acid 109.2 mcg	

selection

Fresh spinach should be dark green, fresh-looking, and free from any evidence of decay. Slightly wilted spinach can be revived to freshness in cold water.

preparation for juicing

Wash organic spinach; soak or spray nonorganic spinach with a biodegradable wash, then rinse. Use a salad spinner to dry. Ball up sprigs of spinach in your hand and then feed into the juicer.

spinach juice recipes

Spinach juice on its own is quite strong; it is wise to mix it with other juices, such as carrot, tomato, and apple. See Beet-Carrot-Spinach (page 125), Brussels Sprouts–Carrot-Spinach (page 131), Carrot-Dandelions-Spinach (page 139), Carrot-Spinach (page 140), Celery-Cucumber-Parsley-Spinach (page 144), Celery-Lettuce-Spinach (page 144), Parsley-Spinach-Tomato (page 171), Everything but the Kitchen Sink (page 199), Go Green Drink (page 202), Popeye's Power Drink (page 207), Potassium Power (page 207), and Super V-7 (page 209). And try this simple combination:

  1 cup spinach   4 tomatoes, quartered

---

sweet potatoes and yams

Sweet potatoes belong not to the potato (Solanaceae) family, but to the morning-glory (Convolvulaceae) family. The sweet potato is native to Mexico and Central and South America. In the United States, we tend to call the darker, sweeter sweet potato a yam, which is inaccurate. True yams are native to Southeast Asia and Africa and differ from the sweet potato in that they have very little carotene.

key benefits

Sweet potatoes are exceptionally rich in carotenes. The darker the variety, the higher the concentration of carotenes. Sweet potatoes are also rich in vitamin C, calcium, and potassium.

nutritional analysis*

1 sweet potato, cooked and then peeled (114 g)		
NUTRIENTS & UNITS	**VITAMINS**	**MINERALS**
Water 79 g	Vitamin A 923 RE	Potassium 342 mg
Calories 160 kcal	Vitamin C 25 mg	Calcium 46 mg
Protein 2 g	Thiamine 0.1 mg	Iron 1 mg
Fat 1 g	Riboflavin 0.08 mg	Magnesium 14 mg
Carbohydrate 37 g	Niacin 0.8 mg	Phosphorus 66 mg
	Vitamin B$_6$ 0.06 mg	Sodium 10 mg
	Folic acid 85 mcg	

*No information is available on raw sweet potatoes, but it is estimated that they would have at least 10 to 15 percent more nutritional value than cooked sweet potatoes.

selection

Use only high-quality sweet potatoes that are firm and display the characteristic features of the variety. Remember, the darker the variety, the higher the carotene content. As a bonus, the darker ones are sweeter and taste better. Avoid wilted, leathery, and discolored sweet potatoes, especially those with a green tint.

preparation for juicing

Wash organic sweet potatoes; soak or spray nonorganic ones with a biodegradable wash, then rinse. Slice into pieces that the juicer can accommodate.

sweet potato juice recipes

If you like to eat sweet potatoes, you may also like the flavor of the juice. I prefer Better Red Than Dead (page 192) to straight sweet potato juice. Also try the Beet–Sweet Potato (page 125) and Carrot–Sweet Potato (page 140).

---

tomatoes

At one time, tomatoes were believed to be poisonous; now they are one of the leading vegetable crops of the world. The tomato, like many other members of the Solanaceae, or nightshade, family, originated in Central and South America. There are numerous varieties of tomatoes, all of which are suitable for juicing.

key benefits

The tomato is packed full of nutrition, especially when fully ripe, as red tomatoes have up to four times the amount of beta-carotene as green tomatoes. Tomatoes are an excellent source of vitamin C, carotenes, biotin, and vitamin K. They are also a very good source of vitamin B_6, pantothenic acid, niacin, folic acid, and dietary fiber.

Tomatoes have received a lot of recent attention because of their lycopene content. This red carotene has been shown to be extremely protective against the major cancers, including breast, colon, lung, skin, and prostate cancer. It has been shown to lower the risk of heart disease, cataracts, and macular degeneration. Lycopene helps prevent these diseases and others by neutralizing harmful oxygen free radicals before they can do damage to cellular structures.[41]

In one of the more detailed studies, Harvard researchers discovered that men who consumed the highest levels of lycopene (6.5 mg per day) in their diet showed a 21 percent decreased risk of prostate cancer compared with those eating the lowest levels. Men who ate two or more servings of tomato sauce each week were 23 percent less likely to develop prostate cancer during the 22 years of the study than men who ate less than one serving of tomato sauce each month.[42] In a study of patients with existing prostate cancer, lycopene supplementation (15 mg per day) was shown to slow tumor growth, shrink the tumor, and lower the level of PSA (prostate specific antigen, a marker of cancer activity) by 18 percent.[43]

The amount of lycopene in tomatoes can vary significantly, depending on the type of tomato and how ripe it is. In the reddest strains, lycopene concentration is close to 50 mg per kilogram, compared with only 5 mg/kg in the yellow strains. Lycopene appears to be relatively stable during cooking and food processing. In fact, you actually get up to five times as much lycopene from tomato paste or tomato juice than you do from raw tomatoes, because processing "liberates" more lycopene from the plant's cells.

nutritional analysis

1 raw tomato (123 g)		
NUTRIENTS & UNITS	**VITAMINS**	**MINERALS**
Water 115 g	Vitamin A 239 RE	Potassium 254 mg
Calories 24 kcal	Vitamin C 21.6 mg	Calcium 8 mg
Protein 1.09 g	Thiamine 0.07 mg	Iron 0.59 mg
Fat 0.26 g	Riboflavin 0.06 mg	Magnesium 14 mg
Carbohydrate 5.34 g	Niacin 0.738 mg	Phosphorus 29 mg
	Vitamin B$_6$ 0.06 mg	Sodium 10 mg
	Folic acid 11.5 mcg	

selection

Good-quality tomatoes are well formed and plump, fully red, firm, and free from bruise marks. Avoid tomatoes that are soft and show signs of bruising or decay.

preparation for juicing

Wash organic tomatoes; soak or spray nonorganic ones with a biodegradable wash, then rinse. Cut them in just small enough wedges to feed into the machine.

tomato juice recipes

Tomato juice is refreshing alone, or use it in any of these tomato-based recipes: Cucumber-Tomato-Parsley (page 147), Cucumber-Tomato-Watercress (page 147), Pepper-Tomato (page 173), Spinach-Tomato (page 180), Cucumber-Celery Cooler (page 196), Everything but the Kitchen Sink (page 199), Potassium Power (page 207), Salad in a Glass (page 208), Some Like It Hot (page 208), and Tomato Zest (page 209).

turmeric

Turmeric (*Curcuma longa*) is a member of the ginger family. It is extensively cultivated in India, China, Indonesia, and other tropical countries. The rhizome (root) with its tough brown skin and a deep orange flesh is the part used. It is usually cured (boiled, cleaned, and sun-dried), polished, and ground into a powder. Turmeric is the major ingredient of curry powder and is also used in prepared mustard as a coloring agent. It is extensively used in foods both for its color and flavor.

Turmeric is used in both the Chinese and Indian systems of medicine as an anti-inflammatory agent and in the treatment of numerous conditions, including flatulence, jaundice, menstrual difficulties, bloody urine, hemorrhage, toothache, bruises, chest pain, and colic.

Curcumin, turmeric's yellow pigment, has demonstrated significant anti-inflammatory activity in a variety of experimental models. In fact, in numerous studies curcumin's anti-inflammatory effects have been shown to be comparable to the potent drugs. Unlike the drugs, which are associated with significant toxic effects (ulcer formation, decreased white blood cell count, intestinal bleeding), curcumin produces no toxicity.[44]

The antioxidant activity of curcumin is superior to antioxidant nutrients like vitamins C and E, as these are effective against only water- and fat-soluble pro-oxidants, respectively. In contrast, curcumin is effective in protecting against both water- and fat-soluble toxins. It also exerts many other additional benefits. Curcumin is particularly helpful in preventing LDL cholesterol from becoming oxidized and damaging arteries. In addition it exerts other effects beneficial in preventing atherosclerosis (hardening of the arteries) including lowering of cholesterol levels, preventing plaque formation, and inhibiting the formation of blood clots by inhibiting platelet aggregation.[45]

As far as slowing down the aging process, there is considerable evidence that curcumin protects against age-related brain damage and, in particular, Alzheimer's disease. Researchers began exploring this effect after noting that elderly (aged 70 to 79) residents of rural India who eat large amounts of turmeric have been shown to have the lowest incidence of Alzheimer's disease in the world: 4.4 times lower than that of Americans. In addition, researchers have also demonstrated that curcumin is able to prevent the development of Alzheimer's brain lesions in mice specifically bred to develop the disease and curcumin may actually untangle the hallmark brain lesions of Alzheimer's.[46]

The anticancer effects of turmeric and curcumin have been demonstrated at all steps of cancer formation: initiation, promotion, and progression. Curcumin acts in an incredible way to protect against damage to DNA. This effect was recently demonstrated in a study in a community with a high content of groundwater arsenic.[47] Arsenic, a metal, is extremely carcinogenic because it causes severe oxidative damage to DNA. Blood samples prior to curcumin supplementation showed severe DNA damage with increased levels of free radicals and lipid peroxidation. Three months of curcumin intervention reduced the DNA damage, retarded free-radical formation and lipid peroxidation, and raised the level of antioxidant activity. In another study, cigarette smokers receiving turmeric demonstrated a significant reduction in the level of urinary-excreted mutagens—an indication of the ability of the body to rid itself of cancer-causing compounds via detoxification mechanisms. For many reasons, curcumin is emerging as a very important agent in the battle against cancer. Data also suggest that curcumin causes cancer to regress.[48]

selection

Turmeric root is becoming more available, but you may have to ask your produce manager to order it for you. Since the color of turmeric varies among varieties, it is not a criterion of quality. Like other root vegetables, make sure that it is fresh without any external discoloration. It is best kept in the refrigerator.

preparation for juicing

Wash organic turmeric; soak or spray nonorganic turmeric with a biodegradable wash, then rinse. Slice into pieces that the juicer can accommodate.

Be careful when juicing turmeric since its deep color can easily stain. To avoid a lasting stain, quickly wash any area with which it has made contact with soap and water. To prevent staining your hands, you might consider wearing kitchen gloves while handling turmeric.

It's best to feed the turmeric in first, before whatever you are juicing it with to ensure that it gets fully processed by the juicer.

turmeric juice recipes

Fresh turmeric has a gingerlike taste and can be used as a replacement for ginger. The simple combination of fresh turmeric with a lemon is a powerful healing drink.

---

turnip greens (see KALE)

---

summary

Vegetables bring us alive and provide the broadest range of nutrients and phytochemicals of any food group. The best way to consume many vegetables is in their fresh, raw form, in which many important phytochemicals are provided in much higher concentrations. Juicing is a phenomenal way to capture the important health benefits that vegetables provide.

7

seventy fabulous juice recipes

It is easy to fall into the habit of making the same juice every day. To help you explore, I offer here some of my favorite juice recipes. And I encourage you to develop your own recipes. Don't be concerned about following the recipe exactly. Be flexible. Have fun! My suggestion is to consume as wide an assortment of fresh fruit and vegetable juices as possible. To make it easier, try to consume the fullest possible spectrum of colors of fruits and vegetables each week. More and more evidence is showing us that the plant pigments contain some of the most important nutritious properties—chlorophyll, carotenes, and flavonoids are all being found to possess some truly remarkable health benefits. So drink a rainbow of fresh fruits and vegetable juices!

some juicing guidelines

Let your taste buds be your guide. If they tell you, for example, that too strong a green drink doesn't taste all that good, you can fix it by mixing in carrots, celery, cucumber, or apples.

The most important guideline is to enjoy yourself. It's fun to experiment and find a combination that is unusually delicious. I had that experience a few years ago when I invented Better Red Than Dead (page 192). It contains carrots, beets, and sweet potatoes. Yes, sweet potatoes—and it is delicious.

Sometimes you may discover a new juice that you don't like. This is fine, too. Why? Because it shows you are willing to at least try something new. I have made some juices that I won't make again, but at least I tried.

Many people say you should not mix fruits and vegetables, but there is little (if any) scientific information to support this contention. There is no physiological basis for any issues in digestion being caused by combining fruits and vegetables in a meal. Nonetheless, some people do seem to have difficulty with combined fruits and vegetables, complaining of gassy discomfort. If you are one of these people, you should avoid mixing fruits and vegetables together. The exceptions to this rule appear to be carrots and apples, as these foods seem to mix well with either a fruit or a vegetable. Again, let your taste buds (and your digestive system) be your guide.

It is best to drink the juice as soon as it is made. This offers the greatest benefit. However, if this is not possible, store the juice in an airtight container in the refrigerator or in a thermos. Do not store the juice for longer than 12 hours. The fresher the juice, the better it is for you.

about the recipes

Each of the recipes should yield 8 to 12 ounces fresh juice. The actual yield will depend on the size of the fruit or vegetable and the quality of your juicer. Unless otherwise noted, all of the recipes call for medium-size fruits and vegetables. I have noted recipes that are particularly helpful for weight loss and detoxification with a symbol (**WL**). These are primarily vegetable juice or low-GL fruit recipes.

apple spice

This is a delicious zesty apple juice that seems to warm you up even though it is a cold drink. I consider it a fall drink and a "live" food alternative to hot apple cider. This drink is good for the liver, as both ginger and cinnamon have been shown to improve liver function. It's also a nice drink before going to bed.

1-inch slice of ginger   ½ teaspoon cinnamon
3 apples, cut into wedges

Juice the ginger, followed by the apples. Pour into a glass, add the cinnamon, and stir.

apple wonder

Here is a drink that is a great example of what happens when you experiment, which often leads to something that you really love. This drink is very refreshing—a fantastic drink in warmer weather.

¼ cup fresh mint leaves	½ lime, peeled
2 Granny Smith apples	2 celery ribs

Juice the mint, followed by the apples, lime, and celery.

apricot-mango ambrosia

This fun drink is nutrition-packed. Apricots and mangoes are extremely good sources of beta-carotenes, while oranges are known as a rich source of vitamin C and flavonoids.

4 apricots, pitted and halved	1 orange, peeled
1 mango, pitted and sliced	

Juice the apricots, followed by the mango and orange. You may need to stir the juice up so that all the flavors mix. It can be a bit thick.

basic carrot-apple

This "basic" juice may be simple, but that doesn't mean it isn't a delicious or nutrient-rich drink. In fact, this drink is called "The Champ" by Jay Kordich, the Juiceman, and it has been his favorite for over 60 years. For good reason—Jay believes this juice saved his life. Basic Carrot-Apple can serve as a base for adding small quantities of more potent vegetables like greens, spinach, radishes, and beets.

4 carrots	2 apples, cut into wedges

Alternate feeding the carrots and apple wedges into the juicer to ensure proper mixing.

berry happy

The health benefits of berries are incredible. The flavonoids they contain impact every body tissue and function. Here is a super berry drink that also takes advantage of the beneficial compounds from pomegranate.

| 1 cup mixed berries (such as blueberries, raspberries, strawberries, blackberries) | ¼ cup pomegranate pips |
| | 1 apple or pear, cut into wedges |

Juice the berries, then the pomegranate pips. Flush through with the apple.

better red than dead ⓦ

This recipe is one of my absolute favorite drinks, especially in the fall. It is rich with carotene, especially the red and orange carotenes. Drinking this juice will give you a year-round tan. I named this drink Better Red Than Dead because one of my professors, Dr. Ed Madison, gave a lecture on the benefits of carotenes with this title. His lecture really made an impression on me, and I have tried to maintain a high carotene intake ever since. As noted earlier, there is a strong correlation between carotene levels and life expectancy. Load up on this drink for a few weeks before going on vacation to a sunny location because the carotenes will be deposited in the skin, where they will protect against sunburn and damage to the skin.

| 1 beet with top | 3 carrots |
| ½ medium sweet potato, cut into strips | |

Juice the beet, followed by the sweet potato strips and carrots.

better red than dead–fruity version

This version is great for those finicky kids (young and old). It takes advantage of the red pigments in berries, cherries, and pomegranate to cover up the beet taste. It provides a different class of red pigments than Better Red Than Dead (above) does, so it is a good idea to alternate this recipe with the other version.

½ cup strawberries	¼ cup pomegranate pips
½ cup pitted cherries	1 apple, cut into wedges
1 beet with top	

Juice the strawberries and cherries, followed by the beet, pomegranate, and apple.

bone builder's cocktail (WL)

This drink provides the key nutrients required for building bone, such as calcium, boron, magnesium, other minerals, and vitamin K_1. This is an extremely nutrient-dense drink in that it provides incredible levels of vitamins and minerals per calorie.

3 or 4 kale leaves	1 cucumber, sliced in half lengthwise
Handful of parsley	
2 carrots	1 red or green bell pepper

Bunch up the kale and parsley and push them through the juicer with the aid of a carrot and the cucumber. Then juice the bell pepper followed by the remaining carrot.

bowel regulator

Pears and apples are excellent sources of water-soluble fibers like pectin, while prunes contain well-known laxative properties. This mixture has a very good tonifying effect on the bowel, improving the functionality of the colon. It is very useful in minor cases of constipation.

2 pitted plums	1 pear, sliced
2 apples, cut into wedges	

Alternate the juicing of the plums, apples, and pear.

cherry pop

Cherries are an excellent source of flavonoids and have been shown to be of great benefit in cases of arthritis, especially gout. This is a delicious drink that parents can serve their children as an alternative to soft drinks or artificially flavored and colored "fruit" drinks.

1 cup pitted cherries	4 ounces sparkling mineral water
1 apple, cut into wedges	

Juice the cherries, then the apple. Pour into a glass with ice, and top it off with the mineral water.

cholesterol-lowering tonic (WL)

If you really want to bring down cholesterol levels quickly, this zesty juice, along with a diet rich in high-fiber foods, can do the trick. It contains a mixture of foods that have been shown to lower cholesterol levels on their own. By combining all of these foods, it is possible that an even greater effect will be produced than if the foods were consumed separately. This effect is referred to as synergistic and reflects a scenario where the whole is greater than the sum of its parts, where 1 + 1 = 3, not 2. My personal experience is that this juice can be very effective in lowering cholesterol levels. The garlic and ginger also work to prevent blood platelets from bunching together, thereby significantly reducing the risk of heart attack and stroke.

¼-inch slice of ginger	2 carrots
1 garlic clove (optional)	4 Red Globe radishes with tops
Handful of parsley	1 apple, cut into wedges

Place the ginger and garlic (if using) in the center of the parsley and feed into the juicer. (This reduces much of the garlic's odor.) Follow with the carrots, radishes, and apple.

cleansing cocktail ⓦ

This is good for a juice fast, because it is nutrient dense and supports detoxification. If wheatgrass is not available, parsley will suffice. Wheatgrass is extremely rich in chlorophyll and antioxidants; look for it at health food stores if you are not familiar with it. It is very good for you.

½ cup wheatgrass or parsley	2 celery ribs
3 carrots	1 beet with top
1 apple, cut into wedges	

Bunch up the wheatgrass and push it through the juicer with the aid of a carrot. Alternate feeding the remaining ingredients into the juicer to ensure proper mixing.

cleansing cocktail extreme ⓦ

This version is for the extreme juicer looking for that extra punch in a detoxification aid.

½ cup wheatgrass or parsley	2 celery ribs
2 carrots	½ large daikon radish cut into lengthwise pieces
½ cup cilantro	1 beet with top
1 green bell pepper, cut into quarters	

Bunch up the wheatgrass and push through the juicer with the aid of a carrot. Alternate feeding the remaining ingredients into the juicer to ensure proper mixing.

color me pink

This recipe is a great way to start the day, especially if you are on a weight-loss program. It is low in calories, but the natural fruit sugars will keep your appetite in check. This drink is particularly rich in flavonoids. Make sure you leave as much of the albido (the white pithy part of the peel) as possible on the grapefruit, as this is rich in flavonoids.

1 cup raspberries	1 large pink grapefruit, peeled

Juice the raspberries, then the grapefruit.

color me red

This recipe is a variant of Color Me Pink (above) and is a great way to add variety to a weight-loss program. Beets are substituted for the raspberries here. Trust me, it tastes great. The beet tops are not used in this recipe, but save them for another juice.

2 medium-large beets	1 large pink grapefruit, peeled

Juice the beet then the grapefruit.

cranberry crush

Cranberries are fantastic for keeping the bladder free from infection. In this drink, the bitter principles of the cranberries are masked by the flavor and natural sweetness of the apples and orange.

1 cup cranberries	1 orange, peeled
2 apples, cut into wedges	

Juice the cranberries, then alternate feeding the apples and orange.

cruciferous surprise

The surprise is just how delicious this drink actually tastes. This is a super-nutrient-dense drink that is rich in the sulfur-containing compounds of the cruciferous family vegetables, which have been shown to enhance the body's ability to detoxify cancer-causing chemicals and eliminate heavy metals. It is also rich in calcium, vitamin C, and carotenes. This is a great drink during a juice fast.

3 or 4 kale leaves	2 carrots
1 cup broccoli florets with stems	1 apple, cut into wedges
½ head of cabbage, cut into wedges	

Juice the kale, followed by the broccoli and cabbage. Then alternate feeding the carrots and apple wedges into the juicer.

cruciferous surprise extreme

This version is a bit spicier and is definitely packed with more power.

3 or 4 kale leaves	2 carrots
1 cup broccoli florets with stems	½ large daikon radish, cut into lengthwise pieces
½ head of cabbage, cut into wedges	

Juice the kale, followed by the broccoli and cabbage. Then alternate feeding the carrots and radish into the juicer.

cucumber-celery cooler

Serve this over ice, or you can juice the tomato the day before and pour it into an ice-cube tray and freeze.

1 tomato, quartered	4 celery ribs
1 cucumber	Parsley sprig, for garnish

Juice the tomato, followed by the cucumber and celery.

cucumber-celery mojito cooler

This drink can be served over ice, or you can juice some celery the day before and pour it into an ice-cube tray and freeze.

½ cup mint leaves	6 celery ribs
1 cucumber	Mint leaf, for garnish

Juice mint leaves, followed by the cucumber and celery. Pour into a glass and garnish with the mint leaf.

digestive delight

This is a fantastic drink for people who have trouble with indigestion. It is packed full of enzymes, and the ginger and mint help ease spastic intestines and promote the elimination of gas.

1-inch slice of ginger	2 kiwifruits with skin
½ cup mint leaves	¼ pineapple with skin, sliced lengthwise

Juice the ginger and mint, followed by the kiwifruit and pineapple.

digestive fire

This recipe is a powerful digestive aid designed to put the fire back into a tired digestive system. It is phenomenal, but it is very strong. It is not for the timid juicer as it is aggressive medicine—both in taste and action.

1-inch slice of ginger	1 kiwifruit with skin
½ large daikon radish cut into lengthwise pieces	¼ pineapple with skin, sliced lengthwise
½ cup mint leaves	

Juice the ginger, followed by the radish, mint, kiwifruit, and pineapple.

diuretic formula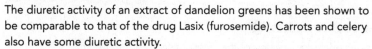

The diuretic activity of an extract of dandelion greens has been shown to be comparable to that of the drug Lasix (furosemide). Carrots and celery also have some diuretic activity.

Handful of dandelion greens or parsley	6 celery ribs
	2 carrots

Juice the greens, followed by the celery and carrots.

diuretic formula plus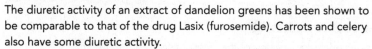

The diuretic activity of daikon radish pumps up the regular formula.

Handful of dandelion greens or parsley	2 carrots
4 celery ribs	½ large daikon radish, cut into lengthwise pieces

Bunch up the greens and push them through the juicer with the aid of a celery rib. Then juice the remaining celery, followed by the carrots and radish.

don juan

Ginger has been shown to possess some mild aphrodisiac effects and has a long history of use as a sexual aid in the Arabic system of medicine. The parsley provides increased energy and awareness.

1-inch slice of ginger	¼ pineapple with skin, sliced
Handful of parsley	

Place the ginger in the middle of the parsley and feed it into the juicer followed by the pineapple.

energizer (WL)

This drink is a popular recipe to increase energy and alertness. It is nutrient-packed yet very low in calories.

Handful of parsley	4 carrots

Bunch up the parsley and push it through the juicer with the aid of a carrot (fat end first). Then juice the remaining carrots.

energizer plus (WL)

For an enhanced version of the classic, add a beet to the mix.

Handful of parsley	1 large beet with tops
3 carrots	

Bunch up the parsley and push it through the juicer with the aid of a carrot. Then juice the beet and the remaining carrots.

enzymes galore

Packed with enzymes, this is a fantastic way to start the day. It is a super breakfast.

2 kiwifruits, peeled

1 orange, peeled

½ papaya, seeded and sliced

¼ pineapple with skin, sliced

Juice the kiwis, followed by the oranges, papaya, and pineapple.

enzymes galore plus

An even more power-packed version.

1-inch slice of ginger

1 large daikon radish, cut into lengthwise pieces, or 4 radishes with tops

1 orange, peeled

2 kiwifruits, peeled

¼ pineapple with skin, sliced

Juice the ginger, followed by the radish, the orange, the kiwifruit, and the pineapple.

everything but the kitchen sink (WL)

Have you ever wondered what it would taste like if you mixed all those summer vegetables you have growing in your garden in a single glass of juice? Well, here is your chance. It tastes good and it's definitely good for me.

Handful of spinach

2 celery ribs

2 radishes with tops

1 apple, cut into wedges

½ cucumber

1 tomato, quartered

½ cup broccoli florets with stems

½ green bell pepper

3 carrots

Bunch up the spinach and push it through the juicer with the aid of a celery rib. Alternate feeding the remaining vegetables into the juicer with a carrot coming last.

femme fatale (WL)

A femme fatale is a woman who attracts men with her aura of charm and mystery. This drink supports the female glandular system. Both fennel and celery contain what are known as phytoestrogens. These plant compounds can occupy binding sites for female hormones and exert hormone-like effects. This drink is helpful in a wide range of conditions specific to women, including menopause and PMS. In addition to the phytoestrogens, this juice packs a nutritional punch with potassium, magnesium, folic acid, and vitamin B.

1 small fennel	4 celery ribs
1 apple, cut into wedges	

Cut the fennel into narrow wedges and feed it into the juicer followed by the apple and celery.

fennel citrus mix

Fennel combines really well with citrus to make a great breakfast or refreshing drink.

1 small fennel	1 orange, peeled
1 large grapefruit, peeled	

Juice the fennel, followed by the grapefruit and orange.

gina's sweet sunshine

This is my wife Gina's specialty. She loves this drink in the morning, and it is one of my favorites as well. It is also a good midafternoon pick-me-up, because of its rich supply of natural sugars. The effervescent qualities of the mineral water seem to enhance the aroma of this juice, which makes this an extremely delicious, refreshing drink.

1 cup green grapes	2 oranges, peeled
½ lemon with skin	4 ounces sparkling mineral water

Juice the grapes, followed by the lemon and oranges. Put into a glass with ice, add the mineral water, and stir.

ginger ale

This is a great drink for children, a super replacement for sugary soft drinks. It is also useful in relieving an upset stomach.

½-inch slice of ginger	1 green apple, cut into wedges
1 lemon wedge with skin	4 ounces sparkling mineral water

Juice the ginger, followed by the lemon and apple. Pour into a glass with ice, add the mineral water, and stir.

ginger hopper (WL)

A classic drink to promote good health and may also help to lower cholesterol.

1-inch slice of ginger
1 apple, cut into wedges
3 carrots

Juice the ginger, followed by the apple and carrots.

ginger hopper plus (WL)

A spicier version of the classic drink.

¼-inch slice of ginger
1 apple, cut into wedges
2 carrots
½ large daikon radish, cut into lengthwise pieces, or 4 radishes with tops

Juice the ginger, followed by the apple, carrots, and radish.

go away gout

Here is a great mix to prevent gout attacks.

1 cup pitted cherries
6 celery ribs

Juice the cherries, followed by the celery.

go away pain

Here is a powerful anti-inflammatory recipe.

1-inch slice of fresh turmeric or ginger
1 cup blueberries
¼ pineapple with skin, sliced
4 celery ribs

Juice the turmeric, followed by the blueberries, pineapple, and celery.

go-go green ⓦ

A little more green goes a long way in this version of a super green drink. It will make you go, go, go with energy.

Handful of parsley or wheatgrass

4 celery ribs

2 kale leaves

1 green bell pepper

Handful of spinach

1 cucumber, cut in half lengthwise

Juice the parsley, followed by the celery, kale, pepper, spinach, and cucumber.

go green drink ⓦ

Have you ever heard the age-old saying "When you are green inside, you are clean inside"? I believe there is some truth to that statement. This is probably one of the healthiest juice recipes available.

Handful of parsley or wheatgrass

1 Granny Smith apple, cut into wedges

2 kale leaves

Handful of spinach

4 celery ribs

Juice the parsley, followed by the apple, kale, spinach, and celery.

green drink for kids

It is tough to get most kids to eat their greens. Fortunately, you can get them to drink them. Here is a great-tasting green drink that your kids will love.

Handful of Swiss chard, kale, spinach, or a combination.

1 pear

1 cup strawberries

½ lemon with skin

1 apple, cut into chunks

Juice the Swiss chard, followed by the pear, strawberries, lemon, and apple.

high c

Often we think of citrus fruits as having the highest vitamin C content, but actually the vegetables in this recipe are higher in vitamin C per serving than citrus.

| 1 cup broccoli florets with stems | 1 red bell pepper |
| 1 green bell pepper | 2 apples, cut into wedges |

Juice the broccoli, followed by the peppers and apples.

immune power fruit

This drink is rich in many nutrients vital to the immune system, and it also abounds in flavonoids and other phytochemicals with demonstrated antiviral and antioxidant effects.

| 1 orange, peeled | ¼ pineapple with skin, sliced |
| 1 cup strawberries | |

Juice the orange, followed by the strawberries and pineapple.

immune power veggie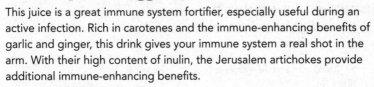

This juice is a great immune system fortifier, especially useful during an active infection. Rich in carotenes and the immune-enhancing benefits of garlic and ginger, this drink gives your immune system a real shot in the arm. With their high content of inulin, the Jerusalem artichokes provide additional immune-enhancing benefits.

2 garlic cloves	3 carrots
¼-inch slice of ginger	1 apple, cut into wedges
Handful of parsley	1 cup Jerusalem artichokes (optional)

Place the garlic and ginger in the center of the parsley, and feed into the juicer with the aid of a carrot. Alternate feeding the remaining carrots, apple, and Jerusalem artichokes (if using) into the juicer.

immune power veggie extreme

This formula is a great weapon against an active upper respiratory tract infection. The daikon radish really helps clear the sinuses and nasal passages.

2 garlic cloves	3 carrots
¼-inch slice of ginger	½ large daikon radish, cut into lengthwise pieces, or 4 radishes with leafy greens
Handful of parsley	

Place the garlic and ginger in the center of the parsley, and feed into the juicer with the aid of a carrot. Juice the radish and the remaining carrots.

iron plus

This is an incredible drink, especially for women prone to anemia and low iron levels. It also has a high content of folic acid, magnesium, vitamins C and E, as well as iron.

1 beet with top	**2 carrots**
2 kale leaves	**1 apple, cut into wedges**
1 cup broccoli florets with stems	

Alternate feeding the ingredients into the juicer.

jicama-carrot-apple ⓌⓁ

This is an example of using carrots and apples as a base for additional vegetables.

½ jicama, cut into lengthwise slices	**2 carrots**
	1 apple, cut into wedges

Alternate feeding the ingredients into the juicer.

kids' favorite ⓌⓁ

Kids absolutely love this drink. It is also a great juice for the dieter (it is low in calories, extremely satisfying, and delicious) and the individual with heart troubles. Plus its high content of vitamin C and flavonoids give the immune system a boost.

½ cantaloupe with skin, sliced	**1 cup strawberries**

Alternate feeding the cantaloupe and strawberries into the juicer.

kill the cold ⓌⓁ

This is a great drink to have when you feel a cold coming on. It is a diaphoretic tea, meaning that it will warm you from the inside and promote perspiration. It's pleasant to drink even if you just want to warm up and feel good.

| 2-inch slice of ginger | 1 cup hot water |
| ½ lemon with skin | |

Juice the ginger and lemon and add it to the water. It's a strong brew. If it's too strong, add more water. Sweeten with a little honey or natural, low-calorie sweeteners like stevia, monk fruit, or xylitol if desired.

liver mover (WL)

This drink is called the Liver Mover because it promotes the flow of bile and fat to and from the liver, which is very beneficial regarding weight loss and liver disorders.

| 1-inch slice of turmeric root or ginger | ½ large daikon radish, cut into lengthwise pieces, or 4 radishes with leafy greens |
| 1 beet with top | 2 apples, cut into wedges |

Juice the turmeric, followed by the beet, radish, and apples.

liver tonic (WL)

A liver tonic is a substance that specifically improves the tone and function of the liver, the most important organ of metabolism and detoxification. If dandelion roots cannot be found, you can substitute 4 radishes with tops or ½ daikon radish.

| 1 dandelion root | 2 carrots |
| 1 beet with top | 1 apple, cut into wedges |

Alternate feeding the ingredients into the juicer.

liver tonic plus (WL)

Turmeric root is a powerful liver aid. It helps with detoxification reactions and increases the flow of bile from the liver to the gallbladder.

1-inch turmeric or ginger	1 beet with top
½ large daikon radish, cut into lengthwise pieces, or 4 radishes with tops	2 carrots
	1 apple, cut into wedges

Alternate feeding the ingredients into the juicer.

mike's favorite

This is my favorite drink not only for flavor but also for what I know it does for my health. It is a great breakfast treat, quite thick and filling.

1-inch slice of ginger
1 cup blueberries

¼ pineapple with skin, sliced

Juice the ginger, followed by the blueberries and pineapple.

mint foam

This is a great drink that is fun-tasting. Mint has a soothing effect on the intestinal tract and also exhibits some antiviral activity.

Handful of mint
2 kiwifruits, peeled

1 green apple, cut into wedges

Juice the mint, followed by the kiwifruits and apple. Pour over ice if desired.

monkey shake

This is another yummy breakfast drink that is filling yet low in calories—it can definitely satisfy a sweet tooth.

½ papaya, peeled, seeded, and sliced
1 orange, peeled

1 banana, peeled
Orange twist, for garnish

Juice the papaya first, then the orange. Pour the mixture into a blender, add the banana, and liquefy. Pour it into a glass and garnish with a twist of orange.

orange aid

A variant of orange juice that is quite pleasing to the taste buds.

¼ pineapple with skin, sliced

2 oranges, peeled

Juice the pineapple, then the oranges.

pineapple-ginger ale

This drink is absolutely delicious and packed full of therapeutic nutrients.

1-inch slice of ginger	½ pineapple with skin, sliced

Juice the ginger, then the pineapple.

popeye's power drink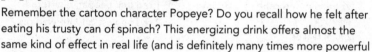

Remember the cartoon character Popeye? Do you recall how he felt after eating his trusty can of spinach? This energizing drink offers almost the same kind of effect in real life (and is definitely many times more powerful than canned spinach).

Handful of parsley	Handful of spinach
3 carrots	2 celery ribs

Bunch up the parsley and push it through the juicer with the aid of a carrot. Repeat this process with the spinach. Feed the remaining carrots and celery through the juicer.

potassium power

This drink provides a whopping 1,800 mg potassium per serving and is packed full of carotenes, vitamins, and other minerals. It's a great drink for people with high blood pressure.

Handful of parsley	4 celery ribs
3 carrots	1 tomato, quartered
Handful of spinach	

Bunch up the parsley and push it through the juicer with the aid of a carrot. Repeat this process with the spinach. Alternate feeding the remaining ingredients into the juicer.

potassium punch

Thick and delicious, this punch is rich not only in potassium but also in vitamin C. It is another great way to start the day.

1 peach, pitted and sliced	½ papaya, seeded and sliced
2 oranges, peeled	1 banana, peeled

Juice the peach, followed by one of the oranges, the papaya, and the second orange. Pour into a blender, add the banana, and liquefy.

purple cow ⓦ

Like milk, this drink is high in calcium (about 150 mg per serving); unlike milk, it contains the added nutrition of vitamin K.

½ head of red cabbage, cut into wedges

2 kale leaves

1 red bell pepper, quartered

2 red apples, cut into wedges

Juice the cabbage, followed by the kale, pepper, and apples.

salad in a glass ⓦ

If you have a hard time eating salads, try juicing one. There are huge nutritional benefits provided in this drink—and it's low in calories.

4 parsley sprigs

3 tomatoes, quartered

½ green bell pepper

½ cucumber

4 celery ribs

1 lemon wedge with skin, for garnish

Bunch up the parsley and feed into the juicer followed by the tomatoes, pepper, cucumber, lemon, celery and lemon. Garnish with lemon wedge if you desire.

some like it hot ⓦ

If you like hot and spicy foods, you will love this drink. The pepper and radish combination is quite invigorating, to say the least.

½ large daikon radish, cut into lengthwise pieces, or 4 radishes with tops

2 tomatoes, quartered

1 green bell pepper, quartered

1 red bell pepper, quartered

4 celery ribs

Alternate feeding the ingredients into the juicer.

spicy jicama fiesta (WL)

This juice is very interesting and possesses significant health benefits because of the combination of ginger and radish. Give it a try for a change of pace.

1-inch slice of ginger

1 jicama, cut into slices

1 pear, cut into slices

½ large daikon radish, cut into lengthwise pieces, or 4 radishes with tops

Juice the ginger, followed by the jicama, pear, and radish.

super v-7 (WL)

If you like V-8, you'll love this drink. It's fresh, it's alive, it's higher in nutrients, and it doesn't taste like it came from a can. This is a great electrolyte replacement drink for athletes in that it is very high in nutrients and low in calories.

Handful of parsley

2 carrots

Handful of spinach

2 tomatoes, quartered

2 celery ribs

½ cucumber

½ green bell pepper

Bunch up the parsley and push it through the juicer with the aid of a carrot. Repeat this process with the spinach. Alternate feeding the remaining ingredients into the juicer.

tomato zest (WL)

A tomato juice cocktail with a pleasant zing to it, this is a great drink to cool you down, especially if served over ice.

4 tomatoes, quartered

2 red bell peppers, quartered

½ large daikon radish, cut into lengthwise pieces, or 4 radishes with tops

Alternate feeding the tomatoes, peppers, and daikon into the juicer. Pour into a glass (ice optional).

tummy tonic (WL)

Fennel, ginger, and peppermint are all carminatives and intestinal antispasmodics. Carminatives are substances that promote digestion and relieve gaseousness; intestinal antispasmodics relieve spastic intestinal muscles. This is an interesting drink, especially worth a try if you have a tummy ache. I also recommend it as a weight-loss drink.

½-inch slice of ginger	½ small fennel
Handful of fresh peppermint or spearmint	1 apple, cut into wedges

Wrap the ginger in the peppermint and feed it through the juicer, followed by the fennel and apple.

vitamin u for ulcer ⓦⓛ

Here are Dr. Garnett Cheney's famous recipe recommendations for treating peptic ulcers. Green cabbage is best, but red cabbage will do.

½ head of green cabbage	4 celery ribs
2 tomatoes, quartered, or 2 carrots	

Cut the cabbage into long wedges and feed through the juicer followed by the tomatoes and celery.

waldorf salad

This drink is delicious and refreshing. It seems to have a relaxing effect and is often recommended for headaches.

4 celery ribs	2 green apples, cut into wedges

Juice the celery, then the apples.

zesty cran-apple

This is a great drink around the holidays and is a healthful alternative to the sugar-filled cranberry drinks available in cans or bottles. This drink is also useful in urinary tract infections and in individuals prone to kidney stones.

½ cup cranberries	½ cup grapes
½ lemon with skin	2 apples, cut into wedges

Juice the cranberries, followed by the lemon, grapes, and apples.

summary

It is easy to fall into the habit of making the same juice every day. Try to consume the fullest possible spectrum of colors of fruits and vegetables each week by juicing a rainbow of fresh fruits and vegetables. Don't be concerned about following a recipe exactly. Be flexible, have fun, and create your own versions. Experiment and find a combination that works for you. The most important guideline is to enjoy yourself.

8

juice as medicine

Hippocrates, the father of Western medicine, said, "Let your food be your medicine and let your medicine be your food." It is amazing how far we have drifted from this sound advice. I remember in the mid-1980s reading the *Sunday Seattle Times* and noticing one of those "Ask the Doctor"–type columns. The doctor was asked, "Does cabbage offer any benefit in the treatment of peptic ulcers?" The doctor's answer was an emphatic no, and he went on to say that in his opinion the promotion of folklore is quackery. His response is a typical knee-jerk reaction based on "opinion" rather than the facts.

First of all, as mentioned earlier, fresh cabbage juice has been well documented in the medical literature as having remarkable success in treating peptic ulcers. Dr. Garnett Cheney at Stanford University's School of Medicine and other researchers in the 1940s and

1950s performed several studies on fresh cabbage juice.[1] The results of these studies demonstrated that fresh cabbage juice is extremely effective in the treatment of peptic ulcers. In fact, the majority of patients experienced complete healing of their ulcers in as little as 7 days. Cabbage juice works by increasing the amount of protective substances that line the intestine. A breakdown in the integrity of this lining is what causes most ulcers. So cabbage juice is able to address the underlying cause of most ulcers.

Another part of the doctor's response that I took exception to was his recommendation of an acid-blocking drug instead. These drugs are divided into two general groups. One group is the older histamine-receptor antagonist drugs like Zantac, Tagamet, and Pepcid AC. The other is the newer and more potent group of drugs called proton-pump inhibitors, including Nexium, Prilosec, Protonix, Prevacid, and Aciphex.

These drugs don't produce a true cure, but they do tend to suppress symptoms. In short, when people start taking these drugs, they tend to become dependent on them. These drugs interfere with the body's natural digestive processes to produce significant disturbances in the gastrointestinal tract, among other more long-term side effects, such as increased risk for osteoporosis, heart arrhythmias, intestinal infections, bacterial pneumonia, and multiple nutrient deficiencies. Most seriously, these drugs may increase the development of various gastrointestinal cancers. Because the body uses gastric acid to release many food nutrients, people taking these acid-blocking drugs run the risk of multiple nutrient deficiencies. In particular, critical nutrients like vitamin B_{12}, magnesium, and iron are generally low in patients when they routinely take acid-blocking drugs.[2]

I recommend a naturopathic approach that eliminates all of these side effects. The first step in treatment is to identify and then eliminate or reduce all factors that can contribute to the development of peptic ulcers: food allergy, cigarette smoking, stress, and drugs such as aspirin and other nonsteroidal analgesics. Once the causative factors have been identified then controlled or eliminated, the focus is directed at healing the ulcers and promoting tissue resistance. This can be accomplished not only by drinking cabbage juice but also by eating a diet high in fiber and low in allergenic foods, avoiding those factors known to promote ulcer formation (such as smoking, alcohol, coffee, and aspirin), and incorporating an effective stress-reduction plan. A naturopath may also utilize a special licorice extract known as DGL (short for deglycyrrhizinated licorice), which promotes the healing of ulcers instead of blocking an important biological process. Like cabbage, DGL works by reestablishing a healthy intestinal lining.

are juices drugs? the importance of a total approach

Many foods and juices do indeed appear to have therapeutic effects, as noted throughout this book. But even though specific juices have been shown to benefit certain health conditions, juices in general should not be viewed as drugs. Instead of looking for a specific juice to cure a specific health condition, we should focus on adopting a diet and a lifestyle that will address the contributing factors of these diseases. You should juice a wide assortment of fruits and vegetables rather than rely on any one juice to remedy a specific medical complaint. This ensures that a broader range of beneficial substances is being delivered to the body.

For an example of how fresh juices can be of benefit in a serious health condition, let's look at their use in arthritis. Many fresh juices contain anti-inflammatory compounds such as enzymes and flavonoids. People suffering with arthritis may get some relief from drinking fresh, raw juices containing these compounds, but if they ignore other important dietary aspects, they will probably not experience long-term results. Ultimately, juicing must be part of a comprehensive and holistic health program if long-term results are desired.

Diet has been strongly implicated in many forms of arthritis for several years, with regard to both cause and cure. Various practitioners have recommended all sorts of specific diets for arthritis, especially the most severe form, rheumatoid arthritis. For example, abstaining from allergenic foods has been shown to offer significant benefit to some individuals with rheumatoid arthritis. Fasting or following a diet designed to eliminate food allergy followed by systematically reintroducing foods is often an effective method of isolating offending foods. Virtually any food can result in an aggravation of rheumatoid arthritis, but the most common offending foods are wheat, corn, milk and other dairy products, beef, and nightshade-family foods (tomato, potato, eggplants, peppers, and tobacco).[3]

A long-term study highlights the effectiveness of juicing (as part of a healthful diet and lifestyle) in the relief of rheumatoid arthritis. In the 13-month study, conducted in Norway at the Oslo Rheumatism Hospital, two groups of patients suffering from rheumatoid arthritis were compared to determine the effect of diet on their condition. One group (the treatment group) followed a therapeutic diet, and the others (the control group) were allowed to eat as they wished.[4]

The treatment group began the therapeutic diet by fasting for 7 to 10 days and then began following a special diet. Dietary intake during the fast consisted of herbal teas, garlic, vegetable broth, decoction of potatoes and parsley, and the juices of carrots, beets, and celery. No fruit juices were allowed.

After the fast, the patients reintroduced a "new" food item every second day. If they noticed an increase in pain, stiffness, or joint swelling within 2 to 48 hours, this item was omitted from the diet for at least 7 days before being reintroduced a second time. If the food caused worsening of symptoms after the second time, it was omitted permanently from the diet.

The study indicated that short-term fasting followed by a vegetarian diet led to a "substantial reduction in disease activity" in many patients. The results implied a therapeutic benefit beyond elimination of food allergies alone. The authors suggested that the additional improvements were due to changes in dietary fatty acids.

Fatty acids are important mediators of inflammation. Manipulation of dietary fat intake can significantly increase or decrease inflammation, depending on the type of fat or oil being manipulated. Arachidonic acid, a fatty acid derived almost entirely from animal sources (such as meat and dairy products), contributes greatly to the inflammatory process through its conversion to inflammatory prostaglandins and leukotrienes. The benefit of a vegetarian diet to those suffering inflammatory conditions like rheumatoid arthritis and asthma presumably results from the decrease in the availability of arachidonic acid for conversion to inflammatory compounds.[5]

Rheumatoid arthritis is a prime example of a very complex "multifactorial" disease. While fresh pineapple juice may be effective in the treatment of some people with rheumatoid arthritis—if we simply use foods or juices for their "druglike" effects—we may not be addressing many of the underlying causes of the disease. Instead of looking for a specific juice to cure a specific health condition, we should focus on adopting a diet and a lifestyle that will address the contributing factors of these diseases.

juicing with fresh herbs and spices

Supplementing your juices with fresh herbs and spices can provide additional health benefits. For example, as noted in chapter 6, garlic has many health-promoting properties—including antibiotic, immune-enhancing, anticancer, cholesterol-lowering, blood-pressure-reducing, and detoxification-enhancement activities.[6] Fresh garlic is much more potent than cooked, dried, or prepared garlic and can be easily included in fresh juices.

Another popular addition to juice is fresh ginger. This is a great idea if a little zest is desired or if an individual is suffering from intestinal spasms, arthritis, or motion sickness. Although most scientific studies have used powdered ginger, fresh ginger at an equivalent dosage is believed to yield even better results because it contains active enzymes. Most studies utilized 1 g powdered ginger. This would be equivalent to approximately 10 g or 1/3 ounce fresh ginger. Fresh ginger is available at most grocery stores.

One of the most powerful spices to add healing effects to fresh juice is turmeric. Although most scientific studies have used curcumin (the yellow pigment of turmeric), juicing fresh turmeric may have some advantages. Normally curcumin is poorly absorbed because it is poorly soluble in water.[7] It is possible that curcumin may be better absorbed in fresh turmeric juice. Newer forms of curcumin are now on the marketplace that have solved the problem of poor absorption. Based on detailed absorption studies, the best available form currently is Theracurmin.[8]

The additions of ginger, turmeric, and garlic are great examples of supplementing your juice with a medicinal herb or spice. Other examples include parsley, peppermint, capsicum (red pepper), onions, and dandelion greens or root.

juice recommendations for common health conditions

The following recommendations are for nutritional support only. Again, juices should not be viewed as drug substitutes or proper medical treatment. Nonetheless, these recommendations may prove beneficial in many instances. For a more complete discussion of the natural approach to common health conditions, consult *The Encyclopedia of Natural Medicine,* which I coauthored with Dr. Joseph Pizzorno. For more information, go to my website, DoctorMurray.com.

acne

> Carrot juice
> Green drinks (page 202)
> Purple Cow (page 208)
> Better Red Than Dead (page 192)

ADDITIONAL RECOMMENDATIONS: Zinc supplementation can be very effective in the treatment of acne. Use a highly absorbable form such as zinc picolinate or citrate at a dosage of 30–45 mg per day for best results.

anemia

> Iron Plus (page 204)
> Everything but the Kitchen Sink (page 199)
> Green drinks (page 202)

ADDITIONAL RECOMMENDATIONS: In the treatment of nutrition-related anemias, it is critical to also supplement with the corresponding nutrient to address the deficiency. For example, supplementing with iron is the treatment for anemia owing to iron deficiency, and vitamin B_{12} is used in treating anemia owing to vitamin B_{12} deficiency. Calf liver is often recommended for anemia as it is rich not only in iron but also in all B vitamins. Some people may respond only to a type of iron known as heme-iron found in calf liver as well as fish and meat.

angina

> Cantaloupe juice
> Pomegranate juice
> Cholesterol-Lowering Tonic (page 193)

Pineapple-Ginger Ale (page 207)
Kids' Favorite (page 204)

ADDITIONAL RECOMMENDATIONS: Try coenzyme Q_{10} (200 mg a day), a vitamin-like compound that has been shown to be quite useful in heart problems. Coenzyme Q_{10} acts like a spark plug in all cells of the body and is critically involved in energy and metabolism. Coenzyme Q_{10} levels are often low in patients with heart problems. Magnesium supplementation is also very much indicated in most cases of angina. Take magnesium citrate or another highly absorbable form at a dosage of 150 to 250 mg three times daily.

anxiety

Potassium Punch (page 207)
Potassium Power (page 207)
Waldorf Salad (page 210)

ADDITIONAL RECOMMENDATIONS: Regular exercise is the best prescription for relieving stress and anxiety. Also, regular deep breathing exercises are often helpful. Simply avoiding caffeine, sugar, alcohol, and food allergens, along with boosting B vitamins, calcium, and magnesium, can go a long way in relieving anxiety. Cutting out caffeine alone often results in complete elimination of symptoms. Supplementation with PharmaGABA—the natural form of the important brain chemical GABA or gamma-aminobutyric acid—can also be quite effective. Take 200 mg up to six times daily.

arthritis

Go Away Pain (page 201)
Pineapple-Ginger Ale (page 207)
Ginger Hopper (page 201)

ADDITIONAL RECOMMENDATIONS: Reduce stress on joints by achieving ideal body weight. Try eliminating nightshade-family vegetables (tomatoes, potatoes, peppers, tobacco), as these foods can often aggravate arthritis. For osteoarthritis, the most common form, glucosamine sulfate has been shown to be very effective at a dosage of 1,500 mg per day.

asthma and hayfever

Apple juice
Berry Happy (page 191)
Cholesterol-Lowering Tonic (page 193)
Salad in a Glass (page 208)
High C (page 202)

ADDITIONAL RECOMMENDATIONS: Food allergies often play a major role, especially in childhood asthma. The most common allergens are wheat, corn, milk and dairy products, citrus, and eggs. A vegetarian diet has been shown to be extremely effective in severe cases. For additional support, try natural products that contain N-acetylcysteine and ivy extract like Lung, Bronchial, and Sinus Health from Natural Factors.

atherosclerosis and high cholesterol levels

Beet juice
Pomegranate juice
Cholesterol-Lowering Tonic (page 193)
Cherry Pop (page 193)
Pineapple-Ginger Ale (page 207)

ADDITIONAL RECOMMENDATIONS: Reducing premature death from heart disease and strokes involves reducing—and ideally—eliminating the following major risk factors: smoking, elevated blood cholesterol levels, high blood pressure, diabetes, physical inactivity, and obesity. There are many natural products that are important considerations in improving heart health. Chief among them is the use of a high-quality fish oil product. Take enough fish oil to provide 1,000 mg each day of EPA+DHA—the key omega-3 fatty acids.

bladder infection (cystitis)

Cranberry Crush (page 195)
Zesty Cran-Apple (page 210)
Immune Power Veggie (page 203)

ADDITIONAL RECOMMENDATIONS: Avoid refined carbohydrates and drink at least 48 ounces of liquids a day. The herb uva ursi has been effectively used to treat urinary tract infections.

boils (faruncles)

Green drinks (page 202)
Cleansing Cocktail (page 194)
Immune Power Veggie (page 203)

ADDITIONAL RECOMMENDATIONS: Apply an Australian tea tree oil ointment topically to inflamed areas.

bronchitis and pneumonia

Pineapple juice
Immune Power Veggie (page 203)
Orange Aid (page 206)
Kill the Cold (page 204)

ADDITIONAL RECOMMENDATIONS: For additional support, try natural products that contain N-acetylcysteine and ivy extract like Lung, Bronchial, and Sinus Health from Natural Factors.

bruising

Blueberry juice
Berry Happy (page 191)
Mike's Favorite (page 206)

Color Me Pink (page 195)
Orange Aid (page 206)

ADDITIONAL RECOMMENDATIONS: Take vitamin C (1 to 3 g per day in incremental dosages) along with grape seed extract (100 to 300 mg per day).

canker sores

Green drinks (page 202)
Vitamin U for Ulcer (page 210)
Potassium Punch (page 207)

ADDITIONAL RECOMMENDATIONS: Allergies to milk and wheat often trigger ulcers and should be avoided. DGL (deglycerrhizinate) can help sooth recurrent inflammations.

carpal tunnel syndrome

Potassium Power (page 207)
Pineapple-Ginger Ale (page 207) or Orange Aid (page 206)
Ginger Hopper (page 201)

ADDITIONAL RECOMMENDATIONS: Vitamin B_6 has been shown to alleviate symptoms. Take 25 to 50 mg three times daily.

cataracts

Blueberry-apple juice
High C (page 202)
Color Me Pink (page 195)

ADDITIONAL RECOMMENDATIONS: High doses of vitamin C (1 to 3 g daily in divided dosages) and other antioxidants like selenium can prevent further damage in individuals with existing cataracts. Lutein, at a dosage of 15 to 30 mg daily, can also help.

common cold

Immune Power Veggie Extreme (page 203)
Immune Power Fruit (page 203)
Kill the Cold (page 204)

ADDITIONAL RECOMMENDATIONS: Rest and drink plenty of liquids. The herb echinacea is often used to bolster the immune system during the height of infection. Also, 250–500 mg vitamin C every 2 hours and the use of zinc-containing lozenges can reduce the severity of symptoms and the duration of the cold.

constipation

Pear juice
Bowel Regulator (page 193)
Go Green Drink (page 202)
Enzymes Galore (page 199)

ADDITIONAL RECOMMENDATIONS: Bulk-forming laxatives like powdered psyllium seed husks, guar, and oat bran may be quite helpful. Increase consumption of whole foods like whole grains, legumes, fruits, and vegetables. Cow's milk consumption was determined to be the cause of constipation in roughly two-thirds of children with constipation according to studies published in the prestigious *New England Journal of Medicine*. Presumably, the same significance holds true for adults as well.

crohn's disease and ulcerative colitis

Vitamin U for Ulcer (page 210)
Go Green Drink (page 202)
Cleansing Cocktail (page 194)
Enzymes Galore (page 199)

ADDITIONAL RECOMMENDATIONS: These are serious disorders. Consult *The Encyclopedia of Natural Medicine* as there is much that can be done from a natural perspective.

diabetes (type 2)

Shot of bitter melon juice
Jerusalem artichoke juice in vegetable-based juices
Super V-7 (page 209)
Salad in a Glass (page 208)

ADDITIONAL RECOMMENDATIONS: The key recommendation for type 2 diabetes is to achieve ideal body weight; being overweight leads to diabetes. Use the supplement PGX (see chapter 10) and follow a low-GL diet. Consult *The Encyclopedia of Natural Medicine* for further information.

diarrhea

Monkey Shake (page 206)
Potassium Punch (page 207)
Tummy Tonic (page 209)

ADDITIONAL RECOMMENDATIONS: If diarrhea lasts more than 24 hours or is quite profuse, consult a physician. To help solidify stools, pectin-rich fruits and vegetables like pears, apples, grapefruit, carrots, potatoes, and beets may offer some benefit. Also, fresh blueberries have a long historical use in diarrhea.

eczema (atopic dermatitis)

Digestive Delight (page 197)
Cleansing Cocktail (page 194)
Immune Power Veggie (page 203)

ADDITIONAL RECOMMENDATIONS: Avoid common food allergens such as wheat, corn, milk and dairy products, citrus, and eggs. In extreme cases, a vegetarian diet can be effective.

fibrocystic breast disease

Liver Mover (page 205)
Liver Tonic (page 205)
Cleansing Cocktail (page 194)

ADDITIONAL RECOMMENDATIONS: Constipation is a contributing factor in many. Iodine, vitamin E, and eliminating caffeine have all been shown to be helpful.

gallstones

Liver Tonic (page 205)
Color Me Pink (page 195)
Digestive Delight (197)

ADDITIONAL RECOMMENDATIONS: For prevention and treatment of gallstones, increase intake of vegetables, fruits, and dietary fiber, especially the gel-forming or mucilaginous fibers (flaxseed, oat bran, guar gum, pectin, etc.); reduce consumption of saturated fats, cholesterol, sugar, and animal proteins; avoid all fried foods; and drink at least six 8-ounce glasses of water each day to maintain the proper water content of the bile.

glaucoma (chronic open-angle)

Mike's Favorite (page 206)
Blueberry-apple juice
Orange juice

ADDITIONAL RECOMMENDATIONS: Taking a high-quality fish oil product can help. Take enough fish oil to provide 1,000 to 3,000 mg each day of EPA+DHA—the key omega-3 fatty acids.

gout

Cherry Pop (page 193)
Go Away Gout (page 201)

Go Away Pain (page 201)
Go Green Drink (page 202)
Pineapple-Ginger Ale (page 207)

ADDITIONAL RECOMMENDATIONS: Gout is easily controlled by diet. Eliminate alcohol and foods high in purines (organ meats, meats, shellfish), reduce fat and refined sugar intake, and increase the consumption of water and liquids to include four to six 8-ounce glasses of water and two 8-ounce glasses of fresh juice a day.

headache

Potassium Power (page 207)
Femme Fatale (page 199)
Ginger Hopper (page 201)

ADDITIONAL RECOMMENDATIONS: Food allergies often play a major role. The most common allergens are wheat, corn, milk and dairy products, citrus, and eggs. Low magnesium levels are common in headache sufferers. Take a highly absorbable form of magnesium, like magnesium citrate, at a dosage of 150 to 250 mg two to three times daily.

hepatitis

Dandelion juice
Liver Tonic (page 205)
Cholesterol-Lowering Tonic (page 193)
Immune Power Veggie (page 203)

ADDITIONAL RECOMMENDATIONS: Silymarin, a compound from the herb milk thistle, has been shown to be extremely effective. Take 240 to 360 mg per day. For more recommendations, see *The Encyclopedia of Natural Medicine*.

high blood pressure

Beet juice
Celery juice
Beet-Carrot-Celery (page 125)
Cholesterol-Lowering Tonic (page 193)
Potassium Power (page 207)
Salad in a Glass (page 208)

ADDITIONAL RECOMMENDATIONS: Eliminate alcohol, caffeine, and tobacco use. Boost potassium levels and lower dietary sodium by avoiding prepared foods and table salt and using potassium chloride salt substitutes such as AlsoSalt, NoSalt, and Nu-Salt instead.

hypoglycemia

Jerusalem artichoke juice in vegetable-based juices
Super V-7 (page 209)
Salad in a Glass (page 208)

ADDITIONAL RECOMMENDATIONS: Dilute fruit juices with a 1:1 water ratio. Eat frequent, smaller meals, and take the supplement PGX (see chapter 10) with every meal.

indigestion

Digestive Delight (page 197)
Pineapple-Ginger Ale (page 207)
Tummy Tonic (page 209)

ADDITIONAL RECOMMENDATIONS: Eat frequent, smaller meals in a relaxed atmosphere. Chew your food thoroughly. Digestive enzyme preparations can be very helpful.

insomnia

Waldorf Salad (page 210)
Immune Power Fruit (page 203)
Potassium Punch (page 207)

ADDITIONAL RECOMMENDATIONS: Eliminate caffeine and alcohol, which disrupt normal sleep processes, and increase exercise. If additional support is needed, try melatonin (3 mg), 5-hydroxytryptophan (50 mg), and L-theanine (100 mg).

irritable bowel syndrome
Tummy Tonic (page 209)
Ginger Hopper (page 201)
Digestive Delight (page 197)

ADDITIONAL RECOMMENDATIONS: Eliminate food allergens, increase fiber content by supplementing the diet with a gel-forming fiber like psyllium or oat bran. Try enteric-coated peppermint oil capsules for additional support.

kidney stones
Zesty Cran-Apple (page 210)
Cranberry Crush (page 195)
Diuretic Formula (page 197)

ADDITIONAL RECOMMENDATIONS: For prevention of kidney stones, increase fluid consumption to dilute urine concentration. A person with a history of kidney stones should consume enough fluids to produce a daily urinary volume of at least 2,000 ml (roughly 2 quarts). Additional amounts of vitamin B_6 (100 mg) and magnesium (300 mg magnesium citrate) will also help prevent recurrences.

macular degeneration
Blueberry-apple juice
High C (page 202)
Color Me Pink (page 195)

ADDITIONAL RECOMMENDATIONS: Lutein supplementation (15 to 30 mg daily) is strongly recommended owing to the serious nature of the condition. Consult *The Encyclopedia of Natural Medicine* for additional information.

menopause (see also OSTEOPOROSIS)

Femme Fatale (page 199)
Bone Builder's Cocktail (page 193)
Color Me Pink (page 195)

ADDITIONAL RECOMMENDATIONS: Herbal support is often helpful, especially for hot flashes. Formulas containing black cohosh (*Cimicifuga racemosa*) are usually the most effective.

menstrual blood loss, excessive (menorrhagia)

Iron Plus (page 204)
Everything but the Kitchen Sink (page 199)
Green drinks (page 202)

ADDITIONAL RECOMMENDATIONS: Low iron stores are a frequent cause of excessive menstrual blood flow. A simple blood test, serum ferritin, can determine iron stores. Low thyroid function can also be a contributing factor. Your doctor can order these tests.

menstrual pain (dysmenorrhea)

Femme Fatale (page 199)
Pineapple-Ginger Ale (page 207)
Potassium Power (page 207)

ADDITIONAL RECOMMENDATIONS: Restrict intake of animal fats, with the exception of fish oils (take 1,000 to 3,000 mg EPA+DHA daily), and take 1 tablespoon flaxseed oil daily.

morning sickness (nausea and vomiting of pregnancy)

Ginger Hopper (page 201)
Tummy Tonic (page 209)
Digestive Delight (page 197)

ADDITIONAL RECOMMENDATIONS: Frequent small meals are typically handled better during pregnancy. The liver is working hard dealing with the hormonal stress of pregnancy. Vitamin B_6, 25 mg three times daily, has been shown to reduce nausea.

osteoporosis

Bone Builder's Cocktail (page 193)
Green drinks (page 202)
Super V-7 (page 209)

ADDITIONAL RECOMMENDATIONS: Cut down on refined sugars, soft drinks, and protein to decrease calcium excretion. Physical fitness is the major determinant of bone density, so stay active. The best bone-building supplement program is Healthy Bones Plus from Natural Factors. See HealthyBonesPlus.com for more information.

periodontal disease

Bone Builder's Cocktail (page 193)
High C (page 202)
Color Me Pink (page 195)

ADDITIONAL RECOMMENDATIONS: Practice proper dental hygiene (regular brushing, flossing, and cleaning). Eliminate refined sugars, especially sticky candies and chocolates.

prostate enlargement (bph)

Pomegranate juice
Cholesterol-Lowering Tonic (page 193)
Don Juan (page 198)
Super V-7 (page 209)

ADDITIONAL RECOMMENDATIONS: Pumpkin seeds provide zinc and essential fatty acids that support prostate function, while the extract of saw palmetto berries (*Serenoa repens*) has been shown to reduce at a dose of 320 mg once or twice daily.

psoriasis

Liver Tonic (page 205)
Immune Power Veggie (page 203)
Pineapple-Ginger Ale (page 207)

ADDITIONAL RECOMMENDATIONS: Restrict intake of animal products, except fish. Higher dosages of fish oils (3,000 mg EPA+DHA daily) have been shown to be effective. Many psoriasis patients also do well on a gluten-free diet.

rheumatoid arthritis

Go Away Pain (page 201)
Pineapple-Ginger Ale (page 207)
Cleansing Cocktail (194)
Ginger Hopper (201)

sports injuries (see ARTHRITIS)

ulcer

Cabbage juice
Vitamin U for Ulcer (page 210)
Green drinks (202)
Potassium Punch (page 207)

ADDITIONAL RECOMMENDATIONS: Reduce or eliminate causative factors such as stress, smoking, and ulcer-causing drugs like aspirin and corticosteroids. Allergies to milk can be a triggering factor. Use DGL (deglycyrrhizinated licorice), available at health food stores.

varicose veins

Blueberry
Berry Happy (page 191)
Orange Aid (page 206)
Mike's Favorite (page 206)
Color Me Pink (page 195)

ADDITIONAL RECOMMENDATIONS: A high-fiber diet is critical in the treatment and prevention of varicose veins (and hemorrhoids) by preventing straining. A diet rich in vegetables, fruits, legumes, and grains promotes peristalsis—the rhythmic contractions that propel food through the gastrointestinal tract during bowel movements. Many fiber components attract water and form a gelatinous mass that keeps the feces soft, bulky, and easy to pass. Also, avoid standing in one place for prolonged periods of time, wear support hose, and get regular exercise. These measures all reduce blood pooling in varicose veins and improve symptoms such as heavy legs or pain.

water retention

Watermelon juice
Diuretic Formula (page 197)
Diuretic Formula Plus (page 197)
Potassium Power (page 207)

ADDITIONAL RECOMMENDATIONS: Reduce sodium intake. Read food labels carefully and keep sodium intake to less than 1,500 mg daily.

9

the juice fast

Substances toxic to our bodies are everywhere—in the air we breathe, the food we eat, and the water we drink. Even our bodies and the bacteria in the intestines produce toxic substances. It should be strongly emphasized that the health of an individual is largely determined by the ability of the body to "detoxify." This ability is based almost entirely on the function of one important organ: the liver.

Our environment is deteriorating as industrialization continues to spread. More and more chemicals that did not exist before are being dumped into the ecosystem and eventually absorbed into our bodies. Our health is not so much being threatened by one individual chemical as it is being undermined by a constant barrage of chemicals: pesticides, herbicides, food additives, lead, mercury, synthetic fertilizers, air pollutants, solvents, and thousands of other compounds.

Now, perhaps more than ever, it is critical for us to support the body's detoxification systems if we desire health. Periodic juice fasting is a healthful way to support your body's ability to deal with toxins.

types of toxic substances
heavy metals

Included in this category are lead, mercury, cadmium, arsenic, nickel, and aluminum. These metals tend to accumulate in the brain, kidneys, and immune system, where they can severely disrupt normal function. Most of the heavy metals in the body are a result of industrial contamination. For example, in the United States alone, industrial sources and cars burning leaded gasoline dump more than 600,000 tons of lead into the atmosphere to be inhaled or, after landing on food crops, in fresh water, and soil, to be ingested.

Common sources of heavy metals, in addition to industrial sources, include lead from the solder in tin cans, pesticide sprays, and cooking utensils; cadmium and lead from cigarette smoke; mercury from dental fillings, contaminated fish, and cosmetics; and aluminum from antacids and cookware.

Early signs of heavy metal poisoning are vague or associated with other problems. They can include headache, fatigue, muscle pains, indigestion, tremors, constipation, anemia, pallor, dizziness, and poor coordination. The person with even mild heavy metal toxicity will experience impaired ability to think or concentrate. As toxicity increases, so does the severity of signs and symptoms.

It is a well-established fact that there is a strong relationship between childhood learning disabilities (and other disorders, including criminal behavior) and body stores of heavy metals. In general, learning disabilities seem to correlate with a general pattern of high hair levels of mercury, cadmium, lead, copper, and manganese. Poor nutrition and elevation of heavy metals go hand in hand, owing to decreased consumption of food factors known to chelate these heavy metals or decrease their absorption.

Every effort should be made to reduce heavy metal levels and promote their excretion. This goal is particularly important to people in professions associated with extremely high exposure, including battery makers, gasoline station attendants, printers, roofers, solderers, dentists, and jewelers.

toxic chemicals, drugs, alcohol, solvents, formaldehyde, everyday toxins, pesticides, herbicides, and food additives

Exposure to food additives, solvents (cleaning materials, formaldehyde, toluene, benzene), pesticides, herbicides, and other toxic chemicals can give rise to a number of symptoms. Most common are psychological and neurological conditions, such as depression, headaches, mental confusion, mental illness, tingling in extremities, abnormal nerve reflexes, and other signs of impaired nervous system function. The nervous system is extremely sensitive to these chemicals. Respiratory tract allergies and increased rates for many cancers are also noted in people chronically exposed to chemical toxins.

The importance of reducing our toxic load by consuming organic produce cannot be overstated. In the United States, each year more than 1.2 billion pounds of pesticides and herbicides are sprayed or added to our crops. Most pesticides in use are synthetic chemicals of questionable safety. The major long-term health risks include the potential to cause cancer and birth defects, while the major health risks of acute intoxication include vomiting, diarrhea, blurred vision, tremors, convulsions, and nerve damage.

microbial compounds

Toxins produced by bacteria and yeast in the gut can be absorbed into the bloodstream, causing significant disruption of body functions. Examples of these types of toxins include endotoxins, exotoxins, toxic amines, toxic derivatives of bile, and various carcinogenic substances.

Gut-derived microbial toxins have been implicated in a wide variety of diseases, including liver diseases, Crohn's disease, ulcerative colitis, thyroid disease, psoriasis, lupus erythematosis, pancreatitis, allergies, asthma, and immune disorders.

In addition to toxic substances being produced by microorganisms, antibodies formed against microbial antigens can cross-react with the body's own tissues, thereby causing autoimmunity. The list of autoimmune diseases that have been linked to cross-reacting antibodies includes rheumatoid arthritis, myasthenia gravis, diabetes, and autoimmune thyroiditis.

To reduce the absorption of toxic substances, a fiber-rich diet is recommended. The water-soluble fibers, such as those found in guar gum, pectin, oat bran, and other vegetables, are particularly valuable. Fiber has an ability to bind to toxins within the gut and promote their excretion. The immune system as well as the liver is responsible for dealing with the toxic substances that are absorbed from the gut.

breakdown products of protein metabolism

The kidneys are largely responsible for the elimination of toxic waste products of protein breakdown (such as ammonia and urea). The kidneys can be supported in their important function by drinking adequate amounts of liquids (especially fresh juices) and avoiding excessive protein intake.

the diagnosis of toxicity

Several special laboratory techniques are useful in detecting toxins in the body. For heavy metals, the most reliable measure of chronic exposure is the hair mineral analysis. Reliable results of hair analysis are dependent on (1) a properly collected, cleaned, and prepared sample of hair and (2) experienced personnel using appropriate analytical methods in a qualified laboratory.

For determining exposure to the second category of toxins, toxic chemicals, a detailed medical history by an experienced physician in these matters is essential. When appropriate, the laboratory analysis for this group of toxins can involve measuring blood and fatty tissue for suspected chemicals. It is also necessary to measure the effect that these chemicals have on the liver. The most sensitive test is the serum bile acid assay. Other tests for liver function (serum bilirubin and liver enzymes) are also important.

Physicians use different laboratory techniques to determine the presence of microbial toxins, including tests for the presence of (1) abnormal microbial concentrations and disease-causing organisms (stool culture) and (2) microbial byproducts (urinary indican test).

The determination of the presence of high levels of breakdown products of protein metabolism and kidney function involves both blood and urine measurement of these compounds.

fasting

Fasting is defined as abstinence from all food and drink except water for a specific period of time, usually for a therapeutic or religious purpose. It is often used as a detoxification method, as it is one of the quickest ways to increase elimination of wastes and enhance the healing processes of the body. This process spares essential tissue (vital organs) while utilizing nonessential tissue (fatty tissue and muscle) for fuel.

Although therapeutic fasting is probably one of the oldest known therapies, it has been largely ignored by the scientific community until relatively recently. There is now considerable scientific support on the use of fasting in the treatment of obesity, chemical poisoning, arthritis, allergies, psoriasis, eczema, thrombophlebitis, leg ulcers, irritable bowel syndrome, impaired or deranged appetite, bronchial asthma, depression, neurosis, and schizophrenia.[1]

One of the most encouraging studies on fasting was published in the *American Journal of Industrial Medicine* in 1984.[2] This study involved patients who had ingested rice oil contaminated with polychlorinated biphenyls, or PCBs. All patients reported improvement in symptoms, and some observed "dramatic" relief, after undergoing 7- to 10-day fasts. This research supports past studies of PCB-poisoned patients and indicates the therapeutic effects of fasting. Caution must be used, however, when fasting after significant contamination with fat-soluble toxins like pesticides. The pesticide DDT has been shown to be mobilized during a fast and may reach blood levels toxic to the nervous system.[3] For this reason, it is a good idea to include those guidelines given below for supporting detoxification reactions while fasting.

the short fast or fresh juice elimination diet

By strict definition, during a fast, only water is consumed. If you are drinking fresh fruit or vegetable juice, this is technically known as an elimination diet rather than a fast, but we will call it a juice fast. Most healthy people do not need to go on a strict water fast to aid in detoxification. In fact, I do not recommend a water fast. Instead, a 3- to 5-day fresh fruit and vegetable juice fast actually provides the greatest benefit. It is important to emphasize that only fresh fruit or vegetable juice be used to aid elimination. As we have noted, fresh juice provides valuable enzymes to our system.

Drinking fresh juice for cleansing reduces some of the side

effects associated with a water fast, such as light-headedness, fatigue, and headaches. While on a fresh juice fast, individuals typically experience an increased sense of well-being, renewed energy, clearer thought, and a sense of purity.

Although a short juice fast can be started at any time, it is best to begin on a weekend or during a time period when adequate rest can be assured and energy can be directed toward healing instead of toward other body functions.

Prepare for a fast on the day before by making the last meal one of only fresh fruits and vegetables (some authorities recommend a full day of raw food to start a fast, even a juice fast).

Only fresh fruit and vegetable juices (ideally prepared from organic produce) should be consumed for the next 3 to 5 days, four 8- to 12-ounce glasses throughout the day.

Virtually any fresh juice provides support for detoxification, but I would recommend Liver Tonic (page 205), Digestive Delight (page 197), Pineapple-Ginger Ale (page 207), Zesty Cran-Apple (page 210), Go Green Drink (page 202), Cleansing Cocktail (page 194), Cruciferous Surprise (page 195), and Potassium Power (page 207).

In addition to the fresh juice, pure water should also be consumed, at least four 8-ounce glasses every day during the fast.

other important guidelines

While fasting, coffee, soft drinks, sports drinks, and any other processed beverage should be eliminated; unsweetened herbal teas may be supplemented in for variety.

Exercise should be reduced while fasting, as conserving energy will allow maximal healing. Short walks or light stretching are useful, but heavy workouts tax the system and inhibit repair and elimination.

Cleansing the skin with lukewarm water is encouraged, but extremes of temperature can be tiring. Deodorants, soaps, sprays, detergents, synthetic shampoos, and exposure to other chemicals should be avoided. These only hinder elimination and add to the body's detoxification and elimination burden.

Rest is one of the most important aspects of a fast. A nap or two during the day is recommended. Less sleep will usually be required at night, since daily activity is lower.

Body temperature usually drops during a fast, as do blood pressure, pulse, and respiratory rate—all measures of the slowing of the metabolic rate of the body. It is important, therefore, to stay warm.

In breaking a fast, as outlined below, an individual is encouraged to eat slowly, chew thoroughly, and not overindulge. While breaking a fast and in the days that follow, it can be very helpful to carefully record what is eaten and note any adverse effects. Many of today's health problems result from food allergies and overeating.

breaking your fast

DAY ONE

BREAKFAST	LUNCH	DINNER
One of the following: melon, nectarine, or pineapple	A different fruit from the breakfast list	8 ounces of any other fruit

DAY TWO

BREAKFAST	LUNCH	DINNER
12 ounces of one type of fresh fruit	14 ounces of whole pears, papaya, or citrus fruit	Raw vegetable salad with leafy greens, tomato, celery, and cucumber or 2 pears, 2 apples, and ¼ avocado

DAY THREE

Resume healthful diet

supporting detoxification reactions while fasting

It is extremely important to support detoxification reactions while fasting. This goal is partly accomplished by electing to go on a fresh juice fast over a water fast; additional nutritional support is needed because stored toxins in our fat cells are released into the system during a fast. I highly recommend that you consider following a focused internal cleansing program like the 7 Day Total Nutritional Cleansing Program from Natural Factors that I co-developed with Michael Lyon, MD. This program comes in a boxed kit with a small booklet that contains detailed, easy-to-follow instructions on how to use the medicinal food powders and supplements in the kit as well as dietary guidelines, menu suggestions, and recipes. It is not a fast—it is a cleansing program designed to feed your body the tools it needs to get rid of the toxins. You can modify the meals suggested by following the guidelines above. For more information on this program and where to get it, go to www.naturalfactors.com.

Or, if you want to provide your own detoxification support, here are some key suggestions:

1. Take a high-potency multiple vitamin and mineral formula to provide general support for detoxification.

2. Take a lipotropic formula, a special formula for supporting the liver that is available at health food stores. These formulas are typically rich in choline and methionine. Take enough of the formula to provide a daily dose of 1,000 mg choline and 1,000 mg either methionine and/or cysteine.

3. Take 1 g vitamin C three times daily.

4. Take 3 to 5 g fiber supplement at night before retiring. The best fiber sources are the water-soluble fibers such as PGX (see chapter 10), powdered psyllium seed husks, guar gum, and pectin.

5. Consider additional liver support by taking a special extract of milk thistle known as silymarin. The dosage is 70 to 210 mg three times daily.

the long view

Detoxification of harmful substances is a continual process in the body. Detoxification does not have to be an unpleasant experience and does not have to be performed only while on a fast. Actually, the best approach may be to detoxify gradually.

A rational approach to aiding the body's detoxification mechanisms can include the use of periodic short juice fasts (3 to 5 days) or longer medically supervised fasts. However, to truly support the body's detoxification processes, a long-term detoxification program is recommended. In particular, you must support the health of your liver. To do so, there are three things you definitely want to stay away from: saturated fats, refined sugar, and alcohol. A diet high in saturated fat increases the risk of developing fatty infiltration and/or cholestasis. In contrast, a diet rich in dietary fiber, particularly the water-soluble fibers, promotes increased bile secretion.

Special foods rich in factors that help protect the liver from damage and improve liver function include high-sulfur-containing foods like garlic, legumes, onions, and eggs; good sources of water-soluble fibers such as pears, oat bran, apples, and legumes; cabbage family vegetables, especially broccoli, Brussels sprouts, and cabbage; artichokes, beets, carrots, dandelion; and many herbs and spices like turmeric, cinnamon, and ginger.

Avoid alcohol if you suffer from impaired liver function and only drink in moderation (no more than two 10-ounce glasses of wine or 24-ounce glasses of beer, no more than 2 ounces hard liquor per day for men, and 1 ounce for women). Alcohol overloads detoxification processes and can lead to liver damage and immune suppression.

summary

The ability to detoxify is one of the critical processes that determine our health. It is amazing just how well the body handles the constant onslaught of modern living. Periodic juice fasting, as well as a long-term approach to detoxification, can be used to support the body's detoxification mechanisms.

10

juicing for weight loss

Why do some people gain weight so easily, while others eat all they want and never seem to put on a pound? And why do so many people find it extremely difficult to lose weight, while others have difficulty keeping weight on? What is the best approach for permanent results? What is the best diet? Researchers have worked for decades to provide answers to these and other questions from the growing number of overweight Americans. Meanwhile, the legions fighting the battle of the bulge have now reached epidemic proportions; data provided by the National Center for Health Statistics indicate that in 2012 nearly 8 out of 10 adults in the United States were overweight or obese.

There are numerous myths and misconceptions about obesity and weight loss. What is undeniable is that successful *permanent* weight loss must incorporate high nutrition, adequate exercise, and a positive mental attitude. *All* the components are critical and inter-related. Improving one facet may be enough to result in some positive changes, but improving all three yields the greatest results.

Hundreds of diets and weight-loss programs claim to be the answer to obesity. While it is true most diets will promote short-term weight loss if followed closely, the reality is that the vast majority of people fail to achieve and maintain their weight-loss goals. Ninety percent of those people gain back more weight than they lost. Statistics from the National Institutes of Health tell us that 94 percent

the weight-loss equation

The basic equation for losing weight is the same for almost everyone. To lose weight, calorie intake must be less than the amount of calories burned. This can be done by decreasing food intake and/or by exercising. Or, ideally, a combination of the two.

To lose 1 pound of fat, a person must take in 3,500 fewer calories than he or she expends. To lose 3 pounds of fat each week, there must be a negative caloric balance of 1,000 calories a day. This can be achieved by decreasing the amount of calories ingested and/or by exercise. To reduce one's caloric intake by 1,000 calories a day by exercise a person would need to jog for 90 minutes, play tennis for 2 hours, or take a brisk 2½-hour walk. The most sensible approach to weight loss is to simultaneously eat less and exercise more.

A successful weight-loss program should provide 1,200 to 1,500 calories a day. This, along with aerobic exercise for 20 to 30 minutes 3 or 4 days a week and resistance training (weight lifting) 3 days per week, will produce optimum weight loss at a rate of 1 to 3 pounds a week. Crash diets usually result in rapid weight loss (largely muscle and water) but cause rebound weight gain. The most successful approach to weight loss is gradual reduction through adopting long-standing dietary and lifestyle modifications.

of people who lose weight by dieting regain it within 5 years. Based upon these statistics, one could actually conclude that dieting is a significant contributor to obesity in the United States.

Diets fail because they result in an increased hunger as you lose weight, making it harder to resist temptation as time goes on. They also result in muscle loss, which lowers your metabolic rate, causing more of your extra calories to turn into fat. Most important, because diets don't help you to make changes that you can live with for the rest of your life, you tend to gradually drift back to your old habits again.

The program I detail in this chapter works—and works for achieving your ideal body weight forever—because it is not a diet, it's a way of life!

preparing your body for weight loss

During the first week of a weight-loss program, you should go on a juice fast or utilize my 7 Day Total Nutritional Cleansing Program (both are discussed in chapter 9). During this week your body will begin ridding itself of stored toxins such as pesticides, heavy metals, and compounds from plastic. Remember that many toxic substances are stored in fat cells, and when you start losing fat these compounds are released into the bloodstream. Be sure to follow the recommendations given in chapter 9 to provide key nutrients that will help your body deal with and eliminate these harmful substances. As weight loss progresses, your body will continue to eliminate these stored toxins and will continue to need the protection of fresh juice, PGX (discussed on pages 256–259), and a high-fiber diet.

the fresh juice advantage for weight loss

Juicing fresh fruits and vegetables provides numerous nutritional advantages that are extremely important to weight loss. Fresh juice offers concentrated nutrition that is easily absorbed, a rich supply of protein, carbohydrate, essential fatty acids, vitamins, and minerals.

As mentioned in chapter 1, diets containing a high percentage of uncooked foods are significantly associated with weight loss, improved blood sugar control, and lower blood pressure. Researchers seeking to determine why raw-food diets produce these effects have concluded the following:

1. A raw-food diet is much more satisfying to the appetite. Cooking can cause the loss of up to 97 percent of water-soluble vitamins (A, D, E, and K). Since uncooked foods such as juices contain more vitamins and other nutrients, they are more satisfying to the body. If the body is not fed, it feels that it is starving. The result: Metabolism will slow down. This means less fat will be burned.

2. The blood-pressure-lowering effect of raw foods is most likely due to healthier food choices, fiber, and potassium. However, the effect of cooking the food cannot be ruled out. When patients are switched from a raw-food diet to a cooked diet (without the content of calories or sodium), there is a rapid increase of blood pressure to prestudy values.

3. A diet in which 60 percent of the calories ingested come from raw foods reduces stress on the body. Specifically, the presence of enzymes in raw foods, the reduced allergenicity of raw foods, and the effects of raw foods on our gut-bacteria ecosystem are thought to be much more healthful than the effects of cooked foods.

Juicing helps the body's digestive process and allows for quick absorption of high-quality nutrition. The result: increased energy levels. This is one of the great advantages of achieving weight loss through improved nutrition. Unlike other plans that leave you feeling tired and lifeless, fresh juices—along with sensible eating—will provide you with energy: energy to burn more calories with physical activity.

While some juice experts promote what is more or less an indefinite juice fast as a strategy to lose weight, I don't think it is sustainable. Excessive juice fasting often leads to rebound weight loss when people eventually start eating food again. The program that I recommend in this chapter has the best chance of helping people lose weight and keep it off.

why is it so hard to lose weight?

Body weight is closely tied to what is referred to as the "set point"—the weight that a body tries to maintain by regulating the amount of food and calories consumed. Research with animals and humans has found that each person has a programmed "set point" weight. The individual fat cells in the abdomen control this set point: When the enlarged fat cells in obese individuals become smaller, they either send powerful messages to the brain to eat or they block the action of appetite-suppressing compounds.

The existence of this set point helps to explain why most diets do not work. Although the overweight individual can fight the impulse to eat for a while, eventually the signals become too strong to ignore. The result is rebound overeating with individuals often exceeding their previous weight. In addition, their set point is now set at a higher level, making it even more difficult to lose weight. This is referred as the ratchet effect and yo-yo dieting.

The key to overcoming the fat cells' set point appears to be increasing the sensitivity of the fat cells to insulin. This sensitivity apparently can be improved, and the set point lowered, by exercise, a specially designed diet, and the use of a special nutritional supplement called PGX (discussed later). The set point theory suggests that a diet that does not improve insulin sensitivity will most likely fail to provide long-term results.

the importance of a low glycemic load

In chapter 2, the importance of eating a low-GL diet was stressed. It is critical to use this practical tool for effective weight loss and blood sugar control. Appendix B provides a list of the GI, fiber content, and GL of common foods. It is provided to help you construct a healthful diet. The following recommendations are essential for weight-loss success:

1. Keep your GL below 20 for any 3-hour period. If you are diabetic or trying to lose weight, keep the value below 15.
2. When drinking juice, keep the amount of high-GL juices like apple, carrot, orange, and most fruit juices to no more than 6 ounces per 3-hour period.
3. Focus on high-nutrient, low-GL fruits and vegetables to juice.
4. Use smaller amounts of higher-GL foods (most fruit and carrots) as a base to add flavor and palatability while focusing on higher nutrient, lower-GL choices.

healthful food choices

Permanent results require permanent changes in choosing what foods to eat and when to eat them. The healthful-diet component of an effective weight-loss program must stress low-GL vegetables; health-promoting fruits, grains, and legumes; and adequate, but not excessive, quantities of protein, and must avoid food components detrimental to health, such as sugar, saturated fats, cholesterol, salt, food additives, alcohol, and agricultural residues like pesticides and herbicides. The healthful foods recommended are divided into the following categories:

- Vegetables
- Fruits
- Whole-grain breads, cereals, and starchy vegetables
- Legumes (beans)

- Protein sources
- Fats
- Sweeteners

vegetables

Vegetables are fantastic "diet" foods because they are very high in nutritional value but low in calories. Vegetables are excellent sources of vitamins, minerals, and health-promoting fiber compounds. In addition to being juiced, the vegetables in table 10.1 can be eaten raw, in salads, or steamed. Those noted with an asterisk (*) are "free foods" and can be eaten in any desired amount because the calories they contain are offset by the number of calories your body burns in the process of digestion. Another effect of these free foods is they help keep you feeling satisfied between meals.

In addition to consuming vegetables as juice, you should eat at least 4 cups of vegetables daily with one of these cups being a dark leafy vegetable. Additional amounts can be eaten if they are chosen from those marked by an asterisk. Buy vegetables that are in season and eat a variety for nutrient diversity. Starchy vegetables like potatoes are included in the Breads, Cereals, and Starchy Vegetables category below.

fruits

Fruits make excellent snacks, because they contain natural sugars that are absorbed slowly into the bloodstream, thereby allowing the body time to utilize them. Fruits are also excellent sources of vitamins and minerals as well as health-promoting fiber compounds and many phytochemicals. However, fruits are typically higher in calories than vegetables, so their intake should be restricted somewhat on a weight-loss plan. Two of the servings of fruit in table 10.2 may be eaten during the day or utilized in juice form.

table 10.1. calories (per cup) from vegetables

*Alfalfa sprouts **20**

Artichokes, steamed heart and leaves **44**

Asparagus, 6 medium spears **21**

Beets **54**

*Bell peppers **22**

*Bok choy **20**

Broccoli **40**

Brussels sprouts **54**

*Cabbage, green or red **24 raw, 31 cooked**

Carrots **46**

*Cauliflower **27**

*Celery **17**

Chard **30**

*Cucumber **16**

Daikon radish **26**

Eggplant **38**

*Endive **10**

*Escarole **10**

Garlic, 1 clove **10**

Greens
  Beet **36**
  Collard **40**
  Mustard **40**
  Turnip **29**

Jicama **49**

Kale **37**

Kohlrabi **40**

Leeks **53**

*Lettuce **10**

*Mushrooms **20**

Okra, 8 pods **36**

Onions **50–60**

Parsley **26**

Peas **106**

*Radishes **20**

Rhubarb **50**

*Spinach **41**

*Sprouted mung beans **21**

String beans, green or yellow **31**

Summer squash, yellow **40**

Tomatoes **23**

*Turnips **36**

Watercress **7**

Zucchini **25**

breads, cereals, and starchy vegetables

Breads, cereals, and starchy vegetables are classified as complex carbohydrates. Chemically, complex carbohydrates are made up of long chains of simple carbohydrates or sugars. This means the body has to digest or break down the large sugar chains into simple sugars. Therefore, the sugar from complex carbohydrates enters the bloodstream more slowly. This means blood sugar levels and appetite are better controlled.

table 10.2. calories from fruits

Apple, 1 large or 2 small **125**

Applesauce, 1 cup unsweetened **100**

Apricots, 8 dried halves **70**

Apricots, 4 fresh medium **70**

Banana, 1 small **100**

Berries:
Blackberries, 1 cup **85**
Blueberries, 1 cup **90**
Cranberries, 1 cup **90**
Raspberries, 1 cup **70**
Strawberries, 1 cup **55**

Cherries 10 large **45**

Dates 4 **100**

Figs, 2 dried **100**

Figs, 2 fresh **100**

Grapefruit, 1 **50**

Grapes, 20 **70**

Mango, 1 small **125**

Melons
Cantaloupe, ½ small **80**
Honeydew, ¼ medium **110**
Watermelon, 2 cups **110**

Nectarines, 2 small **80**

Oranges, 2 small **110**

Papaya, 1 small **110**

Peaches, 2 medium **80**

Persimmons, native, 2 medium **130**

Pineapple, 1 cup **80**

Plums, 4 medium **80**

Prunes, 4 medium **110**

Raisins, ¼ cup **105**

Tangerines, 2 medium **80**

Complex-carbohydrate foods like breads, cereals, and starchy vegetables are higher in fiber and nutrients but lower in calories than foods high in simple sugars like cakes and candies. No more than two servings of the complex carbohydrates in table 10.3 should be eaten per day.

legumes

Legumes are fantastic weight-loss foods. They are rich in important nutrients for proper metabolism. Legumes help improve liver function, as evidenced by their cholesterol-lowering actions. Legumes have also been shown to be effective in improving blood sugar control. Since obesity has been linked to loss of blood sugar control (insulin insensitivity), legumes appear to be extremely important in a weight-loss plan.

table 10.3. calories from breads, cereals, and starchy vegetables

Breads
  Bagel, 1 small **200**
  Dinner roll, 2 **90**
  English muffin, 1 small **120**
  Tortilla, 2 6-inch **90**
  Whole wheat, rye, or
    pumpernickel bread,
    2 slices **200**

Cereals
  Bran flakes, 1 cup **130**
  Cornmeal, dry, ¼ cup **100**
  Cereal, cooked, 1 cup **150**
  Flour, 5 tablespoons **140**
  Grits, cooked, 1 cup **145**
  Pasta, cooked, 1 cup **210**
  Puffed cereal, unsweetened,
    2 cups **120**
  Rice or barley, cooked,
    1 cup **242**
  Wheat germ, ¼ cup **108**
  Other unsweetened cereal,
    1½ cups **160**

Crackers
  Graham, 4 (2½-inch)
    squares **120**
  Matzo, 1 (4-by-6-inch)
    square **111**
  Rye wafers, 4 (2-by-3½-inch)
    wafers **148**
  Saltines, 6 **156**

Starchy Vegetables
  Corn, 1 cup **124**
  Corn on cob, 2 small **120**
  Parsnips, 2 cups **110**
  Potato, mashed, 1 cup **180**
  Potato, white, 1 medium **180**
  Squash, winter, acorn, or
    butternut, 1 cup **84**
  Yam or sweet potato,
    1 cup **100**

One cup of the following cooked beans can be eaten per day:

Black-eyed peas

Chickpeas or garbanzo beans

Kidney beans

Lentils

Lima beans

Pinto beans

Split peas

Tofu

Other dried beans and peas

animal products

To prevent breakdown of muscle during weight loss, it is important that protein intake be adequate. The plant foods recommended above will provide more than enough protein. Although I stress the importance of the previous four food groups, I realize it is necessary to give you some guidelines if you choose to eat some animal protein sources, especially during the transition phase. Certainly you should limit this to no more than twice a week. If one of the following food choices is made, it will be necessary to reduce the fat selection to ½ serving and reduce by half the breads, cereals, and starchy vegetables selection and eliminate the legume selection.

Fish: 6 ounces cod, sole, halibut, salmon, tuna packed in water, red snapper, or perch

Beef: 4 ounces lean cuts of veal, chipped beef, chuck, steak (flank, plate), tenderloin plate ribs, round (bottom, top), all cuts rump, spareribs, or tripe

Lamb: 4 ounces lean cuts of leg, rib, sirloin, loin (roast and chops), shank, or shoulder

Poultry: 4 ounces skinless chicken or turkey

Dairy: 2 cups nonfat milk, 1 cup 2% milk, 1 cup low-fat yogurt, or ½ cup low-fat cottage cheese

fats

Fat intake should be reduced to a minimum, since fats are very dense in calories. Two of the following may be consumed each day:

Avocado, 4-inch diameter, ¼

Vegetable oil, olive, canola, or macadamia oil, flaxseed oil, 1 tablespoon

Olives, 5 small

Almonds, 10 whole

Pecans, 4 large

Peanuts
    Spanish, 20 whole
    Virginia, 10 whole

Walnuts, 6 small

Salad dressings, 1 tablespoon

Mayonnaise, 1 tablespoon

sweeteners

Natural low-calorie sweeteners like stevia, xylitol, or monk fruit (e.g., Nectresse) may be used conservatively. Restrict your intake of natural sweeteners to one of the following each day:

Honey, 1 tablespoon

Jams, jellies, preserves, 1 tablespoon

exercise and weight loss

Regular exercise is a necessary component of a weight-loss program for these reasons:

1. When weight loss is achieved by dieting without exercise, a substantial portion of the total weight loss comes from the lean tissue, primarily as water loss.

2. When exercise is included in a weight-loss program, there is usually an improvement in body composition owing to a gain in lean body weight because of an increase in muscle mass and a concomitant decrease in body fat.

3. Exercise helps counter the reduction in basal metabolic rate (BMR) that usually accompanies calorie restriction alone.

4. Exercise increases the BMR for an extended period of time following the exercise session.

5. Moderate to intense exercise may have an appetite suppressant effect.

6. Those subjects who exercise during and after weight reduction are better able to maintain the weight loss than those who do not exercise.

a daily plan for weight loss

Achieving ideal body weight is not about dieting or food deprivation; it is all about eliminating excessive hunger and increasing the feelings of pleasure and satisfaction from food. Below are sample daily menu options that will help you feel satisfied so that you can effortlessly lose weight. They are basically variations of the following:

BREAKFAST
Before breakfast, take 2.5 to 5 g PGX granules in a glass of water. For breakfast, have one of the recommended juice recipes for weight

pgx—a critical tool for weight loss

This book is about the health benefits of juicing, but I would be remiss if I did not stress the importance of using a new super fiber matrix known as PolyGlycopleX (PGX) for weight loss. In fact, I think PGX is the "Holy Grail" in helping people achieve and maintain their ideal body weight. It is by far the most important aid that I know of in helping people address the underlying issues that lead to insulin resistance, loss of appetite control, obesity, and type 2 diabetes.

The discovery of PGX began when Dr. Michael Lyon and I were working on the book *How to Prevent and Treat Diabetes with Natural Medicine*. We began testing different fiber complexes in helping people control their blood sugar levels. We conducted two years of exhaustive research to create the processes whereby three natural fibers (glucomannan, xanthum gum, and alginate) are used to create PGX.[1] Detailed scientific investigations have proven the novel and unique composition of PGX—it is an entirely new fiber molecule—that has been tested for safety and efficacy. PGX is a safe, all-natural product that improves appetite control by promoting the feeling of satiety. It has no dangerous stimulant activity like many other appetite suppressors.

When we first started using PGX at the Canadian Center for Functional Medicine, not only did we see dramatic improvements in blood sugar control, but many patients started reporting near effortless weight loss. They lost weight because they felt full and consumed fewer calories throughout the day. We decided to do a focused pilot trial of PGX as a weight-loss aid in 2003. Before conducting this trial, I wanted to serve as a human guinea pig to see if the program would be easy to follow and what sort of results participants might expect.

I am glad that I did, because it was a life-changing experience. For nearly 20 years my body weight fluctuated from between 200 and 208 pounds—I am 6 feet 1 inch tall and fairly muscular, so I carried that weight well. On August 18, 2003, I stepped on the scale at 206 pounds with a body fat percentage of 21.3. Four weeks later, I weighed 188—my lowest weight in 15 years! Normally, I would tell people that amount of weight loss is not wise because it usually is associated with loss of muscle mass. But, because my scale also determines body fat percentage, what I observed was that my body fat decreased from 21.3 to 17.8 percent. So most of the weight loss was actually fat loss. As incredible as it was to lose so much weight so rapidly (even though I had only planned on getting down to 195), what was really amazing to me was that the whole process was effortless. What made it so easy was that I felt satisfied all the time. In the 10 years since going on the program, my weight has stabilized between 188 and 190 pounds and amazingly my body fat percentage now fluctuates between 11 and 14 percent. To put this into perspective, I have lost over 28 pounds of fat while actually adding over 10 pounds of muscle. To achieve this sort of effect in someone in his 50s is revolutionary.

I know firsthand that following the program given in this chapter not only helps people lose the weight, but continuing to follow the principles allows them to keep it off and even continue to burn more fat and build lean muscle mass—a key goal for long-term health and vitality.

There are now over 20 published studies on PGX. Human clinical research in has shown PGX to exert the following benefits:

- Reduces appetite and promotes effective weight loss[2]
- Increases insulin sensitivity[3]
- Reduces the GI of food or meals[4]
- Lowers blood cholesterol and triglycerides

In published clinical trials, when participants consumed 5 PGX two to three times per day before meals for 14 weeks they lost between 4.93 and 20.55 pounds with an average of 12.74 pounds. The weight loss consistently experienced on PGX translates into a healthful weight loss of ½ pound to 2 pounds per week over 12 to 14 weeks.

Groundbreaking research by Dr. Lyon has shown that people who are overweight spend much of their day on a virtual "blood sugar roller coaster." Specifically, by using new techniques in 24-hour blood sugar monitoring, it has been shown that excessive appetite and food cravings in overweight subjects are directly correlated with rapid fluctuations in blood glucose throughout the day and night. Furthermore, by utilizing PGX these same subjects can dramatically restore their body's ability to tightly control blood sugar levels, and this accomplishment is powerfully linked to remarkable improvements in insulin sensitivity and reductions in calories consumed.

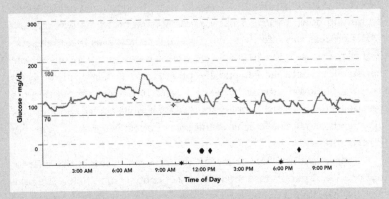

Figure 1. Continuous glucose graph over 24 hours in typical overweight, nondiabetic patient before using PGX. Patient has elevated glycemic volatility (she is on the blood sugar roller coaster). Monitoring for several days showed that this was her consistent pattern even when she ate healthful food. Frequent food cravings were reported to occur at times when blood sugar rapidly dropped over short periods of time. This amounted to several significant food cravings per day. Feelings of hypoglycemia also occurred when blood sugar dropped rapidly, even when blood sugar was above the normal range (i.e., between 70 and 100 mg/dl). This patient was spending most of the day outside this ideal range.

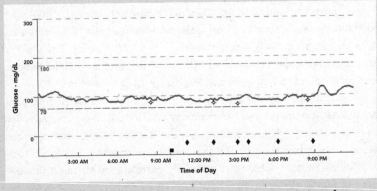

Figure 2. Continuous glucose graph over 24 hours in same patient after 4 weeks of using PGX. Patient now has eliminated glycemic volatility. Appetite and food cravings were dramatically diminished. Hypoglycemic

symptoms no longer occur at all. As well, patient has more energy and mental clarity. Weight loss is progressing on target and with no discomfort. This type of change is very typical when using PGX and it clearly illustrates the remarkable changes that can occur.

To reap the weight-loss benefits of PGX, it is important to ingest 2.5 to 5 g of PGX at major meals and perhaps another dosage about an hour after dinner for those with an evening appetite more difficult to tame. PGX is available in a variety of different forms: soft gelatin capsules, a zero-calorie drink mix, granules to be added into food and beverages, and in a meal replacement drink mix. The key to effective use of PGX is to take it before every meal with a glass of water or juice. Detailed studies in both humans and animals have shown that PGX is very safe and well tolerated. There are no specific drug interactions, but it is advised that it is best to take any medication either an hour before or after taking PGX. PGX products can be found in health food stores throughout North America or via a number of e-tailers on the Internet. To find a store near you, go to PGX.com.

Here is the key point that I make when using PGX along with juicing for weight loss. The PGX granules do not have any taste, so they can always be added to fresh juice if desired. Take 2.5 to 5 g of PGX granules in a glass of water before meals.

what if I don't want to use pgx?

PGX is a tool that can help make weight loss easier, but it is certainly not an absolute necessity to achieve your weight loss goal. My recommending it here in a book on juicing is based on its ability to help people who have struggled with weight loss finally achieve long-term success. If you prefer not to use PGX, simply follow the program below minus the recommendation for PGX.

loss. Alternatively, a weight-loss shake made from the SlimStyles Weight Loss Drink Mix, a meal replacement formula that contains PGX, can be used instead and you can take advantage of fresh juices for the midmorning or midafternoon snack/juice break.

MIDMORNING SNACK OR JUICE BREAK
Snacking is a good habit as long as you keep the portion size small and calorie count low. You are allowed up to two snacks per day to be eaten between breakfast and lunch, and lunch and dinner. Snacks are a good way to keep your metabolism running throughout the day; however, unhealthful snacks or high fat or sugar snack choices lead to weight gain.

Option 1. A 50- to 100-calorie snack focusing on low-GL, high-volumetric foods such as raw, low-calorie vegetables or fruit.

Option 2. An 8-ounce glass of one of recommended juice recipes for weight loss.

LUNCH
Before lunch, take 2.5 to 5 g PGX granules in a glass of water. Lunch is a perfect time to take advantage of high-volume, low-calorie soups and salads. Or you can simply have another glass of juice from the recommended recipes.

SNACK
Option 1. A 50- to 100-calorie snack focusing on low-GL, high-volumetric foods such as raw, low calorie vegetables or fruit.

Option 2. An 8-ounce glass of one of recommended juice recipes for weight loss.

DINNER
Before dinner, take 2.5 to 5 g PGX granules in a glass of water. Dinner should consist of a low-GL, high-volumetric meal. For instance:

One serving (50 to 100 g) of baked chicken breast, salmon, lean meat, or tofu; a medium-size salad with olive oil and natural herbs and spices; one serving (1 to 2 cups) of a cooked nonstarchy vegetable; and 1/2 cup berries for dessert. **NOTE:** As an alternative for dessert, make up 1/2 serving of SlimStyles Weight Loss Drink Mix before dinner and place in fridge. In 40 to 60 minutes, it turns into a delicious and appetite-suppressing pudding!

EVENING PGX AND TEA

If hungry, take 2.5 to 5 g PGX granules in a glass of water. Regardless, enjoy 1 or 2 cups of herbal tea. Most of the major brands of herbal tea (e.g., Celestial Seasons, Bigelow, Republic of Tea, Traditional Medicinals, etc.) provide a sampler pack to help you identify teas that appeal to you. In general, avoid black teas. Try to choose decaffeinated varieties, especially with your nighttime cup of tea. If you feel you need a little caffeine in the morning, go with a cup of regular green tea.

4-day sample menu

To help you get started in planning your daily menus, I am providing you a 4-day program, complete with menus and recipes, that also focuses on taking advantage of the health benefits of fresh juice. I have chosen recipes for lunch and dinner that can be prepared and

recommended juice recipes for weight loss

Juice recipes recommended for weight loss are noted in chapter 7 with a symbol (**WL**). Those recipes without a symbol can still be used, but cut the recipe in half to reduce the calorie count. If you want something a little more filling, cut the recipe in half and dilute it with pure water.

cooked within 30 minutes or less with a short list of ingredients or readily available ingredients and no difficult steps to follow. The recipes provided also allow for substitutions and modifications based on your own tastes. Just try to not alter the caloric content too much in doing so. For example, if a recipe contains a vegetable that you do not like, substitute with one that you do like. The juice recipes are single serving, but the lunch and dinner recipes are based on providing two servings; you can adjust the number of servings up or down as needed (e.g., for four servings simply double the recipe).

I really believe that the secret to long-term success with weight loss is achieving a high degree of satiety—the feeling of satisfaction or feeling full from eating. So you will notice that I am in favor of eating a lot of low-calorie, high-water-content food to fill you up. And I recommend eating smaller quantities throughout the day rather than three large meals. I also think there are benefits from eating a variety of foods and spicing things up a bit with liberal use of ginger, radish, mint, and other pungent agents to help rev up the metabolism.

day 1

breakfast

Before breakfast, take 2.5 to 5 g PGX granules in a glass of water.

1 weight-loss juice recipe, such as Color Me Red (page 195)

midmorning snack or juice break

1 orange

or

1 weight-loss juice recipe, such as Diuretic Formula Plus (page 197)

lunch

Before lunch, take 2.5 to 5 g PGX granules in a glass of water.

field greens salad with healthy oil dressing

4 cups mixed field greens	2 tablespoons Olive/Flaxseed Oil Salad Dressing (recipe follows)

Most supermarkets and grocery stores now have mixed field greens in the produce section or in prepackaged plastic bags. This convenience makes a simple mixed field green salad a perfect quick salad. Your serving size should be 2 cups along with 1 tablespoon olive or flaxseed oil salad dressing. Here is a salad dressing recipe so that you can make your own:

olive/flaxseed oil salad dressing

4 ounces olive or macadamia nut oil	2 garlic cloves, finely minced
4 ounces organic flaxseed oil	1 tablespoon dried Italian herbs
2 tablespoons fresh lemon juice	1 teaspoon NoSalt, Nu-Salt, or AlsoSalt
2 tablespoons balsamic vinegar	1 teaspoon black pepper

Place all ingredients into a blender and blend for 2 to 3 minutes. Store in your refrigerator for up to 1 month. Use no more than 2 tablespoons daily.

midafternoon snack

1 cup celery sticks

or

1 weight-loss juice recipe, such as Cucumber-Celery Mojito Cooler (page 196)

dinner

Before dinner, take 2.5 to 5 g PGX granules in a glass of water.

field greens salad with bell peppers, carrots, and radishes

4 cups mixed field greens	½ cup chopped radishes
1 green bell pepper, chopped	1 tablespoon Olive/Flaxseed Oil
½ cup chopped carrots	Salad Dressing (page 263)

Toss all ingredients in a large bowl with:

minted carrots with pumpkin seeds

3 medium carrots, peeled and cut into round slices	1 tablespoon fresh lemon juice
1 tablespoon fresh chopped parsley	1 tablespoon olive oil
1 tablespoon fresh chopped mint	NoSalt, Nu-Salt, or AlsoSalt and black pepper, to taste
2 tablespoons coarsely chopped pumpkin seeds	

Steam the carrots until still slightly crunchy. Toss the parsley, mint, and pumpkin seeds with the carrots. In a small bowl, whisk the lemon juice and oil, season with NoSalt and pepper, and gently mix with carrots.

steamed broccoli

½ head of broccoli

Slice the broccoli lengthwise or separate out the florets of the head to allow for easy steaming. Steam the broccoli until still slightly crunchy.

asian salmon

2 teaspoons low-sodium soy sauce

1 tablespoon Dijon mustard

1 salmon fillet (8 ounces), cut into 2 pieces

½ cup sliced onion

1 garlic clove, chopped

½ tablespoon minced fresh ginger or ¼ teaspoon dried

2 cups sliced fresh shiitake mushrooms

Preheat the oven to 375 degrees F. Mix the soy sauce into the mustard and coat the salmon with it. Sauté the onion, garlic, ginger, and mushrooms in a medium sauté pan sprayed with olive oil or other vegetable oil for about 5 minutes. Place the salmon in a baking dish and bake for about 7 minutes for each inch of thickness. When cooked, place on bed of mushroom mixture.

fresh raspberries

1 cup fresh raspberries

Vanilla soy milk or nonfat yogurt (optional)

Soak the berries in a little vanilla soy milk or nonfat yogurt, if desired. Serve chilled.

day 2

breakfast

Before breakfast, take 2.5 to 5 g PGX granules in a glass of water.
Feel free to substitute:

1 weight-loss juice recipe, such as Fennel Citrus Mix (page 200)

or

SlimStyles Weight Loss Drink Mix

midmorning snack .

2 tablespoons almonds and 1/2 cup blueberries

or

1 weight-loss juice recipe, such as Tummy Tonic (page 209)

lunch

Before lunch, take 2.5 to 5 g PGX granules in a glass of water.

tuna salad wrap

1 (12-ounce) can or foil pouch of low-sodium, chunk white tuna, in spring water	1 tablespoon chopped fresh parsley
1/4 cup minced onion	1/4 cup Dijon mustard
1 celery rib, chopped	1/2 teaspoon NoSalt, Nu-Salt, or AlsoSalt
1 teaspoon fresh lemon juice	1/2 teaspoon black pepper
1 tablespoon olive oil	2 (6-inch) whole-wheat tortillas

Mix all the ingredients (except the tortillas) in a bowl and spoon
onto the tortilla and wrap. Whole-grain bread may be substituted
for the tortilla to make a sandwich.

midafternoon snack

2 medium plums

or

1 weight-loss juice recipe, such as Tomato Zest (page 209)

dinner

Before dinner, take 2.5 to 5 g PGX granules in a glass of water.

jicama salad

1 cup julienne-cut peeled jicama

1 orange, peeled, sectioned, and cut into chunks

1 cucumber, seeded and thinly sliced

¼ cup chopped green onion

¼ cup chopped fresh cilantro

1 tablespoon chopped fresh mint

¼ cup fresh orange juice

¼ cup fresh lemon or lime juice

¼ teaspoon chili powder

¼ teaspoon NoSalt, Nu-Salt, or AlsoSalt

¼ teaspoon black pepper

Combine the jicama, orange, cucumber, onion, cilantro, and mint in a large bowl. In a small bowl, mix the orange juice, lemon juice, chili powder, salt, and pepper. Pour the juice mixture over the jicama mixture and toss gently. Cover and chill for at least 20 minutes before serving.

black bean chili

1 tablespoon olive oil

½ medium onion, chopped

2 garlic cloves, chopped

1 green bell pepper, diced

1 cup chicken or light vegetable broth

1 (15-ounce) can black beans, drained

1 cup corn kernels, fresh or frozen

1 (4-ounce) can low-sodium tomato sauce

2 tablespoons cumin

2 tablespoons chili powder

2 tablespoons dried Italian herbs

½ teaspoon NoSalt, Nu-Salt, or AlsoSalt

½ teaspoon black pepper

¼ cup chopped fresh cilantro, for garnish

Warm the oil in a medium soup pot over medium-low heat and add the onion, garlic, and bell pepper. Stir frequently for about

5 minutes, or until the onions are translucent. Add the broth, beans, corn, tomato sauce, cumin, chili powder, Italian herbs, No-Salt, and black pepper. Simmer for 15 minutes. Ladle into bowls and garnish with the cilantro. Serve with warmed whole-wheat tortillas.

sliced pineapple

Peel 1 whole pineapple and cut into bite-size pieces. Serve half of the sliced pineapple as a dessert, and reserve the rest in the refrigerator for breakfast the next morning.

day 3

breakfast

Before breakfast, take 2.5 to 5 grams of PGX granules in a glass of water.

Pineapple juice (using the pineapple from Day 2)

or

Mike's Favorite (page 206)

midmorning snack or juice break

1/2 cup blueberries and 2 tablespoons almonds

or

Pineapple juice or Mike's Favorite (page 206)

lunch

Before lunch, take 2.5 to 5 g PGX granules in a glass of water.

italian white bean soup

1 tablespoon olive oil

1/2 onion cut in half and thinly sliced

4 garlic cloves, sliced

2 cups chicken or light vegetable broth

2 cups finely chopped destemmed collard greens or kale

1 (7.5-ounce) can diced tomatoes

2 teaspoons dried Italian herbs

1 (15-ounce) can navy beans, drained

NoSalt, Nu-Salt, or AlsoSalt and black pepper, to taste

Warm the oil in a medium soup pot over medium-low heat and add the onion. Sauté the onion, stirring frequently, for about 5 minutes, or until the onions are translucent. Add the garlic and continue to sauté for another minute. Add the broth, collard greens, tomatoes, and herbs. Simmer for 15 minutes over medium heat. Add the beans, NoSalt, and pepper. Cook for another 5 minutes, until the beans are warmed through.

midafternoon snack or juice break

1 medium red pear

or

1 weight-loss juice recipe, such as Some Like It Hot (page 208)

dinner

Before dinner, take 2.5 to 5 g PGX granules in a glass of water.

orange and fennel salad

1 orange

1 small fennel

1 head of romaine lettuce, cut up

¼ cup chopped fresh parsley

1 tablespoon Olive/Flaxseed Oil Salad Dressing (page 263)

Slice the oranges and fennel and toss them with the lettuce and parsley in a large bowl. Add dressing and toss again to combine.

curried chicken or tofu over brown rice

½ cup uncooked quick brown rice

1 tablespoon olive oil

½ cup chopped onion

1 garlic clove, minced

½ inch fresh ginger, minced

2 teaspoons curry powder

1 cup vegetable or chicken broth

7.5 ounces of firm tofu cut into small cubes or 1 boneless, skinless chicken breast cut into bite-size pieces

1 medium red bell pepper, chopped

½ head of broccoli florets

½ cup coconut milk, well shaken

NoSalt, Nu-Salt, or AlsoSalt and black pepper, to taste

Prepare the rice according to the instructions on the package.
While the rice is cooking, warm the oil in a medium sauté pan
over medium-low heat and add the onion. Sauté the onion, stirring
frequently, for about 5 minutes, or until the onions are translucent.
Add the garlic and ginger and continue to sauté for another minute. Remove the pan from heat and add the curry powder. Mix well.
Return the pan to medium-low heat and add the broth, tofu, bell
pepper, broccoli, and coconut milk. Simmer until the tofu is done,
about 10 minutes. Season with NoSalt and black pepper.

Divide the rice on the plates and top with the curry mixture.

blueberries

1 cup fresh blueberries

Vanilla soy milk or nonfat yogurt (optional)

Soak the berries in a little vanilla soy milk or nonfat yogurt, if desired. Serve chilled.

day 4

breakfast

Before breakfast, take 2.5 to 5 g PGX granules in a glass of water.
SlimStyles Weight Loss Drink Mix

or

Juice of 1/2 large cantaloupe

midmorning snack or juice break

1 medium red apple

or

Juice of 1/2 large cantaloupe

lunch

Before lunch, take 2.5 to 5 g PGX granules in a glass of water.

red bean and tomato soup

1 tablespoon olive oil

1/2 cup chopped onion

1 garlic clove, chopped

1 celery rib, chopped in small chunks

1 (8-ounce) can red kidney beans, drained and rinsed

1 (11-ounce) can low-sodium tomato soup

2 tablespoons dried Italian herbs

NoSalt, Nu-Salt, or AlsoSalt and black pepper, to taste

Warm the oil in a medium soup pot over medium-low heat and add
the onion, garlic, and celery. Sauté, stirring frequently, for about
5 minutes, or until onions are translucent.

In a blender, puree the kidney beans, tomato soup, and Italian
herbs for 2 to 3 minutes and then add to the soup pot. Simmer for

15 minutes, stirring if necessary. Season with NoSalt and pepper and serve hot.

midafternoon snack or juice break

1 cup carrot or celery sticks

dinner

Before dinner, take 2.5 to 5 g PGX granules in a glass of water.

mediterranean salad

1 cup chopped fresh tomato, excess flesh cut out if pulpy

1 cup chopped cucumber

½ cup finely minced green onion

1 garlic clove, finely minced

1 (8-ounce) can garbanzo beans, drained and rinsed

1 tablespoon fresh parsley

1 teaspoon dried Italian herbs

1 tablespoon fresh lemon juice

1 tablespoon olive oil

NoSalt, Nu-Salt, or AlsoSalt and black pepper to taste

In a large bowl, combine the tomato, cucumber, onion, garlic, garbanzo beans, parsley, and Italian herbs. In a small bowl, whisk together the lemon juice, oil, NoSalt, and pepper. Add to the salad and toss to combine. Chill for 15 minutes before serving.

quick acorn squash

1 acorn squash, cut in half with seeds removed

1 tablespoon honey

Dash of cinnamon

Place the squash in a microwave-safe dish, cut side up. Cover and cook in the microwave for 10 to 13 minutes on high, or until fork-tender. Top with the honey and cinnamon.

polenta puttanesca with tofu

1 tablespoon olive oil

1 onion, diced

1 garlic clove, crushed or minced

1 green bell pepper, diced

Bay leaf

1 (12-ounce) can tomato sauce

7.5 ounces firm tofu, cut into small cubes

1 tablespoon dried Italian herbs

1 tablespoon crushed red pepper flakes

2 tablespoons capers, rinsed and drained

4 to 6 pitted Kalamata olives

1 tablespoon finely chopped fresh parsley

¼ teaspoon NoSalt, Nu-Salt, or AlsoSalt

½ teaspoon black pepper

1 cup instant polenta

Warm the oil in a large saucepan over medium heat. Add the onion and garlic and sauté for 3 minutes, or until onions are translucent. Add the bell pepper and sauté for another 3 minutes. Add 1 cup water and the bay leaf and bring to a boil. Cover the pot, reduce heat to medium-low, and simmer for 15 minutes. Add the tomato sauce, tofu, Italian herbs, pepper flakes, capers, olives, parsley, NoSalt, and black pepper. Simmer for 1 hour, stirring occasionally.

While the sauce is simmering, make the polenta according to the package instructions. Divide the polenta between two large bowls or plates. Let it cool about 10 minutes, or until firm. Ladle the sauce on top.

fresh mango slices

Slice up 1 fresh mango for a refreshing dessert.

summary

Permanent weight loss is possible, but it requires a comprehensive system that addresses the underlying factors contributing to weight gain and obesity. The plan described in this chapter focuses on giving the body the quality of nutrition it requires during the weight-loss process. Consuming fresh fruit and vegetable juice and a highly nutritious high-fiber diet is an ideal weight-loss plan that is made even more effective when supplemented with PGX. When you arm your body with improved quality of nutrition, the quantities of calories you consume will be reduced, energy levels will skyrocket, and you will be more prone to exercise. Improved quality of nutrition is an important step to improved quality of life.

11

juicing, immune function, and the cancer patient

One of the most predominant uses of drinking fresh juice is to support the cancer patient, including those undergoing chemotherapy or radiation therapy. Cancer patients are often subjected to a tremendous increase in their free-radical load as a side effect of their medical treatment, and they require the nutritional support and protection that fresh fruit and vegetable juices offer their immune systems.

the immune system: a quick overview

The immune system is composed of the lymphatic vessels and organs (thymus, spleen, tonsils, and lymph nodes), white blood cells (lymphocytes, neutrophils, basophils, eosinophils, monocytes), specialized cells residing in various tissue (macrophages, mast cells), and specialized serum factors. The immune system's prime function is protecting the body against infection and cancer.

the thymus gland: the master gland of the immune system

The thymus is composed of two soft pinkish gray lobes lying in a biblike fashion just below the thyroid gland and above the heart. The thymus gland shows maximum development immediately after birth and undergoes shrinkage, or involution, throughout the aging process. The reason for this involution is that the thymus gland is extremely susceptible to free-radical and oxidative damage caused by stress, drugs, radiation, infection, and chronic illness; when the thymus gland becomes damaged, its ability to function is severely compromised.

The thymus controls many immune system functions, including the production of T lymphocytes, a type of white blood cell responsible for cell-mediated immunity, or immune mechanisms not controlled or mediated by antibodies. Cell-mediated immunity is extremely important in the resistance to infection by mold-like bacteria, yeast (including *Candida albicans*), fungi, parasites, and viruses (including herpes simplex and Epstein-Barr) and is also critical in protecting against the development of cancer and allergies.

In addition to immuno-function, the thymus gland releases several hormones—such as thymosin, thymopoeitin, and serum thymic factor—which regulate many immune functions. Low levels of these hormones in the blood are associated with depressed immunity and an increased susceptibility to infection. Typically, thymic hormone levels are very low in the elderly, those prone to infection, cancer patients, and individuals exposed to undue stress.

Ensuring optimal thymus gland activity, thymic hormone levels, and cell-mediated immunity depends on prevention of thymic shrinkage, use of nutrients that act as cofactors for the thymic hormones, and stimulation of thymus gland activity. Fresh juices can be helpful in achieving all three of these goals, although a comprehensive approach involving herbs, nutritional supplements, special nutritional factors, and other supportive therapies is recommended in more severe cases. For more information, consult *The Encyclopedia of Natural Medicine*.

factors that impair the immune system

The immune system can be adversely affected by a number of factors, including stress, nutritional deficiencies, sugar, obesity, fats in the blood, and alcohol. Each of these is discussed in turn.

stress

Stress causes increases in adrenal gland hormones such as adrenaline and cortisol, which inhibit white blood cells and cause the thymus gland to shrink, leading to a significant suppression of immune function. The level of immune suppression is usually proportional to the level of stress.

Stress results in stimulation of the sympathetic nervous system, which is responsible for the fight-or-flight response. The immune system functions better under parasympathetic nervous system tone—the portion of our autonomic nervous system that assumes control over bodily functions during periods of rest, relaxation, visualization, meditation, and sleep. During the deepest levels of sleep, potent immune-enhancing compounds are released and many immune functions are greatly increased. The value of good-quality sleep, exercise, and relaxation techniques for counteracting the effects of stress and enhancing the immune system cannot be overemphasized.

Stress, personality, attitude, and emotion are causative factors in many diseases and vary among individuals; the variations in response to stress help account for the wide range in severity of stress-induced illnesses.

Perhaps the most important factor in maintaining or attaining a healthy immune system is a consistent positive mental attitude, which usually happens by degrees, subtle changes accumulating one by one. The first step is to take personal responsibility for your own mental state, your life, your current situation, your immune system, and your health. The next step is to take action to make the changes you desire in your life. Last, you need to condition your attitude to be optimistic, positive, and adaptable. Pay attention to your self-talk, the constant internal dialogue that we all have.

nutritional deficiencies

Although historically research relating nutritional status to immune function has concerned itself with severe malnutrition states, attention is now shifting toward marginal deficiencies of single or multiple nutrients and the effects of nutrition excess (e.g., being overweight or obese). There is ample evidence to support the conclusion that any single nutrient deficiency can profoundly impair the immune system.

Nutrient deficiency is not limited to third-world countries. Comprehensive studies sponsored by the U.S. government have revealed that marginal nutrient deficiencies exist in a substantial portion of the American population (approximately 50 percent) and that for some selected nutrients in certain age groups more than 80 percent of the group consumed less than the recommended dietary intake level. While it is theoretically possible that healthy individuals can get all the nutrition they need from foods, the fact is that most do not even come close to meeting all their nutritional needs through diet alone.[1] The significance of these findings to the immune system is substantial, as virtually any nutrient deficiency will result in an impaired immune system, putting an individual at risk for cancer and infections.

sugar

One study showed that the ingestion of 100 g (roughly 3 1/2 ounces) portions of carbohydrate as glucose, fructose, sucrose, honey, and pasteurized orange juice all significantly reduced the ability of a type of white blood cells (neutrophils) to engulf and destroy bacteria.[2] In contrast, the ingestion of 100 g starch had no effect. These effects started in less than 30 minutes after ingestion and lasted for over 5 hours. Typically there was at least a 50 percent reduction in neutrophil activity 2 hours after ingestion. Since neutrophils constitute

60 to 70 percent of the total circulating white blood cells, impairment of their activity leads to depressed immunity.

In addition, ingestion of 75 g glucose has also been shown to depress lymphocyte activity.[3] Other aspects of immune function are also undoubtedly affected by sugar consumption. It has been suggested that the ill effects of high glucose levels are a result of competition between blood glucose and vitamin C for membrane transport sites into the white blood cells.[4] This is based on evidence that vitamin C and glucose appear to have opposite effects on immune function and the fact that both require insulin for membrane transport into many tissues.

Considering that the average American consumes 150 g sucrose and other refined simple sugars each day, the inescapable conclusion is that most Americans likely possess chronically depressed immune systems. It is clear, particularly during an infection or chronic illness like cancer or AIDS, that the consumption of refined sugars is deleterious to immune status.

obesity

Obesity is associated with such conditions as atherosclerosis, hypertension, diabetes mellitus, and joint disorders. It is also associated with compromised immune status, as evidenced by the decreased bacteria-killing activity of neutrophils and increased morbidity and mortality from infections.[5] Cholesterol and lipid levels are usually elevated in obese individuals, which may explain their impaired immune function (see below).

fats in the blood

Increased blood levels of cholesterol, free fatty acids, triglycerides, and bile acids inhibit various immune functions, including the ability of lymphocytes to proliferate and produce antibodies and the ability of neutrophils to migrate to areas of infections and engulf and destroy infectious organisms.[6] Optimal immune function therefore depends on control of these serum components.

alcohol

Alcohol increases the susceptibility to experimental infections in animals, and alcoholics are known to be more susceptible to pneumonia and other infections. Studies of white blood cells show a profound depression after alcohol ingestion. Obviously, alcohol ingestion should be eliminated entirely in the severely ill and anyone seeking a strong immune system.

building optimal immune function

Optimal immune function requires the active pursuit of good health, through a positive mental attitude, a healthful diet, and exercise. A healthful diet is one that (1) is rich in whole, natural foods, such as fruits, vegetables, grains, beans, seeds, and nuts; (2) is low in fats and refined sugars; and (3) contains adequate, but not excessive, amounts of protein. On top of this, an individual should consume 12 to 24 ounces of fresh fruit and vegetable juice a day, drink five or six 8-ounce glasses of water a day, take a good basic multivitamin-mineral supplement, engage in at least 30 minutes of aerobic exercise and 5 to 10 minutes of passive stretching daily, perform daily deep breathing and relaxation exercises (such as meditation or prayer), take time each day to play and enjoy family and friends, and still get at least 6 to 8 hours of sleep daily.

juicing and the cancer patient

There is perhaps no greater need for the benefits of fresh fruit and vegetable juice than in cancer. In many cases the body must deal not just with the stress of cancer but also with the side effects of medical treatment. Specifically, chemotherapy and radiation expose healthy cells, as well as cancer cells, to free-radical damage. The result is a great stress to antioxidant mechanisms and depletion of valuable antioxidant enzymes and nutrients. Cancer patients need higher quantities of antioxidant nutrients.

Juicing not only provides important nutrients that can protect against some of the damaging effects of chemotherapy and radiation, it provides a wide range of phytochemicals as well (see chapter 3) that may exert direct anticancer effects as well as stimulate the immune system.

Furthermore, juicing can help deal with some of the nutritional problems that develop as a result of the cancer or the chemotherapy and radiation. About two-thirds of all people with cancer develop a condition known as cachexia, which is characterized by a loss of appetite, resulting in decreased nutrient intake. This in turn leads to malnutrition, muscle wasting, and impaired immune function. This condition is quite serious, as it greatly reduces the quality of life and contributes greatly to the development of further illness or even the death of the patient. Juicing is used as part of the nutritional support program for the cancer patient at several orthodox cancer treatment centers across the country as well as being featured in many alternative cancer treatments.

specific juicing recommendations for the cancer patient

Virtually every juice recipe in chapter 7 would have some benefit for the cancer patient. But here are my words of advice: I would rather have the cancer patient enjoy the juice than power one down that is going to cause nausea or leave a bad taste in his mouth. Some of the juices are more powerful than others, and it would be counterproductive for the cancer patient to consume what his body might not tolerate.

The most popular juice prepared by cancer patients, for good reason, is carrot juice. It's a nutritional powerhouse, and its flavor/sweetness is both great on its own and blends well with other vegetables. Juicing four carrots along with one apple can mask many of the stronger vegetables, especially some of the more powerful anticancer agents like turmeric root and cabbage-family vegetables.

Another good juice base for the cancer patient is pineapple juice. Believe it or not, juicing kale, spinach, or other greens with pineapple juice is delicious. And juicing 1/4 pineapple along with 1 cup fresh blueberries, raspberries, or strawberries offers the added bonus of the anticancer flavonoids of the berries. Juicing lemons with their peels and making liberal use of cherries and volatile herbs such as fresh peppermint and basil provides powerful anticancer plant terpenes like d-limonene.

Turmeric root contains the incredible anticancer compound curcumin, and ginger is also an important juicing consideration for the cancer patient because of similar compounds. Ginger is also an extremely valuable ally in alleviating the nausea often experienced from chemotherapy and radiation, acting directly on the gastrointestinal system as well as areas in the brain that control nausea. In addition to studies in preventing motion sickness, and nausea and vomiting of pregnancy, several double-blind studies have shown that ginger reduces nausea after surgery and the nausea caused by chemotherapy.[7] The dosage used in these studies is equal to roughly 1/4-inch slice of an average-size root. A juice recipe that is quite soothing to the stomach and intestinal tract is Tummy Tonic (page 209). Homemade ginger ale can also be made with your juice extractor (page 200). Stevia can be used to sweeten if needed. Kill the Cold (page 204) can also be very soothing.

summary

The immune system is responsible for fighting off infection and cancer. The thymus gland is the major gland of the immune system, controlling many aspects of immune function. The health of the thymus gland is largely determined by the status of stress and nutrition. Antioxidant nutrients are critical in protecting the thymus gland from damage as well as enhancing its function. Alcohol, sugar, stress, and high cholesterol levels all inhibit immune function. Fresh fruit and vegetable juices offer nutritional support to the immune system, largely as a result of their high content of antioxidants such as vitamin C, carotenes, and trace minerals. Cancer patients are individuals who would truly benefit from the nutritional support offered by fresh fruit and vegetable juices.

12

answers to common questions on juicing

During the question-and-answer period following my live lectures, I am sometimes asked the same questions more than once. Sometimes we need to hear things several times or hear them in a new light before they sink in. This chapter includes some of the questions

I'm commonly asked as well as topics that were not covered in the preceding chapters.

Q. Why should I juice?

A. It was my goal in writing this book to answer this question. Let me summarize the key benefits of fresh juice:

- Improved energy
- Improved nutritional quality
- Increased intake of health-promoting phytochemicals
- It's fun and tastes great!

Q. When I juice fruits and vegetables, I throw away the fiber, but isn't the fiber an important part of my diet?

A. Definitely, yes. Fiber is an important part of your diet. Think about it: Fiber, the indigestible material found in plants, is the juice that nourishes us. Our body actually converts the food we eat into juice so that it can be absorbed. Juicing helps the body's digestive process and allows for quick absorption of high-quality nutrition. Juicing quickly provides the most easily digestible and concentrated nutritional benefits of fruits and vegetables. The result is increased energy levels.

Juicing fresh fruits and vegetables does provide some fiber, particularly the soluble fiber. It is the soluble fiber that has been shown to lower cholesterol levels and exert other beneficial effects beyond improved bowel function.

Q. Can I do anything with the pulp?

A. Yes. The pulp from many vegetable juices, such as Salad in a Glass (page 208) and Immune Power Veggie (page 203), can make a great soup stock. Carrot or apple pulp can be added to bran muffin or healthful carrot cake recipes to increase the fiber content. If you don't consume it, the pulp can be added to your compost pile and returned to the earth.

Q. What is the difference between a juicer and a blender?

A. A juicer separates the liquid from the fiber. A blender is designed to blend or liquefy food by chopping it up at high speeds. It doesn't necessarily separate the juice from the pulp, so the result is a mushy, globby mess that really doesn't taste very good in most cases.

Blenders can be quite useful in tandem with the juicer. For example, bananas contain very little juice but taste delicious in drinks. You can use a blender to mix freshly extracted juice, such as pineapple juice, along with banana or unsweetened frozen fruits to create a delicious smoothie.

Q. I have heard that you shouldn't mix fruits and vegetables. Why?

A. There is little (if any) scientific information to support this contention. Nonetheless, some people do seem to have difficulty with combined fruits and vegetables, complaining of gassy discomfort. If you are one of these people, you should avoid mixing fruits and vegetables. The exceptions to this rule appear to be carrots and apples, as these foods seem to be able to mix with either a fruit or a vegetable. My advice is to let your body and taste buds be your guide.

Q. How much juice should I drink each day?

A. I recommend up to 12 ounces of fresh fruit juice and up to 24 ounces of fresh vegetable juice a day for most people. I also recommend that people try to drink an assortment of juices. We are learning more and more that the pigments of fruits and vegetables—the carotenes, flavonoids, and chlorophyll—are responsible for many of the benefits, so I tell people to eat a rainbow assortment of fruits and vegetables. Try to consume a variety of colors in your diet.

Q. I am confused. I know that vitamin A is stored in the liver, where it can accumulate to toxic levels and disrupt normal

liver function. Vitamin A toxicity can also lead to severe head-aches, nausea and vomiting, and dry skin. Since beta-carotene is converted to vitamin A in the body, why isn't beta-carotene toxic?

A. Vitamin A is available in the diet either as preformed vitamin A, as found in dairy and other animal products, or as pro–vitamin A carotenes, as found in plant foods. Over 400 carotenes have been characterized, but only 30 to 50 have vitamin A activity. Beta-carotene has been termed the most active of the carotenes owing to its higher pro–vitamin A activity. However, other carotenes exhibit far greater antioxidant and anticancer activities.

The conversion of a pro–vitamin A carotene, like beta-carotene, to vitamin A depends on several factors: level of vitamin A in the body, protein status, thyroid hormones, zinc, and vitamin C. The conversion diminishes as carotene intake increases and when serum vitamin A levels are adequate. Simply stated, if vitamin A levels are sufficient, the beta-carotene is not converted to vitamin A. Instead, it is delivered to body tissues for storage.

Vitamin A and carotenes differ in how they are absorbed by the body and where they are stored. Specifically, vitamin A is stored pri-marily in the liver, while carotenes may be stored in fat cells, other organs (the adrenals, testes, and ovaries have the highest concen-trations), and epithelial cells. Epithelial cells are found in the skin and the linings of the internal organs, including the respiratory tract, gastrointestinal tract, and genitourinary tract.

There have not been any reports of vitamin A toxicity from the ingestion of foods rich in carotenes or supplemental beta-carotene. In addition, beta-carotene has not been shown to possess any significant toxicity despite its use in very high doses in the treatment of numerous medical conditions. Unlike vitamin A, which can cause birth defects if taken at high dosage during pregnancy, carotene is safe during preg-nancy. In fact, carotenes have been shown to prevent genetic damage.

It should be pointed out that though there have been no reports of toxicity stemming from beta-carotene, some evidence indicates that too much carrot juice over a long period of time—1 to 2 quarts of fresh carrot juice a day for several years—may cause a decrease in the number of white blood cells and cessation of menstruation. These effects may be attributable to some other factor in the diet or possibly in carrots themselves. Neither of these effects nor any others have been observed in subjects consuming very high doses of pure beta-carotene—for example, 300,000 to 600,000 IU per day (which is equivalent to 4 to 8 pounds of raw carrots) over long periods of time.

This possible effect of daily consumption of more than a quart of carrot juice over several years can be avoided by utilizing other juices in addition to carrot juice on a regular basis. A wide range of carotene-rich foods should be consumed in the diet. This will provide the greatest benefit.

Q. Why does my skin turn orange when I drink a lot of carrot juice? Is this a sign of toxicity?

A. The storage of carotenes in the skin results in carotenodermia, or the appearance of yellow-orange skin. This is nothing to be alarmed about; it is not associated with any toxicity. In fact, it is probably a very beneficial sign. It simply indicates that the body has a good supply of carotenes. Carotenodermia that is not directly due to dietary intake or supplementation of carotenes, however, may be a sign of a deficiency in a necessary conversion factor, such as zinc, thyroid hormone, vitamin C, or protein.

Q. Does juicing provide greater benefit than beta-carotene supplements or intact carotene-rich foods?

A. Definitely. Juicing ruptures cell membranes, thereby liberating important nutritional compounds like carotenes for easier absorption.

Beta-carotene supplementation, while beneficial, only provides one particular type of carotene, whereas juicing a wide variety of carotene-rich foods will provide a broad range of carotenes, many of which have properties more advantageous than beta-carotene.

Q. If I juice, do I need to take vitamin or mineral pills?

A. The question whether Americans need to supplement their diet with vitamins and minerals is hotly debated. Many experts say supplementation is necessary; others say diet alone can provide all the essential nutrition. Which side is right? They both are right to an extent. It all boils down to what their view of optimum nutrition is.

An expert who believes optimum nutrition simply means no obvious signs of nutrient deficiency or impaired health will answer differently from an expert who thinks of optimum nutrition as the degree of nutrition that will allow an individual to function at the highest level possible with vitality, energy, and enthusiasm for living.

Can an individual get all the nutrition he or she needs from diet alone? Possibly, but it is highly unlikely. During recent years, the U.S. government has sponsored a number of comprehensive studies to determine the nutritional status of the population.[1] These studies indicate the chances of consuming a diet that meets the RDA for all nutrients are extremely remote for most Americans, especially children and the elderly, suggesting dietary supplementation may be extremely beneficial. I am a firm believer in the need for vitamin and mineral supplementation for most people. Even the most dedicated health advocate like myself cannot possibly meet the tremendous nutritional requirements for optimum health through diet alone. In my view, supplementation is essential.

There is a large body of information to support my view. Studies have shown that a multiple vitamin-mineral supplement can improve mental function in children and exert beneficial effects on the immune system in elderly subjects.

With the information available at this time, many experts feel that dietary supplements may be of great benefit to a large number of individuals, especially when combined with a healthful diet and lifestyle. I am in agreement with this position.

Q. When can a baby start drinking juice?

A. My recommendation of no juice until at least 6 months of age is shared by many experts. The digestive tract is just not ready for it, and drinking juice from a bottle is definitely not good for tooth development—it's too high in natural sugars that can literally rot their teeth. After 6 months of age, fresh juices can be introduced slowly. Pay attention for any possible signs of intolerance, like diarrhea or gas. It is recommended that the juices be diluted with an equal amount of water. Good juices for children are the sweeter ones, such as carrot, apple, cantaloupe, and orange. Never let the baby go to sleep with a bottle of juice in his or her mouth or suck on a bottle for prolonged periods of time.

Q. Can I freeze the juices?

A. Yes. You will lose some of the nutritional benefits and enzymes, but it is better than letting the juice go to waste. Also, you can make delicious homemade popsicles. Try freezing the Kids' Favorite (page 204) in an ice tray with some toothpicks.

Q. Do I have to follow the juice recipes exactly?

A. Absolutely not. Juicing is meant to be fun. Recipes are only designed to point you in the right direction. Have fun. Create your own favorites.

Q. Should I juice if I am hypoglycemic?

A. Too much of any simple sugar, including the sugars found in fruit and vegetable juices, can lead to stress of blood sugar control mechanisms, especially if you are hypoglycemic or diabetic. The advantage of the assortment of natural simple sugars in fruits and vegetables over sucrose (white sugar) and other refined sugars is that they are balanced by a wide range of nutrients that aid in the utilization of the sugars. The real problems with carbohydrates begin when they are refined and stripped of these nutrients. Virtually all the vitamin content has been removed from white sugar, white breads and pastries, and many breakfast cereals. Nonetheless, it is often recommended that individuals with faulty blood sugar control consume no more than 8 ounces of juice at any one time. It is also a good idea to focus on vegetable juices and drink the juice with a meal to delay the absorption of the sugars.

Q. I suffer from recurrent kidney stones. Should I avoid juices because many are high in calcium?

A. It is often recommended to people with recurrent calcium oxalate kidney stones that they avoid juices containing spinach, because spinach is rich in both calcium and oxalate. It is probably not a big sacrifice even though it may not be that important in preventing stone formation. Your diet should definitely include other fresh juices. In fact, there are several juices that you should be consuming on a regular basis.

The high rate of kidney stones in the United States has been directly linked to the following dietary factors: low fiber, refined sugar, alcohol, large amounts of animal protein, high fat, high calcium, salt, and vitamin D–enriched foods like milk. The best dietary advice for individuals prone to recurrent kidney stones is to adopt a vegetarian diet. As a group, vegetarians have shown a decreased risk of developing kidney stones. However, studies have demonstrated that even among meat eaters, those who ate higher amounts of fresh fruits and vegetables had a lower incidence of stones. Fiber supplementation, as well as the simple change from white to whole wheat bread, has resulted in lowering urinary calcium excretion.

A beneficial juice for individuals prone to recurrent kidney stones is cranberry juice, which has been shown to reduce the amount of ionized calcium in urine by over 50 percent in patients with kidney stones (high urinary calcium levels greatly increase the risk of developing a kidney stone).

Q. I am concerned about osteoporosis. Can I get the calcium my bones require without drinking milk?

A. Osteoporosis literally means porous bone. It affects more than 20 million people in the United States; 80 percent of them are women. Many factors can result in excessive bone loss, and different variants of osteoporosis exist. Postmenopausal osteoporosis is the most common form and is responsible for nearly 1.5 million fractures each year.

Osteoporosis involves both the mineral (inorganic) and the nonmineral (organic matrix composed primarily of protein) components of bone. This is the first clue that there is more to osteoporosis than a lack of dietary calcium. Recently there has been an incredible push for increasing dietary calcium to prevent osteoporosis. While this appears to be sound medical advice for many, osteoporosis is much more than a lack of dietary calcium. It is a complex condition involving hormonal, lifestyle, nutritional, and environmental factors.

Rather than being fixated on calcium, it would be more beneficial to focus on other lifestyle and dietary factors, such as exercise, sugar, protein, and fresh fruit and vegetable juices.

In fact, physical fitness, not calcium intake, is the major determinant of bone density.[2] One hour of moderate activity three times a week has been shown to prevent bone loss. In fact, this type of exercise has actually been shown to increase the bone mass in postmenopausal women. Walking is probably the best exercise to start with. In contrast to exercise, immobility doubles the rate of calcium excretion, resulting in an increased likelihood of developing osteoporosis.

Coffee, alcohol, and smoking induce a negative calcium balance (more calcium is lost than absorbed) and are associated with an increased risk of osteoporosis. Obviously, these lifestyle factors must be eliminated.

Many general dietary factors have been suggested as a cause of osteoporosis: low calcium–high phosphorus intake, high-protein diet, high-phosphate diet, and trace mineral deficiencies, to name a few. To help slow down bone loss, foods high in calcium are often recommended. You do not need dairy products to meet your body's calcium requirement. Calcium is found in high amounts in many green leafy vegetables and other plant foods. Table 12.1 provides a comparison of calcium content in a variety of foods.

A vegetarian diet, both lacto-ovo and vegan, is associated with a lower risk of osteoporosis. Vegans do not consume dairy products, yet they have a lowered risk for osteoporosis. How can this be? Several factors are probably responsible for this decrease in bone loss observed in vegetarians. Perhaps most important is a reduced intake of protein. A high-protein diet and a diet high in phosphates are associated with increasing the excretion of calcium in the urine. Raising daily protein from 47 to 142 g doubles the excretion of calcium in the urine. A diet this high in protein is common in the United States and may be a significant factor in the growing number of people suffering from osteoporosis in this country.

Another culprit in inducing bone loss is refined sugar. Following sugar intake, there is an increase in the urinary excretion of calcium.

Considering that the average American consumes in one day 150 g sucrose, plus other refined simple sugars, a glass of a carbonated beverage loaded with phosphates, and an elevated amount of protein, it is little wonder that there are so many suffering from osteoporosis in this country. When lifestyle factors are also taken into consideration, it is very apparent why osteoporosis has become a major medical problem.

Juicing offers significant benefit in an osteoporosis-prevention plan. Fresh fruit and vegetable juices provide a rich source of a broad range of vitamins and minerals, such as calcium, vitamin K_I, and boron, which are being shown to be equally important as calcium in bone health. Higher fruit and vegetable intake is associated with better bone quality and reduced fracture rates.[3]

soft drinks and bone loss

The United States ranks first among countries for soft drink consumption, with an average per capita consumption of approximately 15 ounces a day. This high intake of soft drinks may be a big reason osteoporosis is so common in America.

Soft drinks that are high in phosphates and sugar lead to lower calcium and higher phosphate levels in the blood. This leads to the bone breaking down to release calcium into the blood to restore the proper level.

Soft drink consumption among children is also a significant risk factor for poor bone health. It can lead to impaired calcification of growing bones, that can lead to serious issues including an increased risk for breaking a bone as a kid as well as a greater risk for osteoporosis later in life.

The severely negative effect that soft drinks have on bone formation in children was clearly demonstrated in a study that compared 57 children with low blood calcium, aged 18 months to 14 years, with 171 matched controls with normal calcium levels.[4] The goal of the study was to assess whether the intake of at least 1.5 quarts per week of soft drinks containing phosphates is a risk for the development of low blood calcium levels. Of the 57 children with low blood calcium levels, 38 (66.7 percent) drank more than four bottles (12 to 16 ounces) per week, but only 48 (28 percent) of the 171 children with normal serum calcium levels drank as many soft drinks. For all 228 children, a significant inverse correlation between serum calcium level and the amount of soft drinks consumed each week was found.

table 12.1. calcium content of selected foods

Milligrams per 100 g edible portion (100 g = 3.5 ounces)

Kelp **1,093**	Dried apricots **67**
Cheddar cheese **750**	Rutabagas **66**
Carob flour **352**	Raisins **62**
Dulse **296**	Black currants **60**
Collard greens **250**	Dates **59**
Kale **249**	Green snap beans **56**
Turnip greens **246**	Globe artichokes **51**
Almonds **234**	Dried prunes **51**
Brewer's yeast **210**	Pumpkin/squash seeds **51**
Parsley **203**	Cooked dry beans **50**
Dandelion greens **187**	Common cabbage **49**
Brazil nuts **186**	Soybean sprouts **48**
Watercress **151**	Hard winter wheat **46**
Goat milk **129**	Oranges **41**
Tofu **128**	Celery **41**
Dried figs **126**	Cashews **38**
Buttermilk **121**	Rye grain **38**
Sunflower seeds **120**	Carrots **37**
Yogurt **120**	Barley **34**
Wheat bran **119**	Sweet potatoes **32**
Whole milk **118**	Brown rice **32**
Buckwheat **114**	Garlic **29**
Sesame seeds, hulled **110**	Summer squash **28**
Ripe olives **106**	Onions **27**
Broccoli **103**	Lemons **26**
English walnuts **99**	Fresh green peas **26**
Cottage cheese **94**	Cauliflower **25**
Soybeans, cooked **73**	Cucumbers **25**
Pecans **73**	Lentils, cooked **25**
Wheat germ **72**	Sweet cherries **22**
Peanuts **69**	Asparagus **22**
Miso **68**	Winter squash **22**
Romaine lettuce **68**	Strawberries **21**

Millet **20**   Eggplant **12**

Pineapple **17**   Chicken **12**

Grapes **16**   Avocados **10**

Beets **15**   Beef **10**

Cantaloupe **14**   Bananas **8**

Tomatoes **13**   Apples **7**

Source: "Nutritive Value of American Foods in Common Units," USDA Agriculture Handbook No. 456.

Vitamin K_1 is the form of vitamin K found in green leafy vegetables (such as kale, collard greens, parsley, lettuce). A function of vitamin K_1 that is often overlooked is its role in converting inactive osteocalcin to its active form. Osteocalcin is the major noncollagen protein in bone, whose role is to anchor calcium molecules and hold them in place within the bone.

A deficiency of vitamin K leads to impaired mineralization of the bone owing to inadequate osteocalcin levels. Very low blood levels of vitamin K_1 have been found in patients with fractures due to osteoporosis. The severity of fracture strongly correlated with the level of circulating vitamin K. The lower the level of vitamin K, the more severe the fracture. Since vitamin K is found in green leafy vegetables, they may be one of the key protective factors of a vegetarian diet against osteoporosis.

In addition to vitamin K_1, the high levels of many minerals such as calcium and boron in plant foods, particularly green leafy vegetables, may also be responsible for this protective effect. Boron is a trace mineral gaining attention as a protective factor against osteoporosis. It has been shown to have a positive effect on calcium and active estrogen levels in postmenopausal women, the group at highest risk for developing osteoporosis. In one study, supplementing the diet of postmenopausal women with 3 mg boron a day reduced urinary calcium excretion by 44 percent and dramatically increased the levels of the most biologically active estrogen.[5] Boron is required to activate certain hormones involved in bone health, including estrogen and vitamin D. Since fruits and vegetables are the main dietary sources of boron, diets low in these foods may be deficient in boron. Supplementation with boron is not necessary if the diet is rich in fruits and vegetables.

If you are concerned about bone loss, I would recommend that you take Healthy Bones Plus from Natural Factors. This comprehensive formula for bone health is available at health food stores. For more information, go to www.healthybonesplus.com.

Q. I smoked for many years, and even though I quit several years ago, I still have trouble breathing. Will fresh juices help restore my ability to breathe?

A. Perhaps. As you know, the risks of smoking include emphysema and other chronic obstructive pulmonary diseases, such as asthma and chronic bronchitis. Of these, emphysema is the most severe. Cigarette smoking causes emphysema by blocking key enzymes that can prevent damage to the lungs and depleting tissue stores of key antioxidant nutrients like vitamin C.

In Britain and the United States, several studies have shown that individuals who smoke consume less fresh fruit and vegetables than nonsmokers. This greatly increases their risk not only for emphysema but other diseases as well, such as heart disease, cancer, and strokes.

A group of British researchers sought to determine the effect of fresh fruits and fresh fruit juices on respiratory function in both smokers and nonsmokers.[6] They studied the reported frequency of consumption of fresh fruit and juice among 1,502 lifelong nonsmokers and 1,357 current smokers aged 18 to 69 with no history of chronic respiratory disease. The amount of air expelled in 1 second (forced expiratory volume in 1 second, or FEV1) into a spirometer was used as a measurement. Winter fruit consumption was used as an indicator of year-round consumption, the thought being if subjects consumed vegetables during the winter they would likely consume during the other seasons as well.

The results were as expected in smokers: Those who ate fresh fruit or juice had much better respiratory function than those who never drank fresh juice or ate fresh fruit less than once a week (FEV1 values were on average 78 ml lower in the latter group). In nonsmokers, something was discovered that was not expected: Respiratory function was greatest in those who ate fresh fruit or drank fresh fruit juice on a regular basis. They expected this association in smokers, but did not think it would hold true for nonsmokers.

The researchers felt that the observed effects of improved respiratory tract function with fresh fruit and juice consumption may be related more to dietary habits during childhood than to a direct influence of diet on airway function in adult life. They believed the effect of fresh fruit consumption in childhood is even more pronounced than in adults, as fresh fruits may promote improved lung growth and lung capacity.

What the results of these studies on lung health and diet tell us is that consumption of fresh fruit and fruit juice not only protects against chronic respiratory diseases such as emphysema and asthma, but that it can improve lung function in healthy individuals and may promote improved lung growth and capacity if consumed during childhood. From this study, I conclude that fresh fruit and vegetable juices may be of great benefit in helping you restore the health of your lungs.

Q. I've heard that cabbage-family vegetables can cause goiters, yet everybody is telling me to eat them. Should I be concerned?
A. Cabbage-family vegetables do contain compounds that can interfere with thyroid hormone action by blocking the utilization of

iodine. However, there is no evidence that these compounds cause any problems when dietary iodine levels are adequate. Therefore, it is a good idea if large quantities of cruciferous vegetables are being consumed that the diet also contains adequate amounts of iodine. Iodine is found in kelp and other seaweeds, vegetables grown near the sea, iodized salt, and in food supplements.

Q. Can you juice sprouts?

A. Yes. In fact, you can juice virtually any edible plant or food as long as it has a high water content, sprouts included. Sprouts provide a wide range of nutrients and can add flavor to any vegetable juice.

personal message

I hope the information presented in this book not only has made it clear that juicing is an integral part of a healthful diet and lifestyle but has also inspired you to get started. Being healthy takes commitment. The reward is often difficult to see or feel right away. It is usually not until the body fails us in some manner that we realize we haven't taken care of it. Ralph Waldo Emerson said, "The first wealth is health." Don't wait until you have lost your health to realize how important it is to you. Get started right now on living a healthful life.

The reward for most people maintaining a positive mental attitude, eating a healthful diet, and exercising regularly is a life filled with very high levels of energy, joy, vitality, and a tremendous passion for living. This life is my wish for you.

APPENDIX A
acid-base values of selected foods

One of the basic goals of the body in order to function properly is to maintain the proper balance of acidity and alkalinity (pH) in the blood and other body fluids. The acid-alkaline theory of disease is an over-simplification, but it basically states that many diseases are caused by excess acid accumulation in the body. There is accumulating evidence that certain disease states like osteoporosis, rheumatoid arthritis, gout, and many others may be influenced by the dietary acid-alkaline bal-ance. For example, osteoporosis may be the result of a chronic intake of acid-forming foods consistently outweighing the intake of alkaline foods leading to the bones being constantly forced to give up their alkaline minerals (calcium and magnesium) in order to buffer the excess acid.

The dietary goal for good health is simple: Make sure that you have a higher intake of alkaline-producing foods than acid-producing foods. Keep in mind that there is a difference between between acidic foods and acid-forming foods. For example, while foods like lemons and citrus fruits are acidic, they actually have an alkalizing effect on the body. What determines the pH nature of the food in the body is the metabolic end products when it is digested. For example, the citric acid in citrus fruit is metabolized in the body to its alkaline form (citrate) and may even be converted to bicarbonate—another alkaline compound.

In the food table that follows, foods with a negative value exert a base (B), or alkaline, effect and foods with a positive value exert an acid (A) effect. Neutral foodstuffs are labeled with N. The calculation is based on the potential acid load to the kidneys in milliequivalents per 100 g (3.5 ounces) serving.

FOOD	A, B, OR N	POTENTIAL ACIDIC LOAD
BEVERAGES		
Apple juice, unsweetened	B	−2.2
Beer, draft	B	−0.2
Beer, pale	A	0.9

FOOD	A, B, OR N	POTENTIAL ACIDIC LOAD
Beer, stout	B	−0.1
Beetroot juice	B	−3.9
Carrot juice	B	−4.8
Coca-Cola	A	0.4
Cocoa, made with semi-skimmed milk	B	−0.4
Coffee, infusion, 5 minutes	B	−1.4
Espresso	B	−2.3
Fruit tea, infusion	B	−0.3
Grape juice	B	−1.0
Grape juice, unsweetened	B	−1.0
Green tea, infusion	B	−0.3
Herbal tea	B	−0.2
Lemon juice	B	−2.5
Mineral water (Apollinaris)	B	−1.8
Mineral water (Volvic)	B	−0.1
Orange juice, unsweetened	B	−2.9
Red wine	B	−2.4
Tea, Indian, infusion	B	−0.3
Tomato juice	B	−2.8

FOOD	A, B, OR N	POTENTIAL ACIDIC LOAD
Vegetable juice (tomato, beetroot, carrot)	B	−3.6
White wine, dry	B	−1.2
FATS, OILS & NUTS		
Almonds	A	4.3
Butter	A	0.6
Hazelnuts	B	−2.8
Margarine	B	−0.5
Olive oil	N	0.0
Peanuts, plain	A	8.3
Pistachios	A	8.5
Sunflower seed oil	N	0.0
Walnuts	A	6.8
FISH & SEAFOOD		
Carp	A	7.9
Cod, fillets	A	7.1
Eel, smoked	A	11.0
Haddock	A	6.8
Halibut	A	7.8
Herring	A	7.0
Mussels	A	15.3
Prawn	A	15.5
Rosefish	A	10.0

FOOD	A, B, OR N	POTENTIAL ACIDIC LOAD
Salmon	A	9.4
Salted matie (herring)	A	8.0
Sardines in oil	A	13.5
Shrimps	A	7.6
Sole	A	7.4
Tiger prawn	A	18.2
Trout, steamed	A	10.8
Zander	A	7.1
FRUITS		
Apples	B	−2.2
Apricots	B	−4.8
Bananas	B	−5.5
Black currants	B	−6.5
Cherries	B	−3.6
Figs, dried	B	−18.1
Grapefruit	B	−3.5
Grapes	B	−3.9
Kiwifruits	B	−4.1
Lemons	B	−2.6
Mangoes	B	−3.3
Oranges	B	−2.7
Peaches	B	−2.4
Pears	B	−2.9
Pineapples	B	−2.7

FOOD	A, B, OR N	POTENTIAL ACIDIC LOAD
Raisins	B	−21.0
Strawberries	B	−2.2
Watermelon	B	−1.9
GRAINS & FLOURS		
Amaranth	A	7.5
Barley	A	5.0
Buckwheat	A	3.7
Corn (whole grain)	A	3.8
Cornflakes	A	6.0
Dried unripe spelt grains	A	8.8
Millet	A	8.6
Oat flakes	A	10.7
Rice, brown	A	12.5
Rice, white	A	4.6
Rice, white, boiled	A	1.7
Rye flour	A	4.4
Rye flour, whole	A	5.9
Wheat flour, white	A	6.9
Wheat flour whole	A	8.2
PASTAS		
Macaroni	A	6.1
Noodles	A	6.4
Spaetzle (German pasta)	A	9.4
Spaghetti, white	A	6.5

FOOD	A, B, OR N	POTENTIAL ACIDIC LOAD
Spaghetti, whole wheat	A	7.3
BREAD		
Crisp, rye	A	3.3
Pumpernickel	A	4.2
Rye flour	A	4.1
Rye flour, mixed	A	4.0
Wheat flour, mixed	A	3.8
Wheat flour, whole-meal	A	1.8
White wheat	A	3.7
Whole-grain	A	7.2
Whole-wheat, course	A	5.3
LEGUMES		
Beans, green / French beans	B	−3.1
Lentils, green and brown, whole, dried	A	3.5
Peas	A	1.2
Soybeans	B	−3.4
Soy milk	B	−0.8
Tofu	B	−0.8
MEAT & SAUSAGES		
Beef, lean only	A	7.8
Cervelat sausage	A	8.9
Chasseur sausage	A	7.2

FOOD	A, B, OR N	POTENTIAL ACIDIC LOAD
Chicken, meat only	A	8.7
Corned beef, canned	A	13.2
Duck	A	4.1
Duck, lean only	A	8.4
Frankfurters	A	6.7
Goose, lean only	A	13.0
Lamb, lean only	A	7.6
Liver (veal)	A	14.2
Liver sausage	A	10.6
Luncheon meat, canned	A	10.2
Ox liver	A	15.4
Pig's liver	A	15.7
Pork sausage	A	7.0
Pork sausage (Wiener)	A	7.7
Pork, lean only	A	7.9
Rabbit, lean only	A	19.0
Rump steak, lean and fat	A	8.8
Salami	A	11.6
Slicing sausage containing ham	A	8.3
Turkey, meat only	A	9.9
Veal, fillet	A	9.0

FOOD	A, B, OR N	POTENTIAL ACIDIC LOAD
DAIRY PRODUCTS & EGGS		
Buttermilk	A	0.5
Camembert	A	14.6
Cheddar-type, reduced fat	A	26.4
Cheese, rich, creamy, full fat	A	13.2
Cottage cheese, plain	A	8.7
Cream, fresh, sour	A	1.2
Curd cheese	A	0.9
Edam cheese, full fat	A	19.4
Egg, chicken, whole	A	8.2
Egg, white	A	1.1
Egg, yolk	A	23.4
Emmental cheese, full fat	A	21.1
Fresh cheese (Quark)	A	11.1
Gouda	A	18.6
Hard cheese	A	19.2
Ice cream, dairy, vanilla	A	0.6
Ice cream, fruit, mixed	B	−0.6
Kefir cheese, full fat	N	0.0
Milk, whole, evaporated	A	1.1
Milk, whole, pasteurized and sterilized	A	0.7

FOOD	A, B, OR N	POTENTIAL ACIDIC LOAD
Parmesan	A	34.2
Processed cheese, plain	A	28.7
Skimmed milk	A	0.7
Soft cheese, full fat	A	4.3
Whey	B	1.6
Yogurt, whole milk, fruit	A	1.2
Yogurt, whole milk, plain	A	1.5
SWEETS		
Chocolate, bitter	A	0.4
Chocolate, milk	A	2.4
Honey	B	−0.3
Madeira cake	A	3.7
Marmalade	B	−1.5
Nougat hazelnut cream	B	−1.4
Sugar, brown	B	−1.2
Sugar, white	N	0.0
VEGETABLES		
Arugula	B	−7.5
Asparagus	B	−0.4
Broccoli, green	B	−1.2
Brussels sprouts	B	−4.5
Carrots	B	−4.9
Cauliflower	B	−4.0

FOOD	A, B, OR N	POTENTIAL ACIDIC LOAD
Celery	B	−5.2
Chicory	B	−2.0
Cucumber	B	−0.8
Eggplant	B	−3.4
Fennel	B	−7.9
Garlic	B	−1.7
Gherkin, pickled	B	−1.6
Kale	B	−7.8
Kohlrabi	B	−5.5
Lamb's lettuce	B	−5.0
Leeks	B	−1.8
Lettuce	B	−2.5
Lettuce, iceberg	B	−1.6
Mushrooms, common	B	−1.4
Onions	B	−1.5
Peppers, green bell	B	−1.4
Potatoes	B	−4.0
Radish, red	B	−3.7
Sauerkraut	B	−3.0
Spinach	B	−14.0
Tomato	B	−3.1
Zucchini	B	−4.6

FOOD	A, B, OR N	POTENTIAL ACIDIC LOAD
HERBS & VINEGAR		
Apple vinegar	B	−2.3
Basil	B	−7.3
Chives	B	−5.3
Parsley	B	−12.0
Wine vinegar, balsamic	B	−1.6

Source: Table prepared and provided by Professor Jürgen Vormanne, Institute for Prevention and Diet, Ismaning, Germany. Used with permission.

APPENDIX B
glycemic index, carbohydrate content, and glycemic load of selected foods

A complete list of the GI and GL of all tested foods is beyond the scope of this book; it would be a book in itself. This listing will give you a general sense of what are high-GL and low-GL foods. Items are listed by food groups, from low to high GLs. You may notice that certain food groups are not listed. For example, you won't see nuts, seeds, fish, poultry, and meats listed because these foods have little impact on blood sugar levels as they are low in carbohydrates.

FOOD	GI	CARBOHYDRATES (G)	FIBER (G)	GL
BEANS (LEGUMES)				
Soybeans, cooked, ½ cup, 100 g	14	12	7.0	1.6
Peas, green, fresh, frozen, boiled, ½ cup, 80 g	48	5	2.0	2.0
Beans, navy, white, boiled, ½ cup, 90 g	38	11	6.0	4.2
Beans, lima, boiled, ½ cup, 90 g	27	18	7.3	4.8
Peas, split, yellow, boiled, ½ cup, 90 g	32	16	4.7	5.1
Lentils, ½ cup cooked, 100g	28	19	3.7	5.3
Beans, lima, baby, ½ cup cooked, 85 g	32	17	4.5	5.4
Beans, black, canned, ½ cup, 95 g	45	15	7.0	5.7

FOOD	GI	CARBOHYDRATES (G)	FIBER (G)	GL
Beans, pinto, canned, ½ cup, 95 g	45	13	6.7	5.8
Chickpeas, canned, drained, ½ cup, 95 g	42	15	5.0	6.3
Beans, kidney, canned and drained, ½ cup, 95 g	52	13	7.3	6.7
Beans, broad, frozen, boiled, ½ cup, 80 g	79	9	6.0	7.1
Peas, dried, boiled, ½ cup, 70 g	22	4	4.7	8.0
Baked beans, canned in tomato sauce, ½ cup, 120 g	48	21	8.8	10.0
Black-eyed beans, soaked, boiled, ½ cup, 120 g	42	24	5.0	10.0
BREAD				
Multi-grain, unsweetened, 1 slice, 30 g	43	9	1.4	4.0
Oat bran and honey loaf, 1 slice, 40 g	31	14	1.5	4.5
Sourdough, rye, 1 slice, 30 g	48	12	0.4	6.0
Stone-ground whole wheat, 1 slice, 30 g	53	11	1.4	6.0
Wonder, enriched white, 1 slice, 20 g	73	10	0.4	7.0

FOOD	GI	CARBOHYDRATES (G)	FIBER (G)	GL
Sourdough, wheat, 1 slice, 30 g	54	14	0.4	7.5
Pumpernickel, 1 slice, 60 g	41	21	0.5	8.6
Whole wheat, 1 slice, 35 g	69	14	1.4	9.6
Healthy Choice, hearty 7-grain, 1 slice, 38 g	56	18	1.4	10.0
White (wheat flour), 1 slice, 30 g	70	15	0.4	10.5
Healthy Choice, 100% whole grain, 1 slice, 38 g	62	18	1.4	11.0
Gluten-free multigrain, 1 slice, 35 g	79	15	1.8	12.0
French baguette, 30 g	95	15	0.4	14.0
Hamburger bun, 1, 50 g	61	24	0.5	15.0
Rye, 1 slice, 50 g	65	23	0.4	15.0
Light rye, 1 slice, 50 g	68	23	0.4	16.0
Dark rye, black, 1 slice, 50 g	76	21	0.4	16.0
Croissant, 1, 50 g	67	27	0.2	18.0
Kaiser roll, 1, 50 g	73	25	0.4	18.0
Pita, 1, 65 g	57	38	0.4	22.0
Bagel, 1, 70 g	72	35	0.4	25.0

FOOD	GI	CARBOHYDRATES (G)	FIBER (G)	GL
BREAKFAST CEREALS				
Oat bran, raw, 1 tablespoon, 10 g	55	7	1.0	4.0
Bran with psyllium, ⅓ cup, 30 g	47	12	12.5	5.6
Bran, ⅓ cup, 30 g	58	14	14.0	8.0
All-Bran, ½ cup, 40 g	42	22	6.5	9.2
Oatmeal, cooked with water, 1 cup, 245 g	42	24	1.6	10.0
Shredded Wheat, ⅓ cup, 25 g	67	18	1.2	12.0
Kellogg's Frosted Mini-Wheats (whole wheat), 1 cup, 30 g	58	21	4.4	12.0
Cheerios, ½ cup, 30 g	74	20	2.0	15.0
Kellogg's Frosted Flakes, ¾ cup, 30 g	55	27	1.0	15.0
Kellogg's Honey Smacks, ¾ cup, 30 g	56	27	1.0	15.0
Total, 30 g	76	22	2.0	16.7
Puffed wheat, 1 cup, 30 g	80	22	2.0	17.6
Bran flakes, ¾ cup, 30 g	74	24	2.0	18.0
Kellogg's Crunchy Nut, ¾ cup, 30 g	72	25	2.0	18.0
Froot Loops, 1 cup, 30 g	69	27	1.0	18.0

FOOD	GI	CARBOHYDRATES (G)	FIBER (G)	GL
Cocoa Pops, ¾ cup, 30 g	77	26	1.0	20.0
Corn Chex, 1 cup, 30 g	83	25	1.0	20.8
Corn flakes, 1 cup, 30 g	84	26	0.3	21.8
Rice Krispies, 1 cup, 30 g	82	27	0.3	22.0
Rice Chex, 1 cup, 30 g	89	25	1.0	22.0
Oats'n Honey, 1 cup, 45 g	77	31	2.0	24.0
Raisin bran, 1 cup, 45 g	73	35	4.0	25.5
Grape Nuts, ½ cup, 58 g	71	47	2.0	33.3
CAKE				
Angel food, 1 slice, 30 g	67	17	<1.0	11.5
Sponge, 1 slice, 60 g	46	32	<1.0	14.7
Cupcake, with icing and cream filling, 1, 38 g	73	26	<1.0	19.0
Chocolate fudge (Betty Crocker), 73 g cake + 33 g frosting	38	54	<1.0	20.5
Banana, 1 slice, 80g	47	46	<1.0	21.6
Pound, 1 slice, 80 g	54	42	<1.0	22.6

FOOD	GI	CARBOHYDRATES (G)	FIBER (G)	GL
French vanilla (Betty Crocker), 73 g cake + 33 g frosting	42	58	<1.0	24.4
Flan, 1 slice, 80 g	65	55	<1.0	35.8
CRACKERS				
Kavli, 4, 20 g	71	13	3.0	9.2
Breton wheat, 6, 25 g	67	14	2.0	9.4
Ryvita or Wasa (regular), 2, 20 g	69	16	3.0	11.0
Stoned Wheat Thins, 5, 25 g	67	17	1.0	11.4
Premium soda, 3, 25 g	74	17	0.0	12.5
Water, 5, 25 g	78	18	0.0	14.0
Graham, 1, 30 g	74	22	1.4	16.0
Rice cake, 2, 25 g	82	21	0.4	17.0
MILK, SOY MILK, JUICES & SOFT DRINKS				
Milk, full fat, 1 cup, 250 ml	27	12	0.0	3.0
Milk, soy, 1 cup, 250 ml	31	12	0.0	3.7
Milk, skim, 1 cup, 250 ml	32	13	0.0	4.0
Juice, grapefruit, unsweetened, 1 cup, 250 ml	48	16	1.0	7.7

FOOD	GI	CARBOHYDRATES (G)	FIBER (G)	GL
Nesquik chocolate powder, 3 teaspoons in 1 cup (250 ml) milk	55	14	0.0	7.7
Milk, chocolate, low fat, 1 cup, 250 ml	34	23	0.0	7.8
Juice, orange, 1 cup, 250 ml	46	21	1.0	9.7
Gatorade, 1 cup, 250 ml	78	15	0.0	11.7
Juice, pineapple, unsweetened, canned, 1 cup, 250 ml	46	27	1.0	12.4
Juice, apple, unsweetened, 1 cup, 250 ml	40	33	1.0	13.2
Ocean Spray cranberry juice cocktail, 1 cup, 250 ml	68	34	0.0	23.0
Coca-Cola, 12 ounces, 375 ml	63	40	0.0	25.2
Other soft drinks, 12 ounces, 375 ml	68	51	0.0	34.7
Milk, sweetened condensed, ½ cup, 125 ml	61	90	0.0	55.0
FRUIT				
Cherries, 20, 80 g	22	10	2.4	2.2
Plums, 3–4 small, 100 g	39	7	2.2	2.7

FOOD	GI	CARBOHYDRATES (G)	FIBER (G)	GL
Peach, fresh, 1 large, 110 g	42	7	1.9	3.0
Apricots, fresh, 3 medium, 100 g	57	7	1.9	4.0
Apricots, dried, 5–6, 30 g	31	13	2.2	4.0
Kiwifruit, 1 raw, peeled, 80 g	52	8	2.4	4.0
Orange, 1 medium, 130 g	44	10	2.6	4.4
Peach, canned, in natural juice, ½ cup, 125 g	38	12	1.5	4.5
Pear, canned, in natural juice, ½ cup, 125 g	43	13	1.5	5.5
Watermelon, 1 cup, 150 g	72	8	1.0	5.7
Pineapple, fresh, 2 slices, 125 g	66	10	2.8	6.6
Apple, 1 medium, 150 g	38	18	3.5	6.8
Grapes, green, 1 cup, 100 g	46	15	2.4	6.9
Apple, dried, 30g	29	24	3.0	6.9
Prunes, pitted (Sunsweet), 6, 40 g	29	25	3.0	7.3
Pear, fresh, 1 medium, 150 g	38	21	3.1	8.0

FOOD	GI	CARBOHYDRATES (G)	FIBER (G)	GL
Fruit cocktail, canned, in natural juice, ½ cup, 125 g	55	15	1.5	8.3
Apricots, canned, in light syrup, ½ cup, 125 g	64	13	1.5	8.3
Peach, canned, in light syrup, ½ cup, 125 g	52	18	1.5	9.4
Mango, 1 small, 150 g	55	19	2.0	10.4
Figs, dried, tenderized (water added), 50 g	61	22	3.0	13.4
Sultanas, ¼ cup, 40 g	56	30	3.1	16.8
Banana, raw, 1 medium, 150 g	55	32	2.4	17.6
Raisins, ¼ cup, 40 g	64	28	3.1	18.0
Dates, dried, 5, 40 g	103	27	3.0	27.8
GRAINS				
Rice bran, extruded, 1 tablespoon, 10 g	19	3	1.0	0.6
Barley, pearl, boiled, ½ cup, 80 g	25	17	6.0	4.3
Millet, cooked, ½ cup, 120 g	71	12	1.0	8.5
Bulgur, cooked, ⅔ cup, 120 g	48	22	3.5	10.6
Rice, brown, steamed, 1 cup, 150 g	50	32	1.0	16.0

FOOD	GI	CARBOHYDRATES (G)	FIBER (G)	GL
Couscous, cooked, ⅔ cup, 120 g	65	28	1.0	18.0
Rice, white, boiled, 1 cup, 150 g	72	36	0.2	26.0
Rice, Arborio, white, boiled, ½ cup, 100 g	69	35	0.2	29.0
Rice, Basmati, white, boiled, 1 cup, 180 g	58	50	0.2	29.0
Buckwheat, cooked, ½ cup, 80 g	54	57	3.5	30.0
Rice, instant, cooked, 1 cup, 180 g	87	38	0.2	33.0
Tapioca, steamed 1 hour, 100 g	70	54	<1.0	38.0
Tapioca, boiled with milk, 1 cup, 265 g	81	51	<1.0	41.0
Rice, jasmine, white, long grain, steamed, 1 cup, 180 g	109	39	0.2	42.5
ICE CREAM				
Ice cream, low-fat French vanilla, 2 scoops, 50 g	38	15	0.0	5.7
Ice cream, full fat, 2 scoops, 50 g	61	10	0.0	6.1
JAM				
Jam, no sugar, 1 tablespoon, 25 g	55	11	<1.0	6.0

FOOD	GI	CARBOHYDRATES (G)	FIBER (G)	GL
Jam, sweetened, 1 tablespoon, 25 g	48	17	<1.0	8.0
MUFFINS & PANCAKES				
Muffin, chocolate butterscotch, from mix, 50 g	53	28	1.0	15.0
Muffin, apple, oat and sultana, from mix, 50 g	54	28	1.0	15.0
Muffin, apricot, coconut and honey, from mix, 50 g	60	27	1.5	16.0
Muffin, banana, oat and honey, from mix, 50 g	65	28	1.5	18.0
Muffin, apple, 80 g	44	44	1.5	19.0
Muffin, bran, 80 g	60	34	2.5	20.0
Muffin, blueberry, 80 g	59	41	1.5	24.0
Pancake, buckwheat, from dry mix, 1 small, 40 g	102	30	2.0	30.0
Pancake, from dry mix, 1 large, 80 g	67	58	1.0	39.0
PASTA				
Tortellini, cheese, cooked, 1 cup, 180 g	50	21	2.0	10.5
Ravioli, meat filled, cooked, 1 cup, 220 g	39	30	2.0	11.7

FOOD	GI	CARBOHYDRATES (G)	FIBER (G)	GL
Vermicelli, cooked, 1 cup, 180 g	35	45	2.0	15.7
Rice noodles, fresh, boiled, 1 cup, 176 g	40	44	0.4	17.6
Spaghetti, whole grain, cooked, 1 cup, 180 g	37	48	3.5	17.8
Fettucine, cooked, 1 cup, 180 g	32	57	2.0	18.2
Spaghetti, gluten-free, in tomato sauce, 1 small can, 220 g	68	27	2.0	18.5
Macaroni and cheese, packaged, cooked, 220 g	64	30	2.0	19.2
Star pastina, cooked, 1 cup, 180 g	38	56	2.0	21.0
Spaghetti, white, cooked, 1 cup, 180 g	41	56	2.0	23.0
Rice pasta, brown, cooked, 1 cup, 180 g	92	57	2.0	52.0
SUGARS				
Fructose, 1 teaspoon, 10 g	23	10	0.0	2.3
Honey, ½ tablespoon, 10 g	58	16	0.0	4.6
Lactose, 1 teaspoon, 10 g	46	10	0.0	4.6
Sucrose, 1 teaspoon, 10 g	65	10	0.0	6.5

FOOD	GI	CARBOHYDRATES (G)	FIBER (G)	GL
Glucose, 1 teaspoon, 10 g	102	10	0.0	10.2
Maltose, 1 teaspoon, 10 g	105	10	0.0	10.5
SNACKS				
Corn chips, Doritos original, 50 g	42	33	<1.0	13.9
Snickers bar, 59 g	41	35	0.0	14.3
Tofu frozen dessert (nondairy), 100 g	115	13	<1.0	15.0
Real Fruit bar, strawberry, 20 g	90	17	<1.0	15.3
Twix bar (caramel), 59 g	44	37	<1.0	16.2
Pretzels, 50 g	83	22	<1.0	18.3
Mars bar, 60 g	65	41	0.0	26.6
SOUPS				
Tomato, canned, 7/8 cup, 220 ml	38	15	1.5	6.0
Black bean, 7/8 cup, 220 ml	64	9	3.4	6.0
Lentil, canned, 7/8 cup, 220 ml	44	14	3.0	6.0
Split pea, canned, 7/8 cup, 220 ml	60	13	3.0	8.0
VEGETABLES				
Carrots, raw, 1/2 cup, 80 g	16	6	1.5	1.0

FOOD	GI	CARBOHYDRATES (G)	FIBER (G)	GL
LOW-GLYCEMIC VEGETABLES	≈20	≈7	≈1.5	≈1.4
Asparagus, 1 cup cooked or raw				
Bell peppers, 1 cup cooked or raw				
Broccoli, 1 cup cooked or raw				
Brussels sprouts, 1 cup cooked or raw				
Cabbage, 1 cup cooked or raw				
Cauliflower, 1 cup cooked or raw				
Cucumber, 1 cup				
Celery, 1 cup cooked or raw				
Eggplant, 1 cup				
Green beans, 1 cup cooked or raw				
Kale, 1 cup cooked, 2 cups raw				
Lettuce, 2 cups raw				
Mushrooms, 1 cup raw				
Spinach, 1 cup cooked or 2 cups raw				
Tomatoes, 1 cup raw				
Zucchini, 1 cup cooked or raw				

FOOD	GI	CARBOHYDRATES (G)	FIBER (G)	GL
Carrots, peeled, boiled, ½ cup, 70 g	49	3	1.5	1.5
Beets, canned, drained, 2–3 slices, 60 g	64	5	1.0	3.0
Pumpkin, peeled, boiled, ½ cup, 85 g	75	6	3.4	4.5
Parsnips, boiled, ½ cup, 75 g	97	8	3.0	8.0
Corn on the cob, sweet, boiled, 80 g	48	14	2.9	8.0
Corn, canned, drained, ½ cup, 80 g	55	15	3.0	8.5
Sweet potato, peeled, boiled, 80 g	54	16	3.4	8.6
Sweet corn, ½ cup boiled, 80 g	55	18	3.0	10.0
Potato, peeled, boiled, 1 medium, 120 g	87	13	1.4	10.0
Potato, with skin on, boiled, 1 medium, 120 g	79	15	2.4	11.0
Yam, boiled, 80 g	51	26	3.4	13.0
Potato, baked in oven, 1 medium, 120 g	93	15	2.4	14.0
Potatoes, mashed, ½ cup, 120 g	91	16	1.0	14.0

FOOD	GI	CARBOHYDRATES (G)	FIBER (G)	GL
Potatoes, instant mashed, prepared, ½ cup	83	18	1.0	15.0
Potatoes, new, unpeeled, boiled, 5 small, 175 g	78	25	2.0	20.0
Cornmeal (polenta), ⅓ cup, 40 g	68	30	2.0	20.0
French fries, fine cut, small serving, 120g	75	49	1.0	36.0
Gnocchi, cooked, 1 cup, 145 g	68	71	1.0	48.0
YOGURT				
Yogurt, low fat, artificially sweetened, 200 g	14	12	0.0	2.0
Yogurt, with fruit, 200 g	26	30	0.0	8.0
Yogurt, low fat, 200 g	33	26	0.0	8.5

APPENDIX C
pesticide content of popular fruits and vegetables

The Environmental Working Group (EWG) is a nonprofit consumer advocate group composed of professionals in various fields (scientists, engineers, policy experts, lawyers, and computer programmers) bound together to expose threats to our health and the environment and to find solutions.

One of the documents that this organization put together is "EWG's 2013 Shopper's Guide to Pesticides in Produce." In this report, the EWG ranked pesticide contamination for 48 popular fruits and vegetables based on an analysis of over 100,000 tests for pesticides on these foods, conducted by the U.S. Department of Agriculture (USDA) and the Food and Drug Administration. Contamination was measured in six different ways, and crops were ranked based on a composite score from all categories. The six measures of contamination used were:

- **Percentage of the samples tested with detectable pesticides**
- **Percentage of the samples with two or more pesticides**
- **Average number of pesticides found on a sample**
- **Average amount (level in parts per million) of all pesticides found**
- **Maximum number of pesticides found on a single sample**
- **Number of pesticides found on the food in total**

The guide does not present a complex assessment of pesticide risks but simply reflects the overall load of pesticides found on commonly eaten fruits and vegetables. The produce listed in the guide was chosen after an analysis of USDA food consumption data.

MOST CONTAMINATED: THE DIRTY DOZEN
The EWG designated the top 12 foods in pesticide ranking as "the dirty dozen." Eight fruits represented 12 of the most contaminated foods. Among these eight fruits,

- **Nectarines had the highest percentage of samples test positive for pesticides (97.3 percent), followed by pears (94.4 percent) and peaches (93.7 percent).**

- Nectarines also had the highest likelihood of multiple pesticides on a single sample (85.3 percent had two or more pesticide residues), followed by peaches (79.9 percent) and cherries (75.8 percent).
- Peaches and raspberries had the most pesticides detected, with nine pesticides on a single sample, followed by strawberries and apples, each with eight pesticides on a single sample.
- Peaches had the most pesticides overall with 45 pesticides found on the samples tested, followed by raspberries with 39 pesticides, and apples and strawberries, both with 36.

Among vegetables, spinach, celery, potatoes, and sweet bell peppers are the most likely to expose consumers to pesticides. Among these four vegetables,

- Celery had the highest percentage of samples test positive for pesticides (94.5 percent), followed by spinach (83.4 percent) and potatoes (79.3 percent).
- Celery also had the highest likelihood of multiple pesticides on a single vegetable (78 percent of samples), followed by spinach (51.8 percent) and sweet bell peppers (48.5 percent).
- Spinach was the vegetable with the most pesticides detected on a single sample (10), followed by celery and sweet bell peppers (both with 9 on a single sample).
- Sweet bell peppers were the vegetable with the most pesticides overall with 39, followed by spinach at 36, and celery and potatoes, both with 29.

LEAST CONTAMINATED: CONSISTENTLY CLEAN

The five fruits least likely to have pesticide residues on them are pineapples, mangoes, kiwifruit, papaya, and melons (cantaloupe, watermelon, and honeydew melon).

- Fewer than 10 percent of pineapple and mango samples had detectable pesticides on them and fewer than one percent of samples had more than one pesticide's residue.
- Kiwifruit and papaya had residues on 23.6 percent and 21.7 percent of samples, respectively, and just 10.4 percent and 5.6 percent of samples, respectively, had multiple pesticide residues.

The vegetables suitable for juicing least likely to have pesticides on them are cabbage-family vegetables and sweet potatoes.

fruits and vegetables suitable for juicing ranked from worst to best in terms of likely pesticide content

Apples	Tangerines
Strawberries	Summer squash
Grapes	Broccoli
Celery	Winter squash
Peaches	Green onions
Spinach	Oranges
Sweet bell peppers	Tomatoes
Nectarines	Honeydew melon
Cucumbers	Cauliflower
Potatoes	Bananas
Cherry tomatoes	Watermelon
Hot peppers	Sweet potatoes
Blueberries, domestic	Cantaloupe
Lettuce	Grapefruit
Kale or collard greens	Kiwifruit
Cherries	Asparagus
Pears	Mangoes
Plums	Papayas
Raspberries	Cabbage
Blueberries, imported	Pineapples
Carrots	Onions
Green beans	

references

Over the past 30 years, I have painstakingly collected thousands of scientific articles from medical journals on the healing power of foods and food components. The references provided are by no means designed to represent a complete list for all of the studies reviewed or mentioned in *The Complete Book of Juicing.* I have chosen to focus on key studies and comprehensive review articles. In general, these sorts of scientific references are usually of value only to health care professionals.

In addition to the articles listed here, we encourage interested parties to access the Internet site for the National Library of Medicine (NLM) at http://gateway.nlm.nih.gov for additional studies.

The NLM Gateway is a web-based system that lets users search simultaneously in multiple retrieval systems at the NLM. From this site you can access all of the NLM databases including the PubMed database. This database was developed in conjunction with publishers of biomedical literature as a search tool for accessing literature citations and linking to full-text journal articles at websites of participating publishers. Publishers participating in PubMed electronically supply NLM with their citations prior to or at the time of publication. If the publisher has a website that offers the full text of its journals, PubMed provides links to that site as well as sites to other biological data, sequence centers, and so on.

PubMed provides access to bibliographic information, which includes MEDLINE—the NLM's premier bibliographic database covering the fields of medicine, nursing, dentistry, veterinary medicine, the health care system, and the preclinical sciences. MEDLINE contains bibliographic citations and author abstracts from more than 4,000 medical journals published in the United States and 70 other countries. The file contains over 11 million citations dating back to the mid-1960s. Coverage is worldwide, but most records are from English-language sources or have English abstracts (summaries). Conducting a search is quite easy and the site has a link to a tutorial that fully explains the process.

CHAPTER 1: WHY JUICE?

1. K. A. Steinmetz and J. D. Potter, "Vegetables, Fruit, and Cancer. II. Mechanisms," *Cancer Causes and Control* 2 (1991): 427–42.
2. J. Konowalchuk and J. I. Speirs, "Antiviral Effect of Apple Beverages," *Applied and Environmental Microbiology* 36 (1978): 798–801.
3. C. Gerhauser, "Cancer Chemopreventive Potential of Apples,

Apple Juice, and Apple Components," *Planta Medica* 74 (2008): 1608–24.

4. C. Soler, J. M. Soriano, and J. Mañes, "Apple-Products Phyto-chemicals and Processing: A Review," *Natural Product Communications* 4, no. 5 (May 2009): 659–70.

5. E. Bakkalbaşi, O. Menteş, and N. Artik, "Food Ellagitannins-Occurrence, Effects of Processing and Storage," *Critical Reviews in Food Science and Nutrition* 49, no. 3 (March 2009): 283–98.

6. D. P. Jones, R. J. Coates, E. W. Flagg, et al., "Glutathione in Foods Listed in the National Cancer Institutes Health Habits and History Food Frequency Questionnaire," *Nutrition and Cancer* 17 (1995): 57–75.

7. P. L. White and N. Selvey, *Nutritional Qualities of Fresh Fruits and Vegetables* (Mount Kisco, NY: Futura 1974).

8. Ibid.

9. J. M. Douglass, I. M. Rasgon, P. M. Fleiss, et al., "Effects of a Raw Food Diet on Hypertension and Obesity," *Southern Medical Journal* 78 (1985): 841–44.

CHAPTER 2: WHAT'S IN JUICE? THE NUTRIENTS

1. S. M. Kleiner, "Water: An Essential but Overlooked Nutrient," *Journal of the American Dietetic Association* 99 (1999): 200–6.

2. InterAct Consortium, "Consumption of Sweet Beverages and Type 2 Diabetes Incidence in European Adults: Results from EPIC-InterAct," *Diabetologia* April 26, 2013, diabetologia-journal .org.

3. V. S. Malik, B. M. Popkin, G. A. Bray, et al., "Sugar-Sweetened Beverages and Risk of Metabolic Syndrome and Type 2 Diabetes: A Meta-Analysis," *Diabetes Care* 33, no. 11 (2010): 2477–83; and E. S. Eshak, H. Iso, T. Mizoue, et al., "Soft Drink, 100% Fruit Juice, and Vegetable Juice Intakes and Risk of Diabetes Mellitus," *Clinical Nutrition* 32, no. 2 (April 2013): 300–8.

4. A. S. Christensen, L. Viggers, K. Hasselström, et al., "Effect of Fruit Restriction on Glycemic Control in Patients with Type 2 Diabetes—A Randomized Trial," *Nutrition Journal* 12 (2013): 29. doi: 10.1186/1475-2891-12-29; and S. V. Hegde, P. Adhikari, M. N., et al., "Effect of Daily Supplementation of Fruits on Oxidative Stress Indices and Glycaemic Status in Type 2 Diabetes Mellitus," *Complementary Therapies in Clinical Practice* 19, no. 2 (May 2013): 97–100.

5. F. H. Nielsen, "Boron: An Overlooked Element of Potential Nutrition Importance," *Nutrition Today* 23 (January–February 1988): 4–7.
6. K. T. Khaw and E. Barrett-Connor, "Dietary Potassium and Stroke-Associated Mortality," *New England Journal of Medicine* 316 (1987): 235–40; and B. Jansson, "Dietary, Total Body, and Intracellular Potassium-to-Sodium Ratios and Their Influence on Cancer," *Cancer Detection and Prevention* 14 (1991): 563–65.
7. P. K. Whelton and J. He, "Potassium in Preventing and Treating High Blood Pressure," *Seminars in Nephrology* 19 (1999): 494–99; and F. M. Sacks, L. P. Svetkey, W. M. Vollmer, et al., "Effects on Blood Pressure of Reduced Dietary Sodium and the Dietary Approaches to Stop Hypertension (DASH) Diet." *New England Journal of Medicine* 344 (2001): 3–10.

CHAPTER 3: WHAT'S IN JUICE? THE PHYTOCHEMICALS

1. E. Howell, *Enzyme Nutrition* (Wayne, NJ: Avery, 1985); M. I. Grossman, H. Greengard, and A. C. Ivy, "The Effect of Diet on Pancreatic Enzymes," *American Journal of Physiology* 138 (1943): 676–82.
2. S. Taussig and R. Batkin, "Bromelain: The Enzyme Complex of Pineapple (*Ananas comosus*) and Its Clinical Application: An Update," *Journal of Ethnopharmacology* 22 (1988): 191–203.
3. K. Izaka, M. Yamada, T. Kawano, et al., "Gastrointestinal Absorption and Anti-inflammatory Effect of Bromelain," *Japanese Journal of Pharmacology* 22 (1972): 519–34.
4. N. I. Krinsky and E. J. Johnson, "Carotenoid Actions and Their Relation to Health and Disease," *Molecular Aspects of Medicine* 26, no. 6 (2005): 459–516.
5. R. M. Russell, "Physiological and Clinical Significance of Carotenoids," *International Journal of Vitamin and Nutrition Research* 68, no. 6 (1998): 349–53.
6. R. G. Cutler, "Carotenoids and Retinol: Their Possible Importance in Determining Longevity of Primate Species," *Proceedings of the National Academy of Sciences* 81 (1984): 7627–31.
7. J. A. Mares-Perlman, A. E. Millen, T. L. Ficek, et al., "The Body of Evidence to Support a Protective Role for Lutein and Zeaxanthin in Delaying Chronic Disease," *Journal of Nutrition* 132, no. 3 (2002): 518S–24S.
8. A. V. Rao and S. Agarwal, "Role of Antioxidant Lycopene in Cancer and Heart Disease," *Journal of the American College of Nutrition* 19, no. 5 (2000): 563–69.

9. J. H. Weisburger, "Lycopene and Tomato Products in Health Promotion," *Experimental Biology and Medicine* 227, no. 10 (2002): 924–27.

10. A. Bendich, "The Safety of Beta-Carotene," *Nutrition and Cancer* 11 (1988): 207–14.

11. G. Di Carlo, N. Mascolo, A. A. Izzo, et al., "Flavonoids: Old and New Aspects of a Class of Natural Therapeutic Drugs," *Life Sciences* 65 (1999): 337–53; B. H. Havsteen, "The Biochemistry and Medical Significance of the Flavonoids," *Pharmacology and Therapeutics* 96 (2002): 67–202; E. Middleton, Jr., C. Kandaswami, and T. C. Theoharides, "The Effects of Plant Flavonoids on Mammalian Cells: Implications for Inflammation, Heart Disease, and Cancer," *Pharmacological Reviews* 52 (2000): 673–751; and R. J. Nijveldt, E. van Nood, D. E. van Hoorn, et al., "Flavonoids: A Review of Probable Mechanisms of Action and Potential Applications," *American Journal of Clinical Nutrition* 74 (2001): 418–25.

12. M. L. McCullough, J. J. Peterson, R. Patel, et al., "Flavonoid Intake and Cardiovascular Disease Mortality in a Prospective Cohort of US Adults," *American Journal of Clinical Nutrition* 95, no. 2 (February 2012): 454–64.

13. H. A. Rafsky and C. I. Krieger, "The Treatment of Intestinal Diseases with Solutions of Water-Soluble Chlorophyll," *Review of Gastroenterology* 15 (1945): 549–53.

14. M. C. Nahata, C. A. Sleccsak, and J. Kamp, "Effect of Chlorophyllin on Urinary Odor in Incontinent Geriatric Patients," *Drug Intelligence and Clinical Pharmacy* 17 (1983): 732–34.

15. R. Gubner and H. E. Ungerleider, "Vitamin K Therapy in Menorrhagia," *Southern Medical Journal* 37 (1944): 556–58.

16. T. Ong, W. Z. Whong, J. Stewart, et al., "Chlorophyllin: A Potent Antimutagen Against Environmental and Dietary Complex Mixtures," *Mutation Research* 173 (1986): 111–15.

17. S. Ohyama, S. Kitamori, H. Kawano, et al., "Ingestion of Parsley Inhibits the Mutagenicity of Male Human Urine Following Consumption of Fried Salmon," *Mutation Research* 192 (1987): 7–10.

18. J. Sun, "D-limonene: Safety and Clinical Applications," *Alternative Medicine Review* 12, no. 3 (September 2007): 259–64; P. L. Crowell, "Prevention and Therapy of Cancer by Dietary Monoterpenes," *Journal of Nutrition* 129, no. 3 (1999): 775S–78S; and D. M. Vigushin, G. K. Poon, A. Boddy, et al., "Phase I and Pharmacokinetic Study of d-Limonene in Patients with Advanced Cancer," *Cancer Chemotherapy and Pharmacology* 42 (1998): 111–17.

CHAPTER 4: HOW TO JUICE—GETTING STARTED

1. A. Blair and S. H. Zahm, "Agricultural Exposures and Cancer," *Environmental Health Perspectives* 103, no. 58 (1995): 205–8; Y. Mao, J. Hu, A. M. Ugnat, et al., "Non-Hodgkin's Lymphoma and Occupational Exposure to Chemicals in Canada," *Annals of Oncology* 11, no. 51 (2000): 69–73.
2. C. Lu, K. Toepel, R. Irish, et al., "Organic Diets Significantly Lower Children's Dietary Exposure to Organophosphorus Pesticides," *Environmental Health Perspectives* 114, no. 2 (February 2006): 260–63.

CHAPTER 5: A JUICER'S GUIDE TO FRUITS

1. D. A. Hyson, "A Comprehensive Review of Apples and Apple Components and Their Relationship to Human Health," *Advances in Nutrition* 2, no. 5 (September 2011): 408–20.
2. P. Knekt, R. Jarvinen, A. Reunanen, et al., "Flavonoid Intake and Coronary Mortality in Finland: A Cohort Study," *British Medical Journal* 312, no. 7029 (1996): 478–81.
3. Hyson, "Comprehensive Review," 408–20; R. Sable-Amplis, R. Sicart, and R. Agid, "Further Studies on the Cholesterol-Lowering Effect of Apple in Humans: Biochemical Mechanisms Involved," *Nutrition Research* 3 (1983): 325–83.
4. V. Garcia, I. C. Arts, J. A. Sterne, et al., "Dietary Intake of Flavonoids and Asthma in Adults," *European Respiratory Journal* 26, no. 3 (September 2005): 449–52.
5. Hyson, "Comprehensive Review," 408–20.
6. C. Soler, J. M. Soriano, and J. Mañes, "Apple-Products Phytochemicals and Processing: A Review," *Natural Product Communications* 4, no. 5 (May 2009): 459–70.
7. D. Heber, "Multitargeted Therapy of Cancer by Ellagitannins," *Cancer Letters* 269, no. 2 (October 2008): 262–68.
8. D. H. Barch, L. M Rundhaugen, G. D. Stoner, et al., "Structure-Function Relationships of the Dietary Anticarcinogen Ellagic Acid," *Carcinogenesis* 17, no. 2 (1996): 265–69.
9. K. T. Khaw and E. Barrett-Connor, "Dietary Potassium and Stroke-Associated Mortality: A 12-year Prospective Population Study," *New England Journal of Medicine* 316 (1987): 235–40.
10. R. L. Galli, B. Shukitt-Hale, K. A. Youdim, et al., "Fruit Polyphenolics and Brain Aging: Nutritional Interventions Targeting Age-Related Neuronal and Behavioral Deficits," *Annals of the New York Academy of Science* 959 (2002): 128–32.

11. J. A. Joseph, B. Shukitt-Hale, N. A. Denisova, et al., "Reversals of Age-Related Declines in Neuronal Signal Transduction, Cognitive, and Motor Behavioral Deficits with Blueberry, Spinach, or Strawberry Dietary Supplementation," *Journal of Neuroscience* 19, no. 18 (1999): 8114–21.

12. Soler, Soriano, and Mañes, "Apple-Products," 337.

13. S. M. Hannum, "Potential Impact of Strawberries on Human Health: A Review of the Science," *Critical Reviews in Food Science and Nutrition* 44, no. 1 (2004): 1–17.

14. T. Chen, F. Yan, J. Qian, et al., "Randomized Phase II Trial of Lyophilized Strawberries in Patients with Dysplastic Precancerous Lesions of the Esophagus," *Cancer Prevention Research* 5, no. 1 (January 2012): 41–50.

15. S. L. Pinski and J. D. Maloney, "Adenosine: A New Drug for Acute Termination of Supraventricular Tachycardia," *Cleveland Clinic Journal of Medicine* 57 (1990): 383–88.

16. L. W. Blau, "Cherry Diet Control for Gout and Arthritis," *Texas Reports on Biology & Medicine* 8 (1950): 309–11.

17. R. A. Jacob, G. M. Spinozzi, V. A. Simon, et al., "Consumption of Cherries Lowers Plasma Urate in Healthy Women," *Journal of Nutrition* 133, no. 6 (2003): 1826–29.

18. D. S. Kelley, R. Rasooly, R. A. Jacob, et al., "Consumption of Bing Sweet Cherries Lowers Circulating Concentrations of Inflammation Markers in Healthy Men and Women," *Journal of Nutrition* 136, no. 4 (2006): 981–86.

19. Y. Zhang, T. Neogi, C. Chen, et al., "Cherry Consumption and the Risk of Recurrent Gout Attacks," *Arthritis and Rheumatism* 64, no. 12 (2012): 4004–11, doi:10.1002/art.346718.

20. J. T. Belanger, "Perillyl Alcohol: Applications in Oncology," *Alternative Medicine Review* 3, no. 6 (1998).

21. J. Avorn, M. Monane, J. H. Gurwitz, et al., "Reduction of Bacteriuria and Pyruia After Using Cranberry Juice," *Journal of the American Medical Association* 272 (1994): 590.

22. R. J. Kiel, J. Nashelsky, B. Robbins, et al., "Does Cranberry Juice Prevent or Treat Urinary Tract Infection?" *Journal of Family Practice* 52, no. 2 (2003): 154–55.

23. J. Reed, "Cranberry Flavonoids, Atherosclerosis and Cardiovascular Health," *Critical Reviews in Science and Nutrition* 42, no. 53 (2002): 301–16.

24. Ibid.; X. Yan, B. T. Murphy, G. B. Hammond, et al., "Antioxidant Activities and Antitumor Screening of Extracts from Cranberry

Fruit (*Vaccinium macrocarpon*)," *Journal of Agricultural and Food Chemistry* 50, no. 21 (2002): 5844–49.

25. R. C. Robbins, F. G. Martin, and J. M. Roe, "Ingestion of Grapefruit Lowers Elevated Hematocrits in Human Subjects," *International Journal for Vitamin and Nutrition Research* 58 (1988): 414–17.

26. J. Shi, J. Yu, J. E. Pohorly, et al., "Polyphenolics in Grape Seeds—Biochemistry and Functionality," *Journal of Medicinal Food* 6 (2003): 291–99.

27. A. P. Day, H. J. Kemp, C. Bolton, et al., "Effect of Concentrated Red Grape Juice Consumption on Serum Antioxidant Capacity and Low-Density Lipoprotein Oxidation," *Annals of Nutrition and Metabolism* 41, no. 6 (1997): 353–57.

28. J. E. Freedman, C. Parker III, L. Li, et al., "Select Flavonoids and Whole Juice from Purple Grapes Inhibit Platelet Function and Enhance Nitric Oxide Release," *Circulation* 103, no. 23 (2001): 2792–98; and Y. Miyagi, K. Miwa, H. Inoue, et al., "Inhibition of Human Low-Density Lipoprotein Oxidation by Flavonoids in Red Wine and Grape Juice," *American Journal of Cardiology* 80, no. 12 (1997): 1627–31.

29. O. Sommerburg, J. E. Keunen, A. C. Bird, et al., "Fruits and Vegetables That Are Sources for Lutein and Zeaxanthin: The Macular Pigment in Human Eyes," *British Journal of Opthalmology* 82, no. 8 (1998): 907–10.

30. S. Farchi, F. Forastiere, N. Agabiti, et al., "Dietary Factors Associated with Wheezing and Allergic Rhinitis in Children," *European Respiratory Journal* 22, no. 5 (2003): 772–80.

31. J. Sun, "D-Limonene: Safety and Clinical Applications," *Alternative Medical Review* 12, no. 3 (September 2007): 259–64.

32. S. S. Percival, S. T. Talcott, S. T. Chin, et al., "Neoplastic Transformation of BALB/3T3 Cells and Cell Cycle of HL-60 Cells Are Inhibited by Mango (*Mangifera indica* L.) Juice and Mango Juice Extracts," *Journal of Nutrition* 136, no. 5 (May 2006): 1300–4.

33. M. Pandey and V. K. Shukla, "Diet and Gallbladder Cancer: A Case-Control Study," *European Journal of Cancer Prevention* 11, no. 4 (2002): 365–68.

34. B. S. Drammeh, G. S. Marquis, E. Funkhouser, et al., "A Randomized, 4-Month Mango and Fat Supplementation Trial Improved Vitamin A Status Among Young Gambian Children," *Journal of Nutrition* 132, no. 12 (2002): 3693–99.

35. D. I. Thurnham, C. A. Northrop-Clewes, F. S. McCullough, et al., "Innate Immunity, Gut Integrity, and Vitamin A in Gambian and

Indian Infants," *Journal of Infectious Diseases* 182, no. S1 (2000): S23–28.

36. M. Ponce-Macotela, I. Navarro-Alegría, M. N. Martinez-Gordillo, et al., "In Vitro Effect Against Giardia of 14 Plant Extracts," *Revista de Investigacion Clinica* 46 (1998): 343–47.

37. C. Roongpisuthipong, S. Banphotkasem, S. Komindr, et al., "Postprandial Glucose and Insulin Responses to Various Tropical Fruits of Equivalent Carbohydrate Content in Non-Insulin-Dependent Diabetes Mellitus," *Diabetes Research and Clinical Practice* 14, no. 2 (1991): 123–31.

38. E. M. Galati, A. Trovato, S. Kirjavainen, et al., "Biological Effects of Hesperidin, a Citrus Flavonoid. (Note III): Antihypertensive and Diuretic Activity in Rat," *Farmaco* 51, no. 3 (1996): 219–21; and P. Rapisarda, A. Tomaino, R. Lo Cascio, et al., "Antioxidant Effectiveness as Influenced by Phenolic Content of Fresh Orange Juices," *Journal of Agricultural and Food Chemistry* 47, no. 11 (1999): 4718–23.

39. H. R. Maurer, "Bromelain: Biochemistry, Pharmacology and Medical Use," *Cellular and Molecular Life Sciences* 58, no. 9 (2001): 1234–45.

40. M. Stacewicz-Sapuntzakis, P. E. Bowen, E. A. Hussain, et al., "Chemical Composition and Potential Health Effects of Prunes: A Functional Food?" *Critical Reviews in Food Science and Nutrition* 41, no. 4 (2001): 251–86.

41. M. D. Sumner, M. Elliott-Eller, G. Weidner, et al., "Effects of Pomegranate Juice Consumption on Myocardial Perfusion in Patients with Coronary Heart Disease," *American Journal of Cardiology* 96, no. 6 (2005): 810–14; M. Aviram, M. Rosenblat, D. Gaitini, et al., "Pomegranate Juice Consumption for 3 Years by Patients with Carotid Artery Stenosis Reduces Common Carotid Intima-Media Thickness, Blood Pressure and LDL Oxidation," *Clinical Nutrition* 23, no. 3 (2004): 423–33; and A. Esmaillzadeh, F. Tahbaz, I. Gaieni, et al., "Concentrated Pomegranate Juice Improves Lipid Profiles in Diabetic Patients with Hyperlipidemia," *Journal of Medicinal Food* 7, no. 3 (2004): 305–8.

42. C. B. Stowe, "The Effects of Pomegranate Juice Consumption on Blood Pressure and Cardiovascular Health," *Complementary Therapies Clinical Practice* 17, no. 2 (2011): 113–15.

43. V. M. Adhami, N. Khan, and H. Mukhtar, "Cancer Chemoprevention by Pomegranate: Laboratory and Clinical Evidence," *Nutrition and Cancer* 61, no. 6 (2009): 811–15.

CHAPTER 6: A JUICER'S GUIDE TO VEGETABLES

1. O. Manousos, N. E. Day, D. Trichopoulus, et al, "Diet and Colorectal Cancer: A Case-Control Study in Greece," *International Journal of Cancer* 32 (1983): 1–5.

2. P. Bobek, S. Galbavy, M. Mariassyova, "The Effect of Red Beet (*Beta vulgaris* var. *rubra*) Fiber on Alimentary Hypercholesterolemia and Chemically Induced Colon Carcinogenesis in Rats," *Nahrung* 44, no. 3 (2000): 184–87.

3. A. P. Ilnitskii, V. A. Iurchenko, "Effect of Fruit and Vegetable Juices on the Changes in the Production of Carcinogenic N-Nitroso Compounds in Human Gastric Juice," *Vopr Pitan* 4 (1993): 44–46.

4. A. J. Webb, N. Patel, S. Loukogeorgakis, et al., "Acute Blood Pressure Lowering, Vasoprotective, and Antiplatelet Properties of Dietary Nitrate via Bioconversion to Nitrite," *Hypertension* 51, no. 3 (2008): 784–90.

5. G. D. Miller, A. P. Marsh, R. W. Dove, et al., "Plasma Nitrate and Nitrite Are Increased by a High-Nitrate Supplement but Not by High-Nitrate Foods in Older Adults," *Nutrition Research* 32, no. 3 (March 2012): 160–68.

6. L. T. Coles, P. M. Clifton, "Effect of Beetroot Juice on Lowering Blood Pressure in Free-Living, Disease-Free Adults: A Randomized, Placebo-Controlled Trial," *Nutrition Journal* 11 (2012): 106, doi:10.1186/1475-2891-11-106; S. J. Bailey, P. Winyard, A. Vanhatalo, et al., "Dietary Nitrate Supplementation Reduces the O_2 Cost of Low-Intensity Exercise and Enhances Tolerance to High-Intensity Exercise in Humans," *Journal of Applied Physiology* 107, no. 4 (October 2009): 1144–55; K. E. Lansley, P. G. Winyard, J. Fulford, et al., "Dietary Nitrate Supplementation Reduces the O_2 Cost of Walking and Running: A Placebo-Controlled Study," *Journal of Applied Physiology* 110, no. 3 (2011): 591–600; and N. M. Cermak, M. J. Gibala, L. J. van Loon, "Nitrate Supplementation's Improvement of 10-km Time-Trial Performance in Trained Cyclists," *International Journal of Sport Nutrition and Exercise Metabolism* 22, no. 1 (February 2012): 64–71.

7. Bailey, Winyard, Vanhatalo, et al., "Dietary Nitrate Supplementation," 1144–55; Lansley, Winyard, Fulford, et al., "Dietary Nitrate Supplementation," 591–600; Cermak, Gibala, and van Loon, "Nitrate Supplementation's Improvement," 64–71.

8. Cermak, Gibala, and van Loon, "Nitrate Supplementation's Improvement," 64–71.

9. N. Ahmad, M. R. Hassan, H. Halder, et al., "Effect of *Momordica charantia* (Karolla) Extracts on Fasting and Postprandial Serum

Glucose Levels in NIDDM Patients," *Bangladesh Medical Research Council Bulletin* 25, no. 1 (1999): 11–13.

10. L. Foa-Tomasi, G. Campadelli-Fiume, L. Barbieri, et al., "Effect of Ribosome-Inactivating Proteins on Virus-Infected Cells: Inhibition of Virus Multiplication and of Protein Synthesis," *Archives of Virology* 71, no. 4 (1982): 323–32.

11. A. J. Claflin, D. L. Vesely, J. L. Hudson, et al., "Inhibition of Growth and Guanylate Cyclase Activity of an Undifferentiated Prostate Adenocarcinoma by an Extract of the Balsam Pear (*Momardica charantia abbreviata*)," *Proceedings of the Academy of Science USA* 75, no. 2 (1978): 989–93.

12. J. W. Fahey, Y. Zhang, and P. Talalay, "Broccoli Sprouts: An Exceptionally Rich Source of Inducers of Enzymes That Protect Against Chemical Carcinogens," *Proceedings of the National Academy of Sciences USA* 94, no. 19 (1997): 10367–72.

13. K. P. Latté, K. E. Appel, and A. Lampen, "Health Benefits and Possible Risks of Broccoli—An Overview," *Food and Chemical Toxicology* 49, no. 12 (2011): 3287–309.

14. J. W. Fahey, X. Haristoy, P. M. Dolan, et al., "Sulforaphane Inhibits Extracellular, Intracellular, and Antibiotic-Resistant Strains of *Helicobacter pylori* and Prevents Benzo[a]pyrene-Induced Stomach Tumors," *Proceedings of the Academy of Sciences USA* 99, no. 11 (2002): 7610–15.

15. E. M. Rosen and S. Fan, "Inhibitory Effects of Indole-3-carbinol on Invasion and Migration in Human Breast Cancer Cells," *Breast Cancer Research and Treatment* 63, no. 2 (2000): 147–52.

16. Ibid.; J. J. Michnovicz and H. L. Bradlow, "Altered Estrogen Metabolism and Excretion in Humans Following Consumption of Indole-3-carbinol," *Nutrition and Cancer* 16, no. 1 (1991): 59–66; and G. van Poppel, D. T. Verhoeven, H. Verhagen, et al., "Brassica Vegetables and Cancer Prevention: Epidemiology and Mechanisms," *Advances in Experimental Medicine and Biology* 472 (1999): 159–68.

17. G. Cheney, "Anti-peptic Ulcer Dietary Factor," *Journal of the American Dietetic Association* 26 (1950): 668–72; G. Cheney, "Rapid Healing of Peptic Ulcers in Patients Receiving Fresh Cabbage Juice," *California Medicine* 70 (1949): 10–14.

18. S. B. Kritchevsky, "Beta-carotene, Carotenoids and the Prevention of Coronary Heart Disease," *Journal of Nutrition* 129, no. 1 (1999): 5–8.

19. D. S. Michaud, D. Feskanich, E. B. Rimm, et al., "Intake of Specific Carotenoids and Risk of Lung Cancer in 2 Prospective US

Cohorts," *American Journal of Clinical Nutrition* 72, no. 4 (2000): 990–97.

20. M. M. Mathews-Roth, "Neutropenia and Beta-carotene," *Lancet* 2, no. 8291 (1982): 222.

21. M. M. Mathews-Roth, "Amenorrhea Associated with Caroten-emia," *Journal of the American Medical Association* 250 (1983): 731.

22. Q. T. Le and W. J. Elliott, "Hypotensive and Hypocholesterolemic Effects of Celery Oil May Be Due to BuPh," *Clinical Research* 39 (1991): 173A; Q. T. Le and W. J. Elliott, "Dose-Response Relationship of Blood Pressure and Serum Cholesterol to 3-n-butylphthalide, a Component of Celery Oil," *Clinical Research* 39 (1991): 750A.

23. S. Soundararajan and B. Daunter, "Ajvine: Pilot Biomedical Study for Pain Relief in Rheumatic Pain," School of Medicine, University of Queensland, Brisbane, Queensland, Australia, 1991–92; and S. Venkat, S. Soundararajan, B. Daunter, et al., "Use of Ayurvedic Medicine in the Treatment of Rheumatic Illness," Department of Orthopaedics, Kovai Medical Center and Hospitals, Coimbatore, India, 1995.

24. D. Tsi and B. K. Tan, "The Mechanism Underlying the Hypocho-lesterolaemic Activity of Aqueous Celery Extract, Its Butanol and Aqueous Fractions in Genetically Hypercholesterolaemic RICO Rats," *Life Sciences* 66, no. 8 (2000): 755–67; G. Zheng, P. M. Ken-ney, J. Zhang, et al., "Chemoprevention of Benzopyrene-Induced Forestomach Cancer in Mice by Natural Phthalides from Celery Oil," *Nutrition and Cancer* 19 (1993): 77–86; and L. Y. Zhang and Y. P. Feng, "Effect of dl-3-n-butylphthalide (NBP) on Life Span and Neurological Deficit in SHRsp Rats," *Yao Hsueh Hsueh Pao* 31 (1996): 18–23.

25. Y. Peng, J. Sun, S. Hon, et al., "L-3-n-butylphthalide Improves Cognitive Impairment and Reduces Amyloid-beta in a Transgenic Model of Alzheimer's Disease," *Journal of Neuroscience* 16, no. 30 (June 2010): 8180–89.

26. F. Susnik, "Present State of Knowledge of the Medicinal Plant *Taraxacum officinale* Weber," *Medicinski Razgledi* 21 (1982): 323–28.

27. E. Racz-Kotilla, G. Racz, and A. Solomon, "The Action of *Taraxacum officinale* Extracts on the Body Weight and Diuresis of Laboratory Animals," *Planta Medica* 26 (1974): 212–17.

28. D. Spigelski and P. J. Jones, "Efficacy of Garlic Supplementation in Lowering Serum Cholesterol Levels," *Nutrition Reviews* 59, no. 7 (2001): 236–41.

29. C. A. Silagy and A. W. Neil, "A Meta-Analysis of the Effect of Garlic on Blood Pressure," *Journal of Hypertension* 12 (1994): 463–68.

30. G. S. Sainani, D. B. Desai, N. H. Gohre, et al., "Effect of Dietary Garlic and Onion on Serum Lipid Profile in Jain Community," *Indian Journal of Medical Research* 69 (1979): 776–80.

31. A. Grontved, T. Brask, J. Kambskard, et al., "Ginger Root Against Seasickness: A Controlled Trial on the Open Sea," *Acta Otolaryngol* 105 (1988): 45–49.

32. W. Fischer-Rasmussen, S. K. Kjaer, C. Dahl, et al., "Ginger Treatment of Hyperemesis Gravidarum," *European Journal of Ob Gyn Reproductive Biology* 38 (1990): 19–24.

33. K. C. Srivastava and T. Mustafa, "Ginger (*Zingiber officinale*) and Rheumatic Disorders," *Medical Hypotheses* 29 (1989): 25–28.

34. S. Kolida, K. Tuohy, and G. R. Gibson, "Prebiotic Effects of Inulin and Oligofructose," *British Journal of Nutrition* 87, no. S2 (2002): S193–97.

35. K. T. Augusti, "Therapeutic Values of Onion (*Allium cepa* L.) and Garlic (*Allium sativum* L.)," *Indian Journal of Experimental Biology* 34, no. 7 (1996): 634–40.

36. W. Dorsch, M. Ettl, G. Hein, et al., "Antiasthmatic Effects of Onions: Inhibition of Platelet-Activating Factor-Induced Bronchial Obstruction by Onion Oils," *International Archives of Allergy and Immunology* 82, nos. 3–4 (1987): 535–36.

37. S. Ohyama, S. Kitamori, H. Kawano, et al., "Ingestion of Parsley Inhibits the Mutagenicity of Male Human Urine Following Consumption of Fried Salmon," *Mutation Research* 192 (1987): 7–10.

38. R. Edenharder, G. Keller, K. L. Platt, et al., "Isolation and Characterization of Structurally Novel Antimutagenic Flavonoids from Spinach (*Spinacia oleracea*)," *Journal of Agricultural and Food Chemistry* 49, no. 6 (2001): 2767–73.

39. T. He, C. Y. Huang, H. Chen, et al., "Effects of Spinach Powder Fat-Soluble Extract on Proliferation of Human Gastric Adenocarcinoma Cells," *Biomedical and Environmental Sciences* 12, no. 4 (1999): 247–52; and A. Nyska, L. Lomnitski, J. Spalding, et al., "Topical and Oral Administration of the Natural Water-Soluble Antioxidant from Spinach Reduces the Multiplicity of Papillomas in the Tg.AC Mouse Model," *Toxicology Letters* 122, no. 1 (2001): 33–34.

40. M. P. Longnecker, P. A. Newcomb, R. Mittendorf, et al., "Intake of Carrots, Spinach, and Supplements Containing Vitamin A in Relation to Risk of Breast Cancer," *Cancer Epidemiology, Biomarkers and Prevention* 6, no. 11 (1997): 887–92.

41. J. H. Weisburger, "Lycopene and Tomato Products in Health

Promotion," *Experimental Biology and Medicine* 227, no. 10 (2002): 924–27.

42. E. Giovannucci, E. B. Rimm, Y. Liu, et al., "A Prospective Study of Tomato Products, Lycopene, and Prostate Cancer Risk," *Journal of the National Cancer Institute* 94, no. 5 (2002): 391–48.

43. O. Kucuk, F. H. Sarkar, W. Sakr, et al., "Phase II Randomized Clinical Trial of Lycopene Supplementation Before Radical Prostatectomy," *Cancer Epidemiology Biomarkers and Prevention* 10 (2001): 861–68.

44. J. S. Jurenka, "Anti-inflammatory Properties of Curcumin, a Major Constituent of *Curcuma longa:* A Review of Preclinical and Clinical Research," *Alternative Medicine Review* 14, no. 2 (2009): 141–53.

45. W. Wongcharoen and A. Phrommintikul, "The Protective Role of Curcumin in Cardiovascular Diseases," *International Journal of Cardiology* 133, no. 2 (2009): 145–51.

46. E. Sikora, A. Bielak-Zmijewska, G. Mosieniak, et al., "The Promise of Slow Down Ageing May Come From Curcumin," *Current Pharmaceutical Design* 16, no. 7 (2012): 884–92.

47. J. Biswas, D. Sinha, S. Mukherjee, et al., "Curcumin Protects DNA Damage in a Chronically Arsenic-Exposed Population of West Bengal," *Human and Experimental Toxicology* 29, no. 6 (2010): 513–24.

48. A. Shehzad, F. Wahid, and Y. S. Lee, "Curcumin in Cancer Chemoprevention: Molecular Targets, Pharmacokinetics, Bioavailability, and Clinical Trials," *Archiv der Pharmazie* (Weinheim) 343, no. 9 (September 2010): 489–99.

CHAPTER 8: JUICE AS MEDICINE

1. G. Cheney, "Anti-Peptic Ulcer Dietary Factor," *Journal of the American Dietetic Association* 26 (1950): 668–72; G. Cheney, "Rapid Healing of Peptic Ulcers in Patients Receiving Fresh Cabbage Juice," *California Medicine* 70 (1949): 10–14.

2. E. Sheen and G. Triadafilopoulos, "Adverse Effects of Long-Term Proton Pump Inhibitor Therapy," *Digestive Diseases and Sciences* 56, no. 4 (2011): 931–50.

3. L. G. Darlington and N. W. Ramsey, "Clinical Review: Review of Dietary Therapy for Rheumatoid Arthritis," *British Journal of Rheumatology* 32 (1993): 507–14.

4. J. Kjeldsen-Kragh, M. Haugen, C. F. Borchgrevink, et al., "Controlled Trial of Fasting and One-Year Vegetarian Diet in Rheumatoid Arthritis," *Lancet* 338 (1991): 899–902.

5. J. Kjeldsen-Kragh, "Rheumatoid Arthritis Treated with Vegetarian Diets," *American Journal of Clinical Nutrition* 70, no. 53 (1999): 594–600; O. Lindahl, L. Lindwall, A. Spangberg, et al., "Vegan Diet Regimen with Reduced Medication in the Treatment of Bronchial Asthma," *Journal of Asthma* 22, no. 1 (1985): 45–55.
6. Lindahl, Lindwall, and Spangberg, "Vegan Diet Regimen," 45–55.
7. P. Anand, A. B. Kunnumakkara, R. A. Newman, et al., "Bioavailability of Curcumin: Problems and Promises," *Molecular Pharmacology* 4, no. 6 (November–December 2007): 807–18.
8. H. Sasaki, Y. Sunagawa, K. Takahashi, et al., "Innovative Preparation of Curcumin for Improved Oral Bioavailability," *Biological and Pharmaceutical Bulletin* 34, no. 5 (2011): 660–65; and M. Kanai, A. Imaizumi, Y. Otsuka, et al., "Dose-Escalation and Pharmacokinetic Study of Nanoparticle Curcumin, a Potential Anticancer Agent with Improved Bioavailability, in Healthy Human Volunteers," *Cancer Chemotherapy and Pharmacology* 69, no. 1 (2012): 65–70.

CHAPTER 9: THE JUICE FAST

1. A. Goldhamer, S. Helms, and T. K. Salloum, "Fasting," *A Textbook of Natural Medicine,* ed. J. E. Pizzorno and M. T. Murray (London: Churchill Livingstone, 2012), 296–305.
2. M. Imamura and T. Tung, "A Trial of Fasting Cure for PCB Poisoned Patients in Taiwan," *American Journal of Industrial Medicine* 5 (1984): 147–53.
3. R. A. Shakman, "Nutritional Influences on the Toxicity of Environmental Pollutants: A Review," *Archives of Environmental Health* 28 (1974): 105–33.

CHAPTER 10: JUICING FOR WEIGHT LOSS

1. A. S. Abdelhameed, S. Ang, G. A. Morris, et al., "An Analytical Ultracentrifuge Study on Ternary Mixtures of Konjac Glucomannan Supplemented with Sodium Alginate and Xanthan Gum," *Carbohydrate Polymers* 81 (2010): 141–48; S. E. Harding, I. H. Smith, C. J. Lawson, et al., "Studies on Macromolecular Interactions in Ternary Mixtures of Konjac Glucomannan, Xanthan Gum and Sodium Alginate," *Carbohydrate Polymers* 10 (2010): 1016–20.
2. R. A. Reimer, X. Pelletier, I. G. Carabin, et al., "Increased Plasma PYY Levels Following Supplementation with the Functional Fiber PolyGlycopleX in Healthy Adults," *European Journal of Clinical Nutrition* 64, no. 10 (October 2010): 1186–91; and M. R. Lyon and

R. G. Reichert, "The Effect of a Novel Viscous Polysaccharide Along with Lifestyle Changes on Short-Term Weight Loss and Associated Risk Factors in Overweight and Obese Adults: An Observational Retrospective Clinical Program Analysis," *Alternative Medicine Review* 15, no. 1 (April 2010): 68–75.

3. V. Vuksan, J. L. Sievenpiper, R. Owen, et al., "Beneficial Effects of Viscous Dietary Fiber from Konjac-Mannan in Subjects with the Insulin Resistance Syndrome: Results of a Controlled Metabolic Trial," *Diabetes Care* 23 (2000): 9–14.

4. J. C. Brand-Miller, F. S. Atkinson, R. J. Gahler, et al., "Effects of PGX, a Novel Functional Fibre, on Acute and Delayed Postprandial Glycaemia," *European Journal of Clinical Nutrition* 64, no. 12 (December 2010): 1488–93; and A. L. Jenkins, V. Kacinik, M. R. Lyon, et al., "Reduction of Postprandial Glycemia by the Novel Viscous Polysaccharide PGX in a Dose-Dependent Manner, Independent of Food Form," *Journal of the American College of Nutrition* 29, no. 2 (2010): 92–98.

CHAPTER 11: JUICING, IMMUNE FUNCTION, AND THE CANCER PATIENT

1. Centers of Disease Control and Prevention. "National Health and Nutrition Examination Survey," NHANES 2007–2008, accessed May 1, 2013, http://www.cdc.gov/nchs/nhanes/nhanes2007–2008/nhanes07_08.htm.

2. A. Sanchez, J. Reeser, H. Lau, et al., "Role of Sugars in Human Neutrophilic Phagocytosis," *American Journal of Clinical Nutrition* 26 (1973): 1180–84.

3. J. Bernstein, S. Alpert, K. Nauss, et al., "Depression of Lymphocyte Transformation Following Oral Glucose Ingestion," *American Journal of Clinical Nutrition* 30 (1977): 613.

4. G. Mann and P. Newton, "The Membrane Transport of Ascorbic Acid," *Annals of the New York Academy of Sciences* 258 (1975): 243–51.

5. A. Martí, A. Marcos, and J. A. Martínez, "Obesity and Immune Function Relationships," *Obesity Review* 2, no. 2 (May 2001): 131–34.

6. J. Palmblad, D. Hallberg, and S. Rossner, "Obesity, Plasma Lipids and Polymorphonuclear (PMN) Granulocyte Functions," *Scandinavian Journal of Hematology* 19 (1977): 293–303.

7. M. E. Bone, D. J. Wilkinson, J. R. Young, et al., "Ginger Root—A New Antiemetic: The Effect of Ginger Root on Postoperative

Nausea and Vomiting After Major Gynaecological Surgery,"
Anaesthesia 45 (1990): 669–71; S. Phillips, R. Ruggier, and S. E.
Hutchingson, *"Zingiber officinale* (Ginger)—An Antiemetic for
Day Case Surgery," *Anaesthesia* 48 (1993): 715–16; and K. Meyer,
J. Schwartz, D. Craer, et al., *"Zingiber officinale* (Ginger) Used
to Prevent 8-Mop Associated Nausea," *Dermatology Nursing* 7
(1995): 242–44.

CHAPTER 12: ANSWERS TO COMMON QUESTIONS ON JUICING

1. Centers of Disease Control and Prevention. "National Health and
   Nutrition Examination Survey," NHANES 2007–2008, accessed
   May 1, 2013, http://www.cdc.gov/nchs/nhanes/nhanes2007–2008/
   nhanes07_08.htm.
2. N. A. Pocock, J. A. Eisman, M. G. Yeates, et al., "Physical Fitness
   is the Major Determinant of Femoral Neck and Lumbar Spine Density," *Journal of Clinical Investigation* 78 (1986): 618–21.
3. S. A. New, "Intake of Fruit and Vegetables: Implications for Bone
   Health," *Proceedings of the Nutrition Society* 62, no. 4 (November
   2003): 889–99.
4. E. Mazariegos-Ramos, E. Guerrero-Romero, M. Rodriguez-Moran,
   et al., "Consumption of Soft Drinks with Phosphoric Acid as a
   Risk Factor for the Development of Hypocalcemia in Children: A
   Case-Control Study," *Journal of Pediatrics* 126 (1995): 940–42.
5. F. H. Neilsen, C. D. Hunt, L. M. Mullen, et al., "Effect of Dietary
   Boron on Mineral, Estrogen, and Testosterone Metabolism in Postmenopausal Women," *FASEB Journal* 1 (1987): 394–97.
6. D. P. Strachan, B. D. Cox, S. W. Erzinclioglu, et al., "Ventilatory
   Function and Winter Fresh Fruit Consumption in a Random Sample
   of British Adults," *Thorax* 46, no. 9 (1991): 624–29.

index